example in an adjective: **good**, **better**, **best**, or in a verb: **lead**, **led**.

You will find this information after the part of speech. And where a letter should be doubled when changing the form as in **beg**, **begging**, this is also given.

The small figures at the beginning of the words as in [1]**saw**, [2]**saw**, [3]**saw**, show that each similar word has a separate use or meaning, and the most usual is given first. When a word has two main meanings that are the same part of speech, again the most usual appears first.

*Reading, writing, talking, thinking –
everyone needs words, all the time.
Sometimes, however, you may not be quite sure
of the meaning of a particular word, or how to spell it.
And that's when you need a dictionary. In this
Ladybird dictionary you will find nearly 4000 words,
some familiar and some not so familiar,
with their meanings and spellings.*

Acknowledgments

*The Ladybird Dictionary is based on definitions
from Longman Dictionaries and is published by arrangement
with Addison Wesley Longman Ltd.
The publishers wish to thank Heather Gay BSc. PhD.
for her considerable help in the preparation of the first edition,
and Della Summers for the second edition.
Co-ordinating editors Audrey Daly and Zuza Vrbova.*

A catalogue record for this book is available
from the British Library

Published by Ladybird Books Ltd Loughborough Leicestershire UK
Ladybird Books Ltd is a subsidiary of the Penguin Group of companies
First edition © text Longman Group UK Ltd MCMLXXXVIII
This edition © text Addison Wesley Longman Ltd MCMXCVI
Illustrations © Ladybird Books Ltd MCMXCVI
LADYBIRD and the device of a Ladybird are trademarks of Ladybird Books Ltd
All rights reserved. No part of this publication may be reproduced,
stored in a retrieval system, or transmitted in any form or by any
means, electronic, mechanical, photocopying, recording or otherwise,
without the prior consent of the copyright owners.

THE
LADYBIRD
DICTIONARY

illustrations by Peter Massey
and Chris Orr & Associates

a (also **an** *before a vowel sound*) **1** one; **2** each; every: *6 times a day*

abbreviation *noun* a shortened form of a word

ability *noun* power and skill

able *adjective* having the power, skill, knowledge, time, etc, needed to do something

about *adverb, preposition* **1** concerning, of; **2** a little more or less; almost, nearly; **3** here and/or there

above *adverb, preposition* **1** in or to a higher place; higher than; **2** greater or more than

abroad *adverb* to or in another country: *living **abroad***

absent *adjective* not present; away; **absence** *noun*

accept *verb* **1** to take or receive something; **2** to agree to; **acceptable** *adjective*

accident *noun* something, especially something unpleasant or damaging, that happens by chance; **accidental** *adjective*; **accidentally** *adverb*

ache (**say** ayk) *verb* to have a continuous pain; **ache** *noun*

¹acid *noun* a chemical substance that burns

²acid also **acidic** *adjective* having a bitter or sour taste like that of lemons

acorn *noun* the nut of the oak tree

acquaintance *noun* a person you have met but do not know well

acre *noun* a measure of land equal to 4840 square yards or 4047 square metres

acrobat *noun* a person skilled in walking on ropes or wires, balancing, walking on hands, etc, especially at a circus; **acrobatic** *adjective*; **acrobatically** *adverb*

tightrope walker

across *adverb, preposition* **1** from one side to the other; **2** to, at, or on the opposite side

¹act *verb* **1** to play the part of somebody in a play or film; **2** to behave as if playing a part; to pretend; **3** to behave in a certain way: *to **act** bravely*

²act *noun* **1** something done: *an **act** of cruelty*; **2** a law; **3** one of the main parts into which a play is divided

action *noun* **1** movement using force or power for some purpose; **2** something done; **3 out of action** not working properly

active *adjective* always doing things; **actively** *adverb*

activity *noun* **1** the condition of a lot of action; **2** something that is done, especially for interest

actor feminine **actress** *noun* a person who acts a part in a play or film

actual *adjective* real and clear; **actually** *adverb*

add *verb* **1** to put a number, etc with another number; **2** to say something extra; **addition** *noun*; **additional** *adjective*

address *noun* the number of the building, name of the street and town, etc, where a person lives or works

adjective *noun* a word that describes something

admire *verb* to think of with pleasure and respect; to have a good opinion of something or somebody; **admiration** *noun*

admit *verb* **(admitted) 1** to allow somebody to enter; to let in; **2** to confess; **admission** *noun*

adult *noun* **1** a fully grown person, especially a person over 18; **2** a fully grown animal or bird; **adult** *adjective*

advantage *noun* something that may help you to be successful or to get something you want; **advantageous** *adjective*

adventure *noun* an exciting and often dangerous journey, activity, etc; **adventurous** *adjective*

adverb *noun* a word which tells you how, when, or where something is done

advertise *verb* to make something known to a lot of people; **advertisement** *noun*

advice *noun* a suggestion from one person to another on how that other should act

advise *verb* to tell somebody what you think he or she should do

¹**aerial** *noun* a wire, rod, etc, that receives or sends out radio waves

satellite TV dish aerial

²**aerial** *adjective* from or in the air: *an **aerial** view*

aerosol *noun* a small container used to spray liquid, such as paint

afford *verb* to have enough money to be able to buy or pay for something

afraid *adjective* **1** full of fear; **2** sorry for something that has happened or is likely to happen: *I'm **afraid** I've broken your pen*

after *preposition* following in time, place, or order; later than; behind

afternoon *noun* the part of the day between midday and evening

afterwards *adverb* later; after that

again *adverb* **1** once more: *Please say that **again**; **2** now and again** sometimes, but not very often

a

against *preposition* **1** on an opposite side to; **2** next to; touching

age *noun* **1** the period of time a person has lived or a thing has existed; **2** a period of time in history: *the Middle Ages*; **3 ages** a long time; **aged** *adjective*

ago *adjective* back in time from now; in the past

agree *verb* to have the same thoughts, opinions, or feelings as somebody else; **agreement** *noun*

ahead *adverb, adjective* **1** in front; into a forward position; **2** in or into the future

aim *verb* **1** to point or direct something at an object, especially with the intention of hitting it; **2** to intend to do something; **aim** *noun*

¹**air** *noun* **1** the mixture of gases which surrounds the Earth and which we breathe; **2** an appearance or feeling: *an air of excitement*; **3** a tune; ⚠ **heir**

²**air** *verb* **1** to make clothes, sheets, beds, etc, warm or dry; **2** to make a room fresh by letting in air; ⚠ **heir**

aircraft *noun* a flying vehicle, such as a helicopter, plane, or glider

air force *noun* a group of people who use aircraft for fighting or defence

airport *noun* a place where aircraft can land and take off and which is regularly used by passengers

alarm *noun* **1** something such as a bell or flashing light by which a warning of danger is given; **2** a sudden feeling of fear; **alarm** *verb*

alarm clock *noun* a clock that can be set to make a noise at the time that you want to wake up

alarm clock

album *noun* **1** a book which is used for collecting photographs, stamps, etc; **2** a collection of songs on a CD, etc

alcohol *noun* a substance present in wine, beer, etc, that can make people feel drunk if they have too much of it; drinks containing this liquid; **alcoholic** *adjective*

¹**alert** *adjective* ready to act suddenly

²**alert** *noun* a warning to be ready for danger; **alert** *verb*

alike *adjective, adverb* the same or nearly the same

alive *adjective* having life; living

all *adjective, adverb, pronoun* **1** the complete amount, quantity, or number of; the whole of; **2** completely; **3** everybody or everything

American alligator

alligator *noun* a large dangerous reptile that is related to and looks like a crocodile

allow *verb* to let somebody do or have something

all right *adverb, adjective* **1** safe or healthy; **2** good enough; **3** Yes, I/we agree

ally *noun* a person or country that helps or supports you

almost *adverb* very nearly

alone *adjective, adverb* **1** without others; **2** only: *He **alone** knows the secret*

along *preposition, adverb* **1** in the direction of the length of; following the course of; **2** forward; on

aloud *adverb* **1** in a voice that may be heard; **2** in a loud voice

alphabet *noun* the set of letters used in a language, especially when arranged in order; **alphabetical** *adjective*

already *adverb* by or before a particular time

also *adverb* as well; too

although *conjunction* in spite of the fact that

altogether *adverb* completely; considering all things

always *adverb* at all times; for ever

am *see* BE

a m in the morning (short for *ante meridiem*)

amateur *noun* **1** a person who does something, such as acting, painting pictures, or taking part in a sport, for enjoyment and without being paid for doing it; **2** a person who has no skill in doing something; **amateur** *adjective*

amber *noun* **1** a hard yellowish substance used for making ornaments and jewellery; **2** a yellowish colour

ambulance *noun* a motor vehicle for carrying sick or injured people, especially to hospital

among also **amongst** *preposition* in the middle of; surrounded by; between

amount *noun* a quantity or number

amp also **ampere** *noun* a measure of electric current

amplifier *noun* an electronic instrument used in a hearing aid, electric guitar etc, to increase the sound; **amplify** *verb*

amuse *verb* to make somebody laugh or feel cheerful; **amusement** *noun*; **amusing** *adjective*

an *see* A

analyse *verb* **1** to examine something carefully in order to find out what it is made of; **2** to think carefully about the reason for something; **analysis** *noun*

anchor *noun* a heavy metal weight attached to a ship and lowered into the water to keep the ship from moving

ancient (*say* aynshunt) *adjective* in, of, or having existed since times long ago

and *conjunction* as well as; too

angel *noun* a messenger from God, who is usually thought of as a person with large wings and dressed in white; **angelic** *adjective*

anger *noun* a fierce feeling that makes you want to hurt or fight somebody; **angrily** *adverb*; **angry** *adjective*

angle *noun* the shape made by two straight lines that meet at a point; the space between these lines

angling *noun* the sport of catching fish with a hook and line; fishing

animal *noun* a living creature that can move itself when it wants to; any living thing that is not a plant

ankle *noun* the thin part of the leg just above the foot

announce *verb* to make something known; to say in public; **announcement** *noun*

annoy *verb* to make somebody a little angry; **annoyance** *noun*

anorak *noun* a waterproof jacket with a hood

another *pronoun, adjective* **1** one more of the same sort; **2** a different one

answer *noun* **1** the information that tells you what you want to know when you ask a question; **2** a reply to a greeting, letter, etc; **3** something which is discovered as a result of thinking, using numbers, etc; **answer** *verb*

wood ant

ant *noun* a small insect that usually lives on the ground in large groups

antelope *noun* an animal that looks like a deer and runs fast

antenna *noun* (*plural* **antennae** *or* **antennas**) **1** either of two long thin parts on the head of an insect, shrimp, etc, that are used for feeling; **2** an aerial

anticlockwise *adjective, adverb* in the opposite direction to the movement of the hands of a clock; circular movement to the right

anxious (*say* angshus) *adjective* **1** worried or fearful; **2** having a strong wish to do something; **anxiety** *noun*; **anxiously** *adverb*

any *adjective, pronoun* **1** one, some, or all; a number or amount; **2** no matter which, what, where, how, etc; **3 in any case** also **at any rate** whatever may happen

anybody also **anyone** *pronoun* any person

anything *pronoun* **1** any one thing; something; **2** no matter what

anyway *adverb* whatever else is done; no matter what happens

anywhere *adverb* in, at, or to any place

apart *adverb* **1** separate; away from another or others; **2** to pieces: ***take an engine apart***

apartment *noun* a flat

ape *noun* a large monkey without a tail or with a very short tail

apologise *verb* to say that you are sorry; **apology** *noun*

apparatus *noun* equipment used in science

appear *verb* **1** to come into sight; **2** to seem; **appearance** *noun*

appetite *noun* a wish for food

applaud *verb* to praise or show that you like something by clapping or cheering; **applause** *noun*

apple *noun* a hard round fruit with a red, green, or yellow skin

appreciate *verb* to like or be grateful for something; **appreciation** *noun*

approve *verb* to say or think that something is good; **approval** *noun*

apricot *noun* a soft juicy yellowish orange fruit

April *noun* the fourth month of the year

apron *noun* a piece of clothing worn over your other clothes to keep them clean

aquarium *noun* a glass or plastic container for fish; a building containing many of these

arch *noun* a top part, often curved, of a door, bridge, etc, that rests on two supports

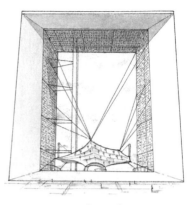

a modern arch –
La Grande Arche de la Défense, Paris

archaeology *noun* the study of the burled remains of ancient times, such as houses, pots, tools, and weapons; **archaeological** *adjective;* **archaeologist** *noun*

are *see* BE

area *noun* **1** a particular space, surface, or part of the world; **2** the measure of a surface: *the **area** of a rectangle*

aren't *see* BE

argue *verb* to disagree in words; to quarrel; **argument** *noun*

arithmetic *noun* the adding, subtracting, multiplying, dividing, etc, of numbers

arm *noun* the part of the body between the shoulder and the hand

armchair *noun* a chair with supporting parts on which you can rest your arms

9

a

15th century German armour

armour *noun* a covering of metal worn by fighting men in old times to protect them

arms *noun* weapons; **armed** *adjective*

army *noun* a large number of people trained for fighting

around *adverb, preposition* **1** on all sides; surrounding; **2** in various directions or places

arrange *verb* **1** to put in order; **2** to make plans or prepare for something; **arrangement** *noun*

arrest *verb* to take somebody prisoner; **arrest** *noun*

arrive *verb* **1** to get to a place, especially after a journey; **2** to happen; come; **arrival** *noun*

arrow *noun* **1** a thin straight pointed stick that is shot from a bow; **2** a mark shaped like an arrow which shows you the way

art *noun* the making of beautiful things by drawing, painting, etc; **artist** *noun*

article *noun* **1** a particular or separate thing or object; **2** a piece of writing in a newspaper, magazine, etc

as *conjunction, preposition* **1** used to compare people or things: *He can run* **as** *fast as I can*; **2** for the reason that; because; **3** while, when; **4** like; similar to; in the same way

¹**ash** *noun* the grey powder left after something has burnt

²**ash** *noun* a tall tree with hard wood

ashamed *adjective* feeling shame or guilt

ask *verb* **1** to put a question; **2** to make a request for or to; **3** to invite

asleep *adjective* sleeping

asteroid *noun* any of the small bodies that move round the sun mainly in the area between Mars and Jupiter

astrology *noun* the skill of understanding the effects that the stars, planets, etc, are supposed to have on our lives; **astrologer** *noun*

astronaut *noun* a person who travels in a spacecraft

astronomy *noun* the scientific study of the sun, moon, stars, etc; **astronomer** *noun*

at *preposition* **1** used to show where or when; **2 at all** in any way

ate *see* EAT

athletics *noun* a branch of sport that includes running, jumping, and throwing

atlas *noun* a book of maps

a

atmosphere *noun* **1** the mixture of gases surrounding any large body in space, especially the Earth; **2** the air; **atmospheric** *adjective*

atom *noun* a very small part of a substance; **atomic** *adjective*

a lithium atom

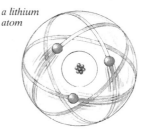

attach *verb* to fix; to fasten; to join; **attachment** *noun*

attack *verb* **1** to be violent towards somebody; to fight, speak, or write against; **2** to harm; **attack** *noun*; **attacker** *noun*

attempt *verb* to make an effort to do something; to try; **attempt** *noun*

attend *verb* **1** to be present at; **2** to listen to or watch carefully; **attendance** *noun*; **attendant** *noun*

attention *noun* the act of fixing the mind on something, especially by watching or listening carefully; **attentive** *adjective*

attic *noun* room at the top of a house, just under the roof

attract *verb* **1** to cause to like, admire, or notice; **2** to draw towards you: *magnets **attract** iron*; **attractive** *adjective*

audience *noun* the people listening to or watching a play, speech, show, etc

audio *adjective* concerned with sound

August *noun* the eighth month of the year

aunt also **auntie, aunty** *noun* the sister of your father or mother; the wife of your uncle

aurora *noun* coloured lights in the sky that can be seen at night in the most northern and southern parts of the world

automatic *adjective* able to work without human help

autumn *noun* the season between summer and winter

avenue *noun* **1** a wide street in a town; **2** a road between two rows of trees

average *adjective* **1** being the amount found by adding together several quantities and then dividing by the number of quantities; **2** usual or ordinary; **average** *noun*

avoid *verb* to keep away from somebody or something

awake *adjective* having woken up; not asleep

away *adverb* from this or that place; to, at, or in another place

awful *adjective* very bad; terrible; shocking; **awfully** *adverb*

awkward *adjective* **1** clumsy; **2** not well made for use; difficult to use; **awkwardly** *adverb*; **awkwardness** *noun*

axe *noun* a tool with a heavy metal blade on the end of a long handle, used to cut wood

Bb

baboon *noun* a large monkey

baby *noun* **1** a very young child, especially one who has not learnt to speak; **2** a very young animal or bird

¹**back** *noun* **1** the part of the body of a human or animal down the middle of which runs the spine; **2** the part that is furthest from the front; **3 at the back (of)** behind; **back** *adjective*

²**back** *adverb* **1** towards or at the back; **2** to or at a place or time where something or somebody was before

³**back** *verb* **1** to go or cause to go backwards; **2** to support; **3** to be or make the back of; **4** to bet money on

background *noun* **1** the place behind someone in a photo; space or colour under a drawing or picture; **2** things that happened before that explain an event; **3** someone's family, education, or where he or she comes from

backward *adjective* **1** directed towards the back, the beginning, or the past; **2** behind in development; **backwardness** *noun*

backwards *adverb* **1** away from your front; towards the back; **2** with the back first; **3** with the back where the front should be; back to front

bacon *noun* salted or smoked meat from the back or sides of a pig, often sold in thin slices

bacteria *noun – plural* (*singular* **bacterium**) very small living things, some of which cause disease; **bacterial** *adjective*

bad *adjective* (**worse, worst**) **1** not good; **2** serious; severe; **badly** *adverb*; **badness** *noun*

badge *noun* a small sign worn to show what you are or what you do

badger *noun* a grey animal that has a white face with two black stripes and lives underground

badminton *noun* a game like tennis played with a shuttlecock instead of a ball

badminton racket and shuttlecock

bag *noun* a container made of soft material, opening at the top

baggage *noun* the bags, cases, etc, you take with you when you travel

bagpipes *noun* (*always plural*) a musical instrument which is played by blowing air into a bag and through pipes

bake *verb* to cook in an oven; **baker** *noun*

¹**balance** *noun* steadiness

²**balance** *verb* to keep yourself or something else steady, especially in a difficult position

12

bald *adjective* with little or no hair; **baldness** *noun*

ball *noun* **1** a round object used in games; anything of a round shape; **2** a large party for dancing

ballet (*say* **balay**) *noun* a form of dancing performed by specially trained dancers whose movements to music tell a story

hot air balloon

balloon *noun* **1** a small rubber bag that can be blown up, used as a toy; **2** a large bag of light material filled with hot air or a light gas to make it rise up in the air

ban *verb* (**banned**) to forbid, especially by law; **ban** *noun*

banana *noun* a long curved fruit with yellow skin

band *noun* **1** a group of musicians; **2** a group of people; **3** a thin flat narrow piece of material for fastening things together: *rubber* **band**; **4** an area into which something can be divided, such as a band of radio waves or a range of frequencies

bandage *noun* a strip of material for covering a wound

bang *noun* **1** a sudden loud noise; **2** a sharp blow; **bang** *verb*

¹**bank** *noun* a place in which money is kept and paid out when you want it: **bank manager, bank note; banker** *noun*

²**bank** *noun* **1** land along the side of a river, lake, etc; **2** a heap of earth, sand, snow, etc

¹**bar** *noun* **1** a long piece of wood or metal; **2** a piece of solid material; **3** a group of notes in music, marked off by lines; **4** a place where drinks are sold

²**bar** *verb* (**barred**) **1** to close with a bar; **2** to block

barber *noun* a person who cuts men's hair

bare *adjective* **1** naked; not covered; **2** empty; with nothing in or on it; **bare** *verb*; ⚠ **bear**

barely *adverb* only just; hardly

¹**bark** *noun* the sound made by a dog; **bark** *verb*

²**bark** *noun* the strong outer covering of a tree

barley *noun* a plant grown for food and making drinks, such as beer

barn *noun* a farm building for storing crops

barrel *noun* **1** the part of a gun that is shaped like a tube; **2** a round wooden container, usually for liquids, with curved sides and a flat top and bottom

base *noun* the bottom of anything

b

baseball *noun* a game played with a bat and ball between two teams of nine players each

basement *noun* the rooms in a house below street level

basin *noun* **1** a shallow container for water; **2** a round container for food

basket *noun* a container made of woven sticks or other such material

basketball *noun* a game in which each team of five players tries to throw a large ball through the other team's basket

bass (*say* **base**) *noun* the lowest part sung or played in music; **bass** *adjective* ⚠ **base**

bassoon *noun* a musical instrument with a low sound, that is played by blowing

bassoon

¹**bat** *noun* a wooden stick used for hitting a ball in various games; **bat** *verb*; **batsman** *noun*; **batter** *noun*

²**bat** *noun* a flying mammal like a mouse, that is active at night

bath *noun* a large water container in which you can wash your whole body; **bath** *verb*

bathe *verb* **1** to go swimming; **2** to pour water or other liquid over; **bathe** *noun*; **bather** *noun*

bathroom *noun* a room where people wash or have a bath

battery *noun* an object that produces or stores electricity

battle *noun* a fight between enemies; a struggle; **battle** *verb*

bay *noun* a part of the shore which curves inwards

be *verb* (**am, are, is, being, was, were, been, aren't, isn't, wasn't, weren't**) **1** to exist; to live; **2** to become; **3** to belong to the group of; **4** to take place; to occur; **5** to have a particular quality, job, purpose, position, cost, etc; ⚠ **bee**

beach *noun* a shore covered in sand or stones and used for swimming and sunbathing; ⚠ **beech**

bead *noun* a small ball of glass or other material which can be threaded onto a string to make a necklace, etc

beak *noun* the hard horny mouth of a bird

¹**beam** *noun* a large long heavy piece of wood, steel, or concrete, used to support a building

²**beam** *noun* a line of light shining from something bright

³**beam** *verb* **1** to send out light; to shine; **2** to smile brightly and happily

bean *noun* **1** the seed of a climbing plant, often used as food; **2** a seed of some other plants, from which food or drink can be made: **coffee bean**; ⚠ **been**

polar bear

¹**bear** *noun* a large and heavy animal with thick rough fur; ⚠ **bare**

²**bear** *verb* (**bears, bearing, bore, borne**) **1** to carry; to support; **2** to give birth; **3** to suffer; ⚠ **bare**

beard *noun* hair on the face mostly below the mouth; **bearded** *adjective*

¹**beat** *verb* (**beats, beating, beat, beaten** *or* **beat**) **1** to do better than; **2** to move regularly; **3** to hit many times

²**beat** *noun* **1** a repeated hit, stroke, or blow; **2** time in music or poetry

beautiful *adjective* very goodlooking; very pleasing; **beautifully** *adverb*; **beauty** *noun*

beaver *noun* a fur covered animal with a broad flat tail, that builds dams across streams

because *conjunction* for the reason that

become *verb* (**becomes, becoming, became, become**) to come to be

bed *noun* **1** an article of furniture to sleep on: **bedroom, bedclothes**; **2** a piece of ground prepared for plants; **3** the bottom of a river, lake, or sea

bee *noun* an insect that makes honey, often lives in groups, and can sting painfully; ⚠ **be**

beech *noun* a tree with a smooth grey trunk, spreading branches, and dark green or copper coloured leaves; ⚠ **beach**

beef *noun* the meat of farm cattle

beehive *noun see* HIVE

been *see* BE; ⚠ **bean**

beer *noun* a drink made from grain

beetle *noun* an insect with hard wing coverings

beetroot *noun* a plant with a large round red root, cooked and eaten as a vegetable

before *preposition, adverb* **1** at an earlier time than; **2** in front of; ahead

beg *verb* (**begged**) to ask for food, money, etc; **beggar** *noun*

begin *verb* (**begins, beginning, began, begun**) to start

behave *verb* to act in a good or bad way; **behaviour** *noun*

behind *preposition, adverb* **1** to or at the back of; where something or somebody was earlier; **2** late

being *noun* a living thing, especially a person

b

b

belief *noun* the feeling that something is true or real; trust; **believable** *adjective*; **believably** *adverb*; **believe** *verb*

bell *noun* a round hollow metal object, that makes a ringing sound when struck

belong *verb* **1** to be your own; **2** to be a part or member of

below *preposition, adverb* in or at a lower place than; underneath

belt *noun* a piece of cloth or leather worn round the waist

bench *noun* a long seat for two or more people

bend *verb* **(bends, bending, bent)** to force something into or out of a curve or angle; **bend** *noun*

beneath *preposition* in or at a lower position than; below

²**best** *noun* **1** something that is the most good; **2** your greatest, highest, or finest effort, state, or performance

bet *verb* **(bets, betting, bet** *or* **betted)** to risk money on the result of a future event; **bet** *noun*

better *see* GOOD, WELL

between *preposition* **1** in the space or at the time separating; **2** as a connection of; **3** with a part for each of

beyond *preposition, adverb* **1** on or to the further side of; **2** later than; **3** out of reach of; much more than

Bible *noun* the holy book of the Christians, consisting of the *Old Testament* and the *New Testament*; **biblical** *adjective*

tandem – a bicycle for two people

beret (*say* **beray**) *noun* a round soft flat hat

berry *noun* a small soft fruit; ⚠ **bury**

berth *noun* **1** a place where a ship can be tied up, as in a harbour; **2** a sleeping place in a ship or a train; ⚠ **birth**

beside *preposition* at or close to the side of

besides *adverb, preposition* as well; also

¹**best** *see* GOOD, WELL

bicycle *also* **cycle** *or* **bike** *noun* a two-wheeled vehicle which you pedal with your feet; **bicyclist** *noun*

big *adjective* **(bigger)** large in size, weight, importance, etc

big bang theory *noun* the idea that everything in the universe began with the explosion of a single piece of material so that the pieces of it are still flying apart

16

bill *noun* **1** a list of things bought and their price; **2** a plan for a new law

billiards *noun* a game played on a cloth-covered table with balls knocked against one another using special sticks (cues)

billion *adjective, noun* the number 1,000,000,000 (a thousand million); **billionth** *adjective, noun* (a billion once meant a million million, but this is no longer in current use)

bin *noun* a large wide container with a lid for bread, flour, etc, or for waste

binary (*say* **bye-nary**) *adjective* using the numbers 0 and 1 only, as computers do

bingo *noun* a game played by covering numbered squares on a card

binoculars *noun (plural)* a pair of special glasses used for looking at objects in the distance

biology *noun* the scientific study of living things; **biological** *adjective*; **biologically** *adverb*; **biologist** *noun*

birch *noun* a tree with smooth wood and thin branches

bird *noun* a creature with wings and feathers that lays eggs

birth *noun* the act or time of being born; ⚠ **berth**

birthday *noun* the date on which you were born

biscuit *noun* any of many types of flat thin dry cake

bishop *noun* a priest in charge of other priests

¹bit *noun* **1** a small piece, quantity, or amount; **2** the smallest piece of information which can be held on a computer

²bit *noun* **1** a metal bar put in the mouth of a horse as part of a bridle and used for controlling its movements; **2** a part of a tool for making holes

bitch *noun* a female dog

¹bite *verb* (**bites, biting, bit, bitten**) to cut or wound with the teeth; ⚠ **byte**

²bite *noun* **1** an act of biting **2** a piece bitten off; **3** a wound made by biting; ⚠ **byte**

an archbishop is in charge of other bishops

b

bitter *adjective* **1** having a sharp, sour taste; **2** very cold; **3** causing anger, pain, or sadness; **bitterly** *adverb*; **bitterness** *noun*

black *noun* **1** the colour of coal; the darkest colour; **2** a person with dark-coloured skin; **black** *adjective*; **blackness** *noun*

black hole *noun* a part of outer space containing a star whose gravity is so strong that not even light can escape from it

blade *noun* **1** the flat cutting part of a knife, sword, or other cutting tool; **2** a long flat leaf of grass

blame *verb* to say that somebody is the cause of something bad; **blame** *noun*

blanket *noun* a thick warm cloth made of wool, used as a cover on a bed

blazer *noun* a jacket, sometimes with the badge of a school, club, etc, on it

bleach *verb* to make something white; **bleach** *noun*

bleed *verb* **(bleeds, bleeding, bled)** to lose blood

bless *verb* **1** to ask God's favour for something; **2** to make holy; **blessing** *noun*

blew *see* BLOW; ⚠ **blue**

¹blind *adjective* unable to see; **blind** *verb*; **blindly** *adverb*; **blindness** *noun*

²blind *noun* a covering for a window, made of cloth or other material

blink *verb* to shut and open the eyes quickly; **blink** *noun*

¹block *noun* **1** a large piece of wood, stone, etc; **2** a large building divided into separate flats or offices; **3** a building or group of buildings between two streets; **4** something that gets in the way

²block *verb* to prevent movement

blond feminine **blonde** *adjective* with light-coloured hair and fair skin

blood *noun* red liquid which carries oxygen to all parts of the body and is pumped round by the heart; **bloody** *adjective*

apple blossom

blossom *noun* the flowers of a flowering tree or bush

¹blot *noun* a mark that spoils something or makes it dirty

²blot *verb* **(blotted) 1** to make blots; **2** to dry or remove with special paper **(blotting paper)**

blouse *noun* a loose piece of clothing for women, reaching from the neck to the waist

¹blow *verb* **(blows, blowing, blew, blown) 1** to move by a current of air; **2** to send air out quickly from your mouth or nose; **3** to force air into or through something; **4 blow up** to break by exploding

b

[2]**blow** *noun* **1** a hard hit with the hand, a weapon, etc; **2** a shock

blue *noun* the colour of the clear sky on a fine day; **blue** *adjective*; **blueness** *noun*; **bluish** *adjective*; ⚠ **blew**

blunt *adjective* **1** not sharp; **2** rough and plain, without trying to be polite or kind; **bluntness** *noun*; **bluntly** *adverb*

blush *verb* to become red in the face because you feel shy

[1]**board** *noun* **1** a thin flat piece of cut wood; **2** a stiff flat surface used for a special purpose: **chessboard, dartboard, noticeboard; 3** a group of people with a special job, like running a company; **4** the cost of meals; **5 on board** or **aboard** in or on a ship or public vehicle

[2]**board** *verb* **1** to go on board a ship or public vehicle; **2** to cover with wooden boards; **3** to get or supply meals and somewhere to live for payment; **boarder** *noun*

boast *verb* to praise yourself; **boaster** *noun*; **boastful** *adjective*

boat *noun* a small open ship

body *noun* **1** the whole of a person or animal, but not the mind; **2** this without the head or limbs; **3** a dead person or animal; **4** a number of people who do something together; **5** a person: **anybody, nobody, somebody**

bog *noun* an area of soft wet ground

[1]**boil** *noun* a painful swelling under the skin

[2]**boil** *verb* **1** to make liquid so hot that it gives off steam; **2** to cook food in boiling water

bold *adjective* daring; brave; without fear; **boldly** *adverb*; **boldness** *noun*

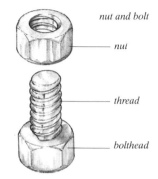

nut and bolt

nut

thread

bolthead

[1]**bolt** *noun* **1** a metal bar that slides across to fasten a door or window; **2** a screw with no point

[2]**bolt** *verb* **1** to fasten with a bolt; **2** to swallow quickly; **3** to run away suddenly, as if frightened

[1]**bomb** *noun* a hollow container filled with materials that will explode

[2]**bomb** *verb* to attack with bombs, especially by dropping them from aircraft

bone *noun* one of the hard white parts of the body, round which are the flesh and skin; **boneless** *adjective*; **bony** *adjective*

bonfire *noun* a large fire built in the open air

bonnet *noun* **1** a metal lid over the front of a car; **2** a round hat tied under the chin

¹**book** *noun* a collection of sheets of paper fastened together as a thing to be read, or to be written in: **bookcase, bookmark, book token**

²**book** *verb* to arrange to have or do something later; **bookable** *adjective*; **booking** *noun*

riding boots

boot *noun* **1** a shoe of leather, rubber, etc, with a part that covers the ankle; **2** a space at the back of a car for luggage

border *noun* **1** an edge; **2** the dividing line between two countries; △ **boarder**

¹**bore** *verb* to make somebody feel not interested, by something dull; **boredom** *noun*; **boring** *adjective*

²**bore** *noun* a person or thing that is dull or uninteresting

³**bore** *verb* to make a round hole or passage in or through something; **borer** *noun*

⁴**bore** *see* BEAR

born *adjective* **1** given life; **2** at birth; originally; △ **borne**

borne *see* BEAR; △ **born**

borrow *verb* to get the use of something which you are going to give back later; **borrower** *noun*; **borrowing** *noun*

botany *noun* the scientific study of plants; **botanist** *noun*

both *pronoun, adjective* the two; this one and the other

bottle *noun* a tall round container, usually of glass or plastic, with a narrow neck

bottom *noun* **1** the base on which something stands; the lowest part; **2** the part of the body on which you sit

bough (*say like* how) *noun* a branch of a tree; △ **bow**

bought *see* BUY

bounce *verb* **1** to spring back or up again from the ground or something hard; to make something do this; **2** to jump or spring up and down; **bounce** *noun;* **bouncily** *adverb;* **bounciness** *noun;* **bouncy** *adjective*

¹**bound** *adjective* **1** fastened; **2** certain to; sure to; **3** going towards

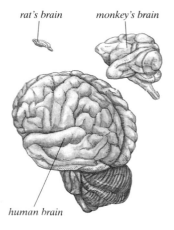

rat's brain   *monkey's brain*

human brain

²bound *verb* to jump or bounce

¹bow (*say like* **how**) *verb* to bend the head or upper part of the body forward to show respect; **bow** *noun*; **bowed** *adjective*; ⚠ **bough**

²bow (*say like* **go**) *noun*
1 a piece of wood held in a curve by a tight string and used for shooting arrows; **2** a knot with loops; **3** a long thin piece of wood with stretched horsehairs fastened along it, used for playing stringed instruments

¹bowl *noun* a deep round container for holding liquids, flowers, sugar, etc; **bowlful** *noun*

²bowl *verb* **1** to throw the ball towards the batsman in cricket or rounders; **2** to play the games of **bowls** or **bowling**

¹box *noun* a container made from wood, cardboard, plastic, or metal, with stiff sides and a lid

²box *verb* to fight somebody or hit with the fists; **boxer** *noun*; **boxing** *noun*

boy *noun* a young male person; ⚠ **buoy**

bra *noun* a piece of women's underwear worn to support the breasts

bracelet *noun* a band or ring worn round the wrist or arm as an ornament

bracket *noun* **1** a piece of metal or wood put on a wall to support something; **2** a pair of signs (—) or [—] used round a piece of information

¹brain *noun* the organ inside the head with which you think and feel

²brain *verb* (slang) to hit hard on the head

¹brake *noun* something for slowing down or stopping a car, bicycle, train, etc; ⚠ **break**

²brake *verb* to use brakes; ⚠ **break**

¹branch *noun* **1** a stem growing from the trunk of a tree or from another stem; **2** a part of a company, shop, etc

²branch *verb* to become divided into two parts

brass *noun* **1** a very hard bright yellow metal; **2** musical instruments made of this metal, such as a trumpet

brave *adjective* having courage and ready to go through danger or pain; **bravely** *adverb*; **bravery** *noun*

bread *noun* a common food made of baked flour

breadth *noun* the distance from side to side; width

¹break *verb* **(breaks, breaking broke, broken) 1** to cause to fall to pieces; **2** to fall to pieces; ⚠ **brake**

²break *noun* **1** an opening made by breaking or being broken; **2** a pause for rest; ⚠ **brake**

breakfast *noun* the first meal of the day

breast *noun* **1** either of the two parts of a woman's body that produce milk; **2** the upper front part of the body between the neck and the stomach

breath *noun* air taken into and let out of the body; **breathless** *adjective:* out of breath

breathe *verb* to take air into the body and let it out; **breathing** *noun*

¹breed *verb* **(breeds, breeding, bred) 1** to produce young; **2** to keep animals so that they will produce young ones

²breed *noun* a type of animal

brick *noun* a hard piece of baked clay used for building

bridge *noun* something built over a valley, river, etc, so that people, a road, etc, can go over it

bridle *noun* leather bands on a horse's head for controlling it

brief *adjective* lasting a short time

bright *adjective* **1** giving out or throwing back light very strongly; **2** having a strong clear colour; **3** clever; quick at learning; **brightly** *adverb*; **brightness** *noun*

bring *verb* **(brings, bringing, brought) 1** to fetch, carry, or take with you; **2** to cause or lead to

broad *adjective* wide **broadly** *adverb*; **broadness** *noun*

broadcast *verb* to send out by radio or television; **broadcast** *noun*; **broadcaster** *noun*

broke *see* BREAK

broken *adjective* **1** in pieces; **2** not working

brooch *noun* an ornament worn on women's clothes, fastened by a pin

broom *noun* a brush with a long handle

brother *noun* a boy or man with the same parents as another person

brought *see* BRING

brown *noun, adjective* the colour of earth; **brownish** *adjective*

a suspension bridge –
Pont de Normandie, France

bruise *noun* a mark left on the skin where it has been hit; **bruise** *verb*

¹**brush** *noun* an object for cleaning, smoothing, or painting, made of sticks, stiff hair, nylon, etc; hairbrush

²**brush** *verb* to clean or smooth with a brush

¹**bubble** *noun* a hollow ball of liquid containing air or gas; **bubbly** *adjective*

²**bubble** *verb* to make bubbles

buck *noun* the male of certain animals, such as the deer and the rabbit

bucket *noun* a round open metal or plastic container with a handle, for holding or carrying water, coal, etc

buckle *noun* a fastener for joining the ends of two straps

bud *noun* a flower or leaf before it opens

budgerigar

budgerigar also **budgie** *noun* a small brightly coloured bird often kept in a cage

buffalo *noun* a large wild ox that is black and has long curved horns

bug *noun* **1** a small insect; **2** a mistake or fault in a computer program

buggy *noun* a light folding chair with wheels for taking a baby or child out

build *verb* (**builds, building, built**) to make by putting pieces together; **builder** *noun*; **building** *noun*

bulb *noun* **1** a round root of certain plants; **2** the glass part of an electric lamp that gives out light

bull *noun* the male form of cattle and some other animals

bulldozer *noun* a powerful machine used for pushing heavy objects, earth, etc, out of the way

bullet *noun* a type of shot fired from a gun

bully *noun* somebody who likes to hurt or frighten weaker people; **bully** *verb*

¹**bump** *verb* to hit or knock against something

²**bump** *noun* **1** a sudden hit or knock; **2** a raised round swelling; **bumpy** *adjective*

bun *noun* a small round sweet cake

bunch *noun* a number of things fastened or growing together

bundle *noun* a number of things tied together

bungalow *noun* a house all on ground level

bunk also **bunk bed** *noun* a bed fixed to the wall (as on a ship); **bunk beds** *noun* two beds one above the other

b

b

buoy *noun* a floating object fastened to the bed of the sea to show ships where there are rocks; ⚠ **boy**

burglar *noun* a thief who breaks into houses, shops, etc; **burglary** *noun*

¹**burn** *verb* (**burns, burning, burnt** *or* **burned**) **1** to be on fire; **2** to hurt, damage, or destroy by fire

²**burn** *noun* a hurt place produced by burning

burrow *noun* a hole in the ground made by an animal, in which it lives or hides

burst *verb* (**bursts, bursting, burst**) **1** to break suddenly because of the pressure inside; **2** to do something suddenly

bury *verb* **1** to put a dead person into the ground; **2** to hide away; ⚠ **berry**

bus *noun* a large motor vehicle for carrying passengers

bush *noun* a small low tree; **bushy** *adjective*

business *noun* **1** a person's work; **2** trade and the getting of money: **businessman, businesswoman**; **3** an activity, such as a shop, that earns money; **4** a personal or private thing that concerns you; **businesslike** *adjective*

busy *adjective* having a lot to do; **busily** *adverb*

but *conjunction* only; except that

butcher *noun* a person in a shop who sells meat

butter *noun* **1** yellow fat made from milk; **2** a substance like butter: **peanut butter**; **buttery** *adjective*

buttercup *noun* a yellow wild flower

butterfly *noun* an insect with four often beautifully coloured wings

Red Admiral butterfly

Peacock butterfly

button *noun* **1** a small usually round or flat thing fixed to a piece of clothing and passed through a **buttonhole** to act as a fastener; **2** a knob or object like a button, for starting, stopping, or controlling a machine

buy *verb* (**buys, buying, bought**) to get something by giving money; **buyer** *noun;* ⚠ **by**

buzz *verb* to make a low steady noise, as bees do; **buzz** *noun;* **buzzer** *noun*

by *preposition* **1** near; beside; **2** by way of; through; ⚠ **buy**

byte *noun* an amount of information stored in a computer, equal to eight bits; ⚠ **bite**

Cc

cabbage *noun* a large round vegetable with thick green leaves used as food

cabin *noun* **1** a small room on a ship; **2** a small wooden house

cable *noun* **1** a thick, heavy strong rope, wire, or chain; **2** a set of wires laid underground and used for carrying electricity, telephone calls, and television programmes: **cable TV**

cactus *noun* (*plural* **cacti** or **cactuses**) a prickly plant with thick leaves and stems, that grows in hot dry places

café (*say* **caffay**) *noun* a small restaurant where you can buy drinks and light meals

cage *noun* a box made of wires or bars in which animals or birds may be kept

cake *noun* a food made by mixing flour, eggs, sugar, etc, and baked

Scottish medieval cannon – Mons Meg

calculate *verb* to work out by using numbers; **calculation** *noun*; **calculator** *noun*

calendar *noun* a set of tables or sheets of paper showing the days, weeks, and months of the year

calf *noun* (*plural* **calves**) the young of the cow or some other large animals

¹**call** *verb* **1** to name; **2** to shout; to cry out; **3** to make a short visit; **4** to telephone somebody

²**call** *noun* **1** a telephone conversation; **2** a shout; **3** a short visit

calm *adjective* peaceful; quiet; not worried; **calmly** *adverb*; **calmness** *noun*

came *see* COME

camel *noun* a large long-necked animal used for riding or carrying goods in desert countries. The *dromedary* has one hump and the *Bactrian camel* has two humps.

camera *noun* an instrument for taking photographs or filming

¹**camp** *noun* a place with tents or huts where people live for a short time or spend their holidays

²**camp** *verb* **1** to make a camp; **2** to sleep in a tent; **camper** *noun*; **camping** *noun*

¹**can** *verb* (**could, cannot, can't**) to know how to; to be able to

²**can** *noun* a tin in which foods are stored

canal *noun* a man-made river

canary *noun* a small yellow bird often kept as a pet

candle *noun* a wax stick with a string in the middle which gives light when it burns

cannon *noun* a large and powerful gun

cannot can not

canoe *noun* a long light narrow boat, pointed at both ends, and moved by a paddle; **canoeist** *noun*

can't *see* CAN

cap *noun* **1** a soft flat hat; **2** a covering for the end of a bottle or tube

capital *noun* **1** the chief city of a country, where the government is; **2** a large letter, such as A, B, or C

captain *noun* **1** the leader of a team or group; **2** the person in command of a ship or aircraft; **3** an officer in the armed forces

caravan *noun* **1** a small house on wheels which can be pulled by a car or horse; **2** a group of people travelling together through desert areas

card *noun* **1** also **playing card** one of a pack of 52 small sheets of stiffened paper marked to show number and suit and used for various games; **2** a piece of stiffened paper, usually with a picture on the front and a message inside, sent to a person on a birthday, at Christmas, etc; a **postcard**

cardboard *noun* a stiff material like thick paper, used for making boxes, book covers, etc; cardboard city: where the homeless live

cardigan *noun* a knitted woollen jacket with sleeves

¹**care** *noun* **1** looking after somebody or something; protection; **2** thought; serious attention; **3** something that makes you worried or sad; **careful** *adjective*; **carefully** *adverb*; **careless** *adjective*; **carelessly** *adverb*; **carelessness** *noun*

²**care** *verb* **1** to be worried or concerned about something; to look after somebody; **2** to like; to want

carol *noun* a religious song sung especially at Christmas

carpenter *noun* a person who makes and repairs wooden objects; **carpentry** *noun*

carpet *noun* a piece of heavy woven material for covering the floor of a room

carriage *noun* **1** a vehicle with wheels that is pulled by horses; **2** a part of a train in which you sit; **3** the way in which people stand, sit or move

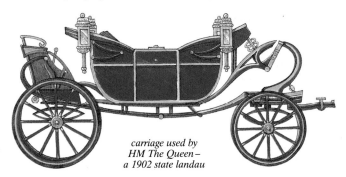

*carriage used by
HM The Queen –
a 1902 state landau*

carrot *noun* a vegetable with a long orange-red root

carry *verb* to take up somebody or something in your arms, on your back, etc, and move them from one place to another; **carrier** *noun*

cart *noun* a wooden vehicle pulled by an animal and used for carrying goods

cartoon *noun* **1** a funny drawing; **2** a film made by photographing a set of drawings

cartridge *noun* **1** a metal or paper tube containing explosive for use in a gun; **2** a small plastic container that holds ink for use in a *cartridge pen*

carve *verb* **1** to cut wood or stone in order to make a special shape; **2** to cut meat into pieces or slices; **carver** *noun*

¹**case** *noun* **1** an example of something; a particular occasion; a state or condition; **2** a question to be decided in a court of law; the facts and arguments used on each side

²**case** *noun* a container in which things can be stored or moved; a **suitcase** or **packing case**

cassette *noun* a small flat plastic case containing tape for use in a tape recorder or *cassette recorder*

¹**cast** *noun* **1** all the actors and actresses in a play, film, etc; **2** an act of throwing

²**cast** *verb* **1** to make a spell and put it into effect; **2** to throw or drop; to throw off; **3** to make an object by pouring hot metal or plastic into a special shape *(mould)*

castle *noun* a large strong building with thick walls and towers

casual *adjective* **1** not planned or arranged; **2** clothing worn when people are not at work or school; **casual** *adverb*

cat *noun (young* **kitten***)* a small animal with soft fur and sharp teeth and claws, often kept as a pet

¹**catch** *verb* **(catches, catching, caught) 1** to get in your hand and hold; **2** to run after and take hold of an animal, person, or thing; **3** to get an illness; **catcher** *noun*

²**catch** *noun* **1** something that is caught; **2** a hook or fastener for a door, window, etc

hawkmoth caterpillar

caterpillar *noun* an early stage in the life of a butterfly or moth which is like a small worm with short legs

cathedral *noun* the chief church of a city

cattle *noun* large four-legged animals, especially cows

caught *see* CATCH; △ **court**

cauliflower *noun* a vegetable with green leaves around a large white head of flowers

cause *noun* a person, thing, or event that makes something happen; a reason; **cause** *verb*

cave *noun* a deep hollow place in the side of a cliff or hill or underground

CD *noun* a thin plastic disc used to play recorded music: a **CD** *player*

CD-ROM *noun* a thin plastic disc used to store computer information and for computer games

ceiling *noun* the inside of the top of a room

celery *noun* a vegetable with greenish white stems used as food

cellar *noun* an underground room used for storing goods; ⚠ **seller**

cello (*say* **chello**) *noun* a large violin with a deep sound, that is played held between the knees

cello

Celsius *adjective* the scale of temperature in which water freezes at 0° and boils at 100°; compare FAHRENHEIT

cement *noun* a grey powder that becomes like stone when mixed with water and allowed to dry

cent *noun* a coin worth 0.01 of a dollar; ⚠ **scent, sent**

centimetre *noun* a measure of length equal to 0.01 metres or 0.394 inches

centipede *noun* a creature like an insect, with a long body and many pairs of legs

central heating *noun* a way of heating a building in which heat is produced in one place and carried by pipes to the other parts of the building

centre *noun* **1** the middle; **2** a place where a lot of people come for a special purpose: **Health Centre, shopping centre; central** *adjective*

century *noun* a period of 100 years

cereal *noun* **1** any kind of grain, such as wheat, oats, and rice; **2** food made from grain, usually eaten at breakfast; ⚠ **serial**

ceremony *noun* a special set of actions used for marking an important event, occasion, or happening

¹**certain** *adjective* sure; **certainly** *adverb*

²**certain** *adjective* some

chain *noun* a length of metal rings joined to one another

chair *noun* a piece of furniture to sit on, which usually has a back, seat, four legs, and sometimes arms: **rocking chair**

chalk *noun* **1** a soft white material formed from the shells of very small sea animals; **2** a piece of this material, white or coloured, used for writing or drawing; **chalky** *adjective*

challenge *verb* **1** to offer to fight or play a game against; **2** to test or question; **challenge** *noun*

chance *noun* **1** an opportunity; a time when something may be done; **2** something which happens without cause; luck; **3** something which may or may not happen; **4** a risk

¹**change** *verb* **1** to make or become different; **2** to give, take, or put something in place of something else; **3** to put on different clothes

²**change** *noun* **1** something that has become different; **2** the money returned when you give too much for something

channel *noun* **1** a narrow piece of water joining two seas; **2** a way along which water can flow; **3** a band of television or radio waves

chapel *noun* a small church, or part of a church

character *noun* **1** the qualities and nature of somebody or something; **2** a person in a book, play, etc

¹**charge** *verb* **1** to ask money for; **2** to say that a person has done something wrong; **3** to run or hurry

²**charge** *noun* **1** a price asked for something; **2** a statement that a person has done wrong; **3** a hurried attack; **4** *in charge of* responsible for; caring for or looking after

chase *verb* to run after; **chase** *noun*

cheap *adjective* costing only little money; **cheaply** *adverb*

¹**cheat** *noun* **1** a dishonest person; **2** a trick

²**cheat** *verb* to trick somebody; to do something which is dishonest

¹**check** *verb* to make sure that something is right; ⚠ **cheque**

²**check** *noun* **1** an act of checking; **2** a pattern of squares; ⚠ **cheque**

cheek *noun* **1** the fleshy part of the face on either side under the eyes; **2** rudeness

cheer *verb* **1** to shout because you are pleased; **2** to make happy; **cheer** *noun*

cheerful *adjective* happy; **cheerfully** *adverb*; **cheerfulness** *noun*

Dutch Gouda cheese

cheese *noun* solid food made from milk

cheetah *noun* a spotted wild animal of the cat family, that can run very fast

chef (*say* **shef**) *noun* a head cook in a hotel or restaurant

chemist (*say* **kemist**) *noun* a person who owns or runs a shop where medicines are sold

chemistry *noun* a science which studies substances like gases, liquids, metals, etc; **chemical** *adjective, noun*

cheque *noun* a specially printed order form to a bank to pay money; ⚠ **check**

cherry *noun* a small red round fruit with a seed like a stone; the tree on which this grows

chess *noun* a game for two players, with 16 pieces, or **chessmen** each, which are moved across a square **chessboard** with 64 black and white squares

chest *noun* **1** the upper front part of the body; **2** a large strong box

chestnut *noun* **1** a reddish brown nut; the tree on which this grows; **2** a reddish brown colour

chest of drawers *noun* a piece of furniture with drawers

chew *verb* to crush food with the teeth

chick *noun* the young of a bird, especially a chicken

chicken *noun* a bird kept by people for its eggs and meat

chicken pox *noun* a disease, caught especially by children, causing fever and spots

¹**chief** *noun* a leader; a ruler; the head of a party, group, etc

²**chief** *adjective* the most important; **chiefly** *adverb*

child *noun* (*plural* **children**) a boy or girl; a son or daughter; **childhood** *noun;* **childish**, **childlike** *adjective*

chimney *noun* a hollow passage for taking away smoke from a fireplace

chimpanzee

chimpanzee *noun* a large ape

chin *noun* the front part of the face below the mouth

china *noun* **1** a hard white substance made by baking fine clay at high temperatures; **2** plates, cups, etc, made from this

chip *noun* **1** a small piece of brick, wood, paint, etc, broken off; **2** a long thin piece of potato cooked in deep fat; **3** a tiny piece of metal or plastic used in computers to store information or make the computer work; **chip** *verb*

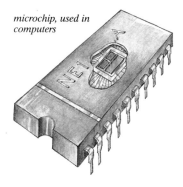
microchip, used in computers

chocolate *noun* a sweet or food made from cocoa

choice *noun* the act of choosing; somebody or something chosen

choir (*say* **kwire**) *noun* a group of people who sing together

choke *verb* to have difficulty or stop breathing because of something blocking your throat

choose *verb* (**chooses, choosing, chose, chosen**) to pick out from a number of things or people the one you want

¹chop *verb* (**chopping**) to cut with an axe or sharp knife

²chop *noun* a slice of meat containing a bone

chose *see* CHOOSE

chosen *see* CHOOSE

Christian *noun* a person who believes in Jesus Christ; **Christianity** *noun*

Christmas also **Christmas Day** *noun* 25th December; the day on which Jesus Christ is said to have been born

church *noun* a building in which Christians meet to pray to God

cider (*say* **syder**) *noun* a drink made from apple juice

cigarette *noun* a narrow tube of thin paper filled with finely cut tobacco for smoking

cinema *noun* a building in which films are shown

circle *noun* **1** a perfectly round, closed, curved line; a ring; **2** a group of people; **circle** *verb*; **circular** *adjective*

circuit (*say* **sir-kit**) *noun* the path of an electric current

circus *noun* a show given by performers and trained animals, often in a large tent

city *noun* a large and important town, often having a cathedral

claim *verb* **1** to ask for something that you say belongs to you; **2** to say that something is true; **claim** *noun*

¹clap *verb* (**clapping**) to hit the palms of your hands together loudly when you are pleased by a musical performance, etc

²clap *noun* **1** the sound of clapping; **2** a loud noise: *a **clap** of thunder*

clarinet *noun* a musical instrument that you blow

class *noun* **1** a group of people who are taught together or the time during which they are taught: **classroom**; **2** a group of people or things of the same kind

claw *noun* a sharp curved nail on the toe of an animal or bird; **claw** *verb*

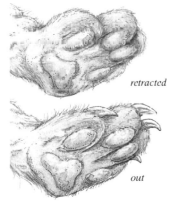

cat's claws

retracted

out

31

clay *noun* heavy earth, used for making bricks, pots, etc, when baked

¹**clean** *adjective* not dirty; **cleanness** *noun*; **cleanly** *adverb*

²**clean** *verb* to make or become clean; **cleaner** *noun*

¹**clear** *adjective* **1** easy to see through: **clear** *glass*; **2** easily heard, seen, read, or understood; **3** open; not having anything in the way; **4** bright; sunny and not cloudy; **clearly** *adverb*; **clearness** *noun*

²**clear** *verb* **1** to make or become clear; **2** to take things away

clever *adjective* quick at learning and understanding; **cleverly** *adverb*; **cleverness** *noun*

cliff *noun* a high steep piece of land close to the sea

climb (*say* **clime**) *verb* to go up, over, or through using the hands and feet; **climb** *noun*; **climber** *noun*

cling *verb* (**clings, clinging, clung**) to hold on tightly

¹**clip** *noun* a small plastic or metal object for holding things together

²**clip** *verb* **1** to hold with a clip; **2** to cut with scissors or another sharp instrument

clock *noun* an instrument for measuring and showing time

clockwise *adjective, adverb* in the same direction as the movement of the hands of a clock; circular movement to the left

¹**close** (*say like* **doze**) *verb* to shut

²**close** (*say like* **dose**) *adjective* near; not far away; **closely** *adverb*; **closeness** *noun*

cloth *noun* **1** material made from wool, cotton, etc, by weaving, and used for making clothes, covers, etc; **2** a piece of this used for a special purpose: **tablecloth, dishcloth**

clothes *noun* the things you wear

clothing *noun* clothes worn together on different parts of the body

cumulus clouds mean fine weather

cloud *noun* **1** a mass of very small drops of water floating high in the sky; **2** a mass of dust, smoke, etc, which floats in the air; **cloudy** *adjective*

clown *noun* a person, especially in the circus, who makes people laugh

club *noun* **1** a group of people who join together for sport, amusement, etc; **2** a heavy wooden stick; **3** a playing card with one or more three-leafed figures printed on it in black (♣)

clue *noun* something that helps to find an answer to a question, difficulty, etc

clumsy *adjective* knocking things over; awkward or careless; **clumsily** *adverb*; **clumsiness** *noun*

clung *see* CLING

¹**coach** *noun* **1** a bus used for long-distance travel; **2** a railway carriage; **3** a large four-wheeled vehicle pulled by horses; **4** somebody who trains sports people, students, etc

²**coach** *verb* to train or teach a person or group

coal *noun* a black or dark brown material dug out of the earth, that can be burned to give heat

coarse *adjective* not fine or smooth; rough; **coarsely** *adverb*; **coarseness** *noun*; ⚠ **course**

coast *noun* the land next to the sea

coat *noun* **1** a piece of clothing with long sleeves, worn for warmth; **2** an animal's fur, wool, hair, etc

cobweb *noun* a very fine net of sticky threads made by a spider to catch insects

garden spider's web

cock *noun* a fully grown male bird, especially a chicken

cocoa *noun* **1** a dark brown powder made by crushing the cooked seeds of the *cacao tree*, used for giving foods and drinks a chocolate flavour; **2** a drink made from hot milk or water mixed with this powder

coconut *noun* a large brown nut with a thick hard shell, white flesh, and a hollow centre filled with a milky juice

cod *noun* a type of large sea fish used for food

code *noun* a way of using words, letters, numbers, etc, to keep messages secret

coffee *noun* **1** a brown powder made by crushing the beans of the coffee tree, used for making drinks or flavouring food; **2** a drink made by adding hot water and/or milk to this powder

coffin *noun* a box in which a dead person is buried

¹**coil** *verb* to wind into a set of rings one above the other

²**coil** *noun* **1** a connected set of rings into which a rope, wire, etc, can be wound; **2** a single one of these rings

coin *noun* a flat round piece of metal, made by a government for use as money

¹**cold** *adjective* having very little heat; not warm; **coldly** *adverb*; **coldness** *noun*

²**cold** *noun* **1** the absence of heat; cold weather; **2** an illness of the nose and/or throat

c

collar *noun* **1** the part of a shirt, dress, or coat that stands up or folds down round the neck; **2** a leather or metal band round an animal's neck

collect *verb* to gather together; **collection** *noun*; **collector** *noun*

college *noun* a place where people study after they have left school

come *verb* (**comes, coming, came, come**) **1** to move towards the person speaking, or a particular place; **2** to arrive; **3** to happen; **4** to become; **5 come to** to reach; to add up to something; **6 come from** to be made by; to be born or live in

comedian feminine **comedienne** *noun* a person who tells jokes, does amusing things, or acts in funny plays and films

Halley's comet can be seen from Earth about every 76 years

¹**colour** *noun* **1** the quality which allows the eyes to see the difference between (for example) a red and a blue flower of the same size and shape; **2** red, blue, green, black, yellow, white, etc; **colourful** *adjective*; **colouring** *noun*; **colourless** *adjective:* without colour

²**colour** *verb* to put colour into a drawing

comb (*say like* **home**) *noun* a piece of bone, metal, plastic, etc, with thin teeth, used for tidying the hair; **comb** *verb*

comet *noun* an object in space, with a bright head and a long, burning tail, that moves round the sun

¹**comfort** *noun* **1** freedom from pain, trouble, etc; **2** help, kindness, etc, given to somebody who is sad, ill, in pain, etc; **comfortable** *adjective*; **comfortably** *adverb*

²**comfort** *verb* to give comfort to; to cheer up; **comforter** *noun*

comic *noun* **1** a magazine for children containing stories told in drawings; **2** a person who is amusing; a comedian

comma *noun* the mark (,) used in writing and printing to separate parts of a sentence

¹command *verb* **1** to order; **2** to be in charge of; **commander** *noun*

²command *noun* **1** an order; **2** power; control

common *adjective* **1** ordinary; usual; **2** belonging to or shared by two or more people; **3** found or happening often and in many places

communicate *verb* to make known; to pass on or send information

communication *noun* **1** the sending on of a piece of information, news, etc; **2 communications** roads, railways, phones, television, or other ways of sending information, moving goods, or travelling to other places

community *noun* a group of people who live together or near one another and/or who may share the same interests or beliefs

compact disc *noun* a CD or CD ROM

company *noun* **1** a group of people doing business; a firm; **2** people to be with

compare *verb* to see if things are alike or different; **comparison** *noun*; ⚠ **compere**

compass *noun* an instrument for showing direction, usually with a needle which always points to the north

compere *noun* a person who introduces the acts in a show; **compere** *verb*; ⚠ **compare**

competition *noun* a test of strength, skill, etc, to show who is best at something; **compete** *verb*; **competitor** *noun*

complain *verb* to say that you are angry, unhappy, or sad about something; to say that something is not good; **complaint** *noun*

complement *verb* to add to something in a good way; to go with ⚠ **compliment**

¹complete *adjective* whole; with nothing left out; **completeness** *noun*

²complete *verb* to make whole or perfect; to finish; **completely** *adverb*; **completion** *noun*

complicated *adjective* difficult to understand or deal with

compliment *noun* something nice said about somebody ⚠ **complement**

computer *noun* an electronic machine that can store information and make calculations at very high speeds

concentrate *verb* to keep all your thoughts, attention, etc, on one thing; **concentration** *noun*

concern *verb* **1** to make unhappy or troubled; to worry; **2** to be about something; **concern** *noun*

bearing compass, used by hikers and mountaineers

concert *noun* music played by a number of singers and/or musicians

concrete *noun* a building material made by mixing sand, small stones, cement, and water

condition *noun* **1** the state that somebody or something is in; **2** something that is said to be necessary or that must happen before something else happens

conductor *noun* **1** a person who controls a group of people playing music; **2** a person who collects fares on a bus or train

cone *noun* a shape or object with a round base and a point at the top: **ice cream cone, fir cone**

confess *verb* to admit a fault or something you have done wrong; **confession** *noun*

conscience *noun* part of your mind that judges whether what you do is good or bad, and makes you feel guilty

conscious *adjective* awake, able to understand what is happening; **consciously** *adverb*; **consciousness** *noun*

conservation *noun* saving and protecting trees, the Earth, etc

consider *verb* to think about

considerable *adjective* fairly large

consist *verb* to be made up of

consonant *noun* any of the letters of the English alphabet, or their sounds, except a, e, i, o, or u; compare VOWEL

constant *adjective* happening all the time; **constantly** *adverb*

constellation *noun* a large group of stars

the Great Bear constellation, sometimes called the Plough

confuse *verb* to mix up in your mind; **confusion** *noun*

conjunction *noun* a word that joins two parts of a sentence

conjuror or **conjurer** *noun* a person who does clever tricks which seem magical, usually by very quick movement of the hands; **conjure** *verb*

connect *verb* to join; **connected** *adjective*; **connection** *noun*

contain *verb* to have inside; to hold; **container** *noun*

content *adjective* satisfied; happy; **contented** *adjective*

contents *noun* what is contained in an object or a book

continent *noun* any of the seven main masses of land on the Earth; **continental** *adjective*

continual *adjective* happening often; repeated; **continually** *adverb*

continue *verb* to go on happening or speaking

continuous *adjective* never stopping; **continuously** *adverb*

¹**control** *verb* (**controlled**) **1** to have power over somebody or something; **2** to direct; to guide

²**control** *noun* **1** the ability to control; power; **2** an instrument, knob, switch, etc, for controlling a machine: **volume control**

convenient *adjective* **1** near; easy to get to; **2** easy to use; helpful; **convenience** *noun*; **conveniently** *adverb*

conversation *noun* a talk

cook *verb* to prepare food for eating by using heat; **cook** *noun*; **cooker** *noun*

cool *adjective* **1** neither warm nor cold; **2** calm; not excited; **cool** *verb*; **coolly** *adverb*, **coolness** *noun*

copper *noun* a soft reddish metal that is easily shaped and allows heat and electricity to pass through it readily

¹**copy** *noun* **1** a thing made to be exactly like another; **2** a single example of a magazine, book, etc

²**copy** *verb* to make or do something exactly the same as something else

cord *noun* a thick string or thin rope

cork *noun* **1** a soft light material that comes from the bark of a tree; **2** a round piece of this used to seal a bottle

corn *noun* the seed of grain plants, such as wheat

corner *noun* **1** the point at which two lines, surfaces, or edges meet; **2** the place where two roads meet

¹**correct** *adjective* right; **correctly** *adverb*; **correctness** *noun*

²**correct** *verb* to make right; to mark the mistakes in; **correction** *noun*

corridor *noun* a long narrow part of a building; a passage off which rooms open

¹**cost** *noun* the price you pay when you buy something

²**cost** *verb* (**costs, costing, cost**) to have as a price

costume *noun* the clothes typical of a certain time in history, a country, etc; the clothes worn by an actor or actress

cot *noun* a small bed for a young child

cottage *noun* a small house in the country

cotton *noun* **1** cloth used to make sheets and clothes; **2** the plant grown to make this; **3 cotton wool** soft white stuff used to put medicine on cuts, etc

cotton plant

couch *noun* a sofa

cough (*say* **coff**) *verb* to push air out from the throat suddenly, with a rough sharp noise because you are ill; **cough** *noun*

could (**couldn't**) *see* CAN

council *noun* a group of people who are chosen to make laws, rules, or decisions or to give advice; **councillor** *noun*; ⚠ **counsel, counsellor**

counsel *noun* advice; **counsel** *verb*; **counsellor** *noun*; ⚠ **council, councillor**

count *verb* **1** to find out how many there are; **2** to say the numbers in order; **3** to add up; **count** *noun*

counter *noun* **1** a narrow table or flat surface on which goods are shown or at which people in a shop, bank, etc, are served; **2** a small flat object used in playing games

country *noun* **1** an area of land that has its own government; **2** the land outside cities or towns: **countryside**

couple *noun* **1** two things of the same kind; **2** a man and a woman together, especially a husband and wife

courage *noun* the feeling of not being afraid; bravery; **courageous** *adjective*

course *noun* **1** the direction taken by somebody or something; **2** an area of land or water on which a race is held or certain types of sport played; **3** a set of lessons; **4** any of the several parts of a meal; **5 of course** *adverb* certainly; as everyone knows or must agree; ⚠ **coarse**

court *noun* **1** a place where somebody is questioned about a crime, and where people decide whether or not he or she is guilty; **2** the officials, servants, etc, who attend a king and queen; **3** an open space where games are played: **tennis court**; ⚠ **caught**

cousin *noun* the child of your uncle or aunt

¹**cover** *verb* to place or spread something upon, over, or in front of something else

²**cover** *noun* **1** anything that protects by covering: **bed cover, book cover**; **2** a lid; a top

covering *noun* something that covers or hides

cow *noun* (*male* **bull**, *young* **calf**) the fully grown female form of cattle, elephants, and certain other large animals

coward *noun* a person who avoids danger or pain because he or she has no courage; **cowardly** *adjective*; **cowardice** *noun*; **cowardliness** *noun*

cowboy *noun* a man who rides a horse and looks after cattle in America

CPU *noun* **central processing unit;** the main part of a computer, which deals with the programs and controls other parts

crab *noun* a sea animal with five pairs of legs and a hard shell

fiddler crab

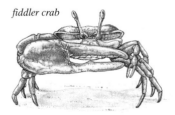

¹**crack** *verb* **1** to break without dividing into separate parts; **2** to make a sudden sharp sound

²**crack** *noun* **1** a thin line or split where something is broken; **2** a loud sharp sound

cracker *noun* **1** a small thin biscuit; **2** a paper toy which bangs when its ends are pulled, used especially at Christmas

cradle *noun* a small rocking bed for a baby

cream *noun* the thick fatty part of milk which rises to the top; **creaminess** *noun*; **creamy** *adjective*

creature *noun* an animal of any kind

creep *verb* (**creeps, creeping, crept**) to move slowly and quietly

crew *noun* the people working on a ship, plane, etc

¹**cricket** *noun* an outdoor game played with a ball and bat, by two teams of eleven players each; **cricketer** *noun*

²**cricket** *noun* a type of small insect which makes a noise by rubbing its forewings together

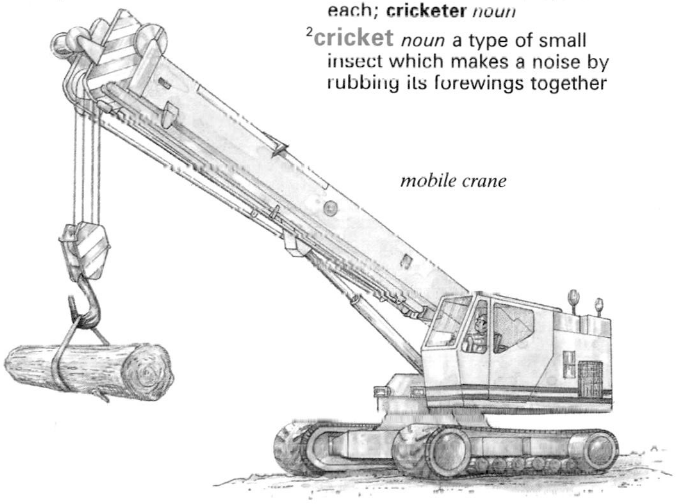

mobile crane

crane *noun* a machine for lifting and moving heavy objects

crash *noun* **1** a sudden loud noise; **2** a violent vehicle accident; **3** a sudden failure of a computer or a computer program; **crash** *verb*

crawl *verb* to move slowly with your body close to the ground, or on your hands and knees

cried *see* CRY

crime *noun* something that is wrong and can be punished by law; **criminal** *noun*

¹**crisp** *adjective* **1** hard and dry; easily broken; **2** firm; fresh; **crispy** *adjective*

²**crisp** *noun* a thin piece of potato cooked in hot fat, dried, and sold in packets

Nile crocodile – crocodiles look very like alligators, except that the big teeth in the lower jaw can be seen even when the mouth is closed

crocodile *noun* a large reptile that lives on land and in lakes and rivers in the hot wet parts of the world

crooked *adjective* not straight; bent; **crookedly** *adverb*; **crookedness** *noun*

crop *noun* **1** a plant or part of a plant such as grain, fruit, or vegetables grown by a farmer; **2** the amount of grain, vegetables, etc, cut and gathered at one time

¹**cross** *noun* **1** a figure or mark formed by one straight line crossing another; anything shaped like x or +; **2** an animal or plant that is a mixture of breeds

²**cross** *verb* **1** to go, pass, or reach over or across; **2** to cause an animal or plant to breed with one of another kind; **crossing** *noun*

³**cross** *adjective* angry; bad-tempered; **crossly** *adverb*

crow *noun* a large shiny black bird with a loud rough cry

crowd *noun* a large number of people gathered together; **crowded** *adjective*

crown *noun* a circle of gold with jewels in it, worn on the head by a king or queen at special times

cruel *adjective* liking to hurt other people or animals; unkind; **cruelly** *adverb*; **cruelty** *noun*

crumb *noun* a very small piece of dry food, such as bread or cake

crush *verb* to press heavily; to hurt or damage by doing this

crust *noun* the hard part on the outside of bread or some other things; **crusty** *adjective*

¹**cry** *verb* **(cries, crying, cried)** **1** to produce tears from your eyes; **2** to make loud sounds because of fear, sadness, etc

²**cry** *noun* a loud call; a shout

cub *noun* the young of various types of wild animals, such as the lion, bear, etc

cube *noun* a solid object that has six equal square sides

cuckoo *noun* **1** a grey bird that lays its eggs in other birds' nests; **2** the call of this bird

cucumber *noun* a long green vegetable which is usually eaten raw with cold food

cue *noun* a long straight wooden stick, slightly thicker at one end than the other, used for hitting the ball in snooker, billiards, etc; ⚠ **queue**

cup *noun* **1** a small round container, usually with a handle, from which liquids are drunk: **cupful; 2** a specially shaped bowl, usually made of gold or silver, given as a prize in a competition

cupboard *noun* a piece of furniture with space inside where things may be stored

¹**cure** *verb* to make somebody better when they have been ill; to make a disease, illness, etc, go away

²**cure** *noun* a way of making somebody or something better; a drug or medicine that cures an illness, disease, etc

curious *adjective* **1** wanting to know or learn about things or people, **2** odd, strange, peculiar; **curiosity** *noun*

¹**curl** *verb* to twist into or form a round or curved shape

²**curl** *noun* **1** a roll or round shape; **2** a small piece of twisted hair; **curliness** *noun*; **curly** *adjective*

currant *noun* **1** small dried seedless grape; **2** a small bush or the small fruits in bunches on it; ⚠ **current**

current *noun* a flow of water, gas, electricity, etc; ⚠ **currant**

curtain *noun* a piece of hanging cloth that can be drawn to cover a window or door or to divide a room

curve *verb* to bend into a smooth round shape; **curve** *noun*

cushion *noun* a bag filled with a soft substance which you put on a chair to make it more comfortable

custard *noun* a thick sweet yellow sauce

customer *noun* a person who buys something

cut *verb* (**cuts, cutting, cut**) to make an opening in, separate, or remove something with a knife, scissors, etc; **cut** *noun*

¹**cycle** *noun* a bicycle or motorcycle

²**cycle** *verb* to bicycle; **cyclist** *noun*

cygnet (*say* signet) *noun* a young swan

cymbals *noun* a musical instrument consisting of a pair of round thin metal plates struck together to make a loud ringing noise; ⚠ **symbols**

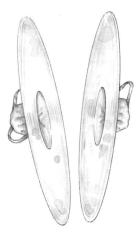

cymbals – a percussion instrument (that is, one that is played by being struck)

Dd

dad, daddy *noun* father

daddylonglegs *noun* a large fly with very long legs

daffodil *noun* a yellow flower that grows in the spring

dagger *noun* a short pointed knife used as a weapon

daily *adjective, adverb* happening or done once every day

dairy *noun* a place where milk, butter, and cheese are made

daisy *noun* a small wild or garden flower, yellow in the centre and white round the edge

daisies

dam *noun* a wall or bank built to keep back water; **dam** *verb*

¹damage *noun* harm, especially to things

²damage *verb* to cause damage to; to hurt

damp *adjective, noun* slightly wet; not properly dry; **dampness** or **damp** *noun*

¹dance *verb* to move to music; **dancer** *noun*

²dance *noun* **1** a set of movements performed to music; **2** a party for dancing; **3** a piece of music for dancing

dandelion *noun* a small yellow wild flower

dangerous *adjective* not safe; likely to cause harm or damage; **danger** *noun*; **dangerously** *adverb*

dare *verb* **1** to be brave or rude enough to do or say something; **2** to challenge; **dare** *noun*

dark *adjective* without light; nearly black; **dark** *noun*; **darkness** *noun*

dart *noun* a small pointed arrow thrown at a round board in the game of **darts**

dash *noun* **1** a sudden quick run; **2** a mark (–) used in writing or printing; **dash** *verb*

data *noun* measurements, facts, and information that can be put into a computer

database *noun* information in a computer, organised so that you can find things quickly

¹date *noun* **1** time shown by the number of the day, the month, and the year; **2** an arrangement to meet at a particular time and place especially between a boy and a girl

²date *noun* a small brown sweet fruit with a long stone

daughter *noun* a person's female child

dawn *noun* the time of day when light first appears and the sun rises

day *noun* **1** the time when it is light: **daytime, daylight**; **2** twenty four hours

dead *adjective* **1** no longer alive; **2** unable to feel

deaf *adjective* unable to hear or hear well; **deafness** *noun*

42

deal *verb* (**deals, dealing, dealt**)
1 to give out a share of
something; **2 deal with** to
do what is necessary with
something or somebody;
deal *noun*; **dealer** *noun*

dear *adjective* **1** much loved;
2 a term used to begin a letter;
3 costing a lot of money;
⚠ **deer**

death *noun* the end of life

decay *verb* to go bad; **decay** *noun*

deceive *verb* to cause
somebody to accept as true or
good what is false or bad

December *noun* the twelfth and
last month of the year

decide *verb* to arrive at an
answer or make a choice about
something; **decision** *noun*

¹**decimal** *adjective* having to do
with the number ten

²**decimal** *noun* a number like
0.5, 0.375, etc

deck *noun* **1** a floor of a ship or
bus, **2** a machine for playing
records or tapes: **record deck,
tape deck**

decorate *verb* to make
something more beautiful or
colourful; **decoration** *noun*

deep *adjective* **1** going far down;
2 going a long way in; **3** strong
and dark (colour), **4** low (voice);
deeply *adverb*; **deepness** *noun*;
depth *noun*

deer *noun* (*plural* **deer**)
(*male* **buck**, *female* **doe** *or* **hind**,

*fallow deer
fawns*

young **fawn**) a large wild animal
that eats grass and can run very
fast; ⚠ **dear**

degree *noun* a unit for
measuring temperature or
the size of an angle

delay *verb* **1** to put off until later;
2 to make late; **3** to act slowly;
delay *noun*

*truffle – an underground
fungus that is thought
of as a delicacy*

delicacy *noun* something that is
good to eat but is rare or costs
a lot of money

delicate *adjective* **1** easily
harmed or broken; **2** beautiful
and pleasing but small and not
strong; **delicately** *adverb*

delicious *adjective* nice to smell
or taste

delight *verb* to give great
pleasure; **delight** *noun*;
delightful *adjective*

deliver *verb* **1** to send or take
something to a particular place;
2 to help somebody to have a
baby; **3** to say; to read aloud;
delivery *noun*

den *noun* **1** the home of a wild
animal; **2** a secret or private
place

dentist also **dental surgeon**
noun a person who looks after
your teeth

dependant *noun* a person who
depends on another;
dependent *adjective*

depend on *verb* **1** to rely on someone or something; to need; **2** to be influenced by; to be a result of

depth *see* DEEP

describe *verb* to say what something is like; **description** *noun*

¹**desert** (*say dez*-ert) *noun* a large sandy piece of land where there is hardly any rain and very few plants or animals; ⚠ **dessert**

²**desert** (*say* de-*zert*) *verb* to leave completely; ⚠ **dessert**

deserve *verb* to be worthy of something good, or bad, by doing something good or bad

desk *noun* a table, often with drawers, at which you read, write, etc

dessert (*say* de-zert) *noun* a sweet dish you eat at the end of a meal; ⚠ **desert**

destroy *verb* to ruin or wreck; **destruction** *noun*

detect *verb* to find out or discover; **detection** *noun*; **detector** *noun*

detective *noun* a police officer who finds out about crimes

determined *adjective* having made up your mind to do something; **determination** *noun*

develop *verb* to make or become larger, more active, more complete, etc; to grow; **developer** *noun*; **development** *noun*

devil *noun* **1** an evil spirit or person; **2 Devil** the most evil spirit; the enemy of God

dew (*say* dyoo) *noun* small drops of water which form on the ground during the night; ⚠ **due**; **dewy** *adjective*

diagram *noun* a drawing that explains something or shows how its parts are arranged

diamond
noun **1** a very hard valuable jewel; **2** a shape with four equal sides that stands on one of its points (♦); **3** a playing card which has these shapes in red

the Star of Africa – one of the largest cut diamonds in the world

diary *noun* a book with separate spaces for each day of the year, in which you write down things you have done or will do

dice *see* DIE

dictionary *noun* a book that gives the meanings and spelling of words

did *see* DO

didn't *see* DO

¹**die** *verb* (**dies, dying, died**) to stop living

²**die** *noun* (*plural* **dice**) a small cube, with a different number of spots from one to six on each side, that is used in many games

different *adjective* not of the same kind; **difference** *noun*; **differently** *adverb*

difficult *adjective* not easy; hard to do, understand, etc; **difficulty** *noun*

dig *verb* (**digs, digging, dug**) **1** to break up and move earth; **2** to make a hole by taking away earth or soil

digger *noun* somebody or something that digs; a tool or machine for digging the earth

digit *noun* **1** any number from nought to nine; **2** a finger or toe; **digital** *adjective*

dining room *noun* a room in which you eat meals

dinner *noun* a main meal, eaten either at midday or in the evening

dinosaur *noun* any of several types of reptiles, some very large, that lived millions of years ago

disappoint *verb* to become sad or make somebody sad because what was expected or hoped for did not happen; **disappointed** *adjective*; **disappointing** *adjective*; **disappointment** *noun*

disapprove *verb* to have a bad opinion of somebody or something; **disapproval** *noun*

disarm *verb* to give up or reduce the number of weapons or soldiers that you have

a recently discovered Chinese dinosaur – a yingshanosaurus

¹**direct** *verb* **1** to tell somebody the way; **2** to control or manage; **director** *noun*

²**direct** *adjective* straight towards or straight after or behind; **directly** *adverb*

direction *noun* **1** the course or way in which a person or thing moves; **2 directions** information that tells you where to go or what to do

dirt *noun* soil, mud, dust, or anything that is not clean

dirty *adjective* **1** covered with dirt; **2** making you, or your clothes, unclean; **dirtily** *adverb*; **dirtiness** *noun*

disagree *verb* not to agree; **disagreement** *noun*

disappear *verb* to go out of sight; **disappearance** *noun*

disc *noun* **1** round flat thing, **2** a flat piece of plastic on which music or electronic information is stored

disciple *noun* somebody who is faithful to or follows a leader

discipline *noun* good behaviour and the obeying of rules; the training of somebody to behave in this way

disco *noun* a place where people dance to pop music

discover *verb* to find out or find something, especially for the first time; **discoverer** *noun*; **discovery** *noun*

disease *noun* an illness; **diseased** *adjective*

dish *noun* **1** a large, flat, and often round plate on which your food is served; **2** prepared food of one kind

scuba diver (scuba stands for self contained underwater breathing apparatus)

dishonest *adjective* not honest; **dishonestly** *adverb*; **dishonesty** *noun*

disk *noun* a computer DISC

dislike *verb* not to like; **dislike** *noun*

distance *noun* **1** the amount of space between two places; **2 in the distance** far away; **distant** *adjective*

ditch *noun* a long narrow not very deep channel dug in the ground for water to drain into

dive *verb* **1** to jump head first into water; **2** to move quickly or suddenly; **dive** *noun*

diver *noun* a person who works under water and wears a special **diving suit** to help him or her to breathe

divide *verb* **1** to separate into smaller parts or groups; to share; **2** to find out how many times one number will go into another number

division *noun* **1** one of the parts or groups into which something is divided; **2** dividing sums

do *verb* (**does, doing, did, done, doesn't, don't, didn't**) **1** to carry out; to act; **2** to deal with something; **3** to be suitable for something; to be enough; **4 That will do!** That's enough!; **5 How do you do?** a form of words used when introduced to somebody; **6 make do with** to use something even though it may not be perfect or enough

dock *noun* a place where ships are loaded or repaired

doctor *noun* a person whose job is to look after sick people

doe *noun* the female of any animal of which the male is called a buck, such as the deer or the rabbit △ **dough**

does *see* DO

doesn't *see* DO

dog *noun* (*female* **bitch**, *young* **puppy**) a common four-legged animal, kept as a pet or for hunting, working, etc

doing *see* DO

doll *noun* a toy made to look like a person

dollar *noun* the money used in America, Australia, and some other countries. There are one hundred cents to one dollar and its sign is $.

bottle-nosed dolphin

dolphin *noun* a sea animal which swims in groups and is very intelligent

done *adjective* **1** finished; **2** *see* DO

donkey *noun* an animal like a horse but smaller, with longer ears and a rough coat

don't *see* DO

door *noun* **1** a flat surface that opens and closes the entrance to a building, room, or piece of furniture; **2** the opening for a door: **doorway**; **3 answer the door** to go and open the door to see who is there

dot *noun* a small round spot; **dot** *verb*; **dotted** *adjective*

¹**double** *adjective* **1** having two parts; **2** made for two; **double** *adverb*

²**double** *noun* **1** something that is twice as much as another; **2** a person who looks like another; **3 doubles** a game of tennis, badminton, etc, for two pairs of players

³**double** *verb* **1** to multiply a number or amount by two; **2** to fold or bend sharply or tightly over

double bass *noun* a musical instrument with a deep sound, like a very big violin

double-decker *adjective* having two layers or two floors

doubt *verb* not to be sure about something; **doubt** *noun*

dough (*say* doe) *noun* a thick mixture of flour and water used for making bread, cakes, etc; ⚠ **doe**

¹**down** *adverb, preposition, adjective* **1** to or in a lower place or position; **2** along

²**down** *noun* small soft feathers on a bird

downhill *adjective, adverb* towards the bottom of a hill

downstairs *adverb, adjective* on or to a lower floor of a building; **downstairs** *noun*

downwards *adverb* **1** from a higher to a lower place; **2** towards the ground or floor

dozen *noun* (*plural* **dozen** *or* **dozens**) **1** a group of twelve; **2 dozens of** lots of; **dozen** *adjective*

drag *verb* (**dragged**) **1** to pull a heavy thing along; **2** to move along slowly; **3** to look for something by pulling a heavy net along the bottom of a lake or river

Welsh heraldic dragon

dragon *noun* an imaginary animal in stories that is said to breathe fire

d

¹**drain** *verb* **1** to make a liquid, usually water, flow away; **2** to make or become gradually dry or empty

²**drain** *noun* a pipe, tube, etc, that drains something away

drake *noun* a male duck

mallard drake

drank *see* DRINK

draught *noun* air blowing into a room

draughts *noun* a game for two, each with twelve round pieces, on a board of 64 squares

¹**draw** *verb* (**draws, drawing, drew, drawn**) **1** to make pictures with a pencil, pen, etc; **2** to pull; to pull up or out; **3** to move; **4** to attract; **5** to end a game, battle, etc, without either side winning; **6 draw the curtain** to close or open the curtain

²**draw** *noun* a game, battle, etc, which neither side wins

drawer *noun* a sliding container, like a box without a top, that fits into a piece of furniture

drawing *noun* **1** making pictures; **2** a picture done by pencil, pen, etc

drawn *see* DRAW

¹**dream** *noun* **1** thoughts that you have or pictures that you see when you are asleep; **2** something not real that you hope for or imagine

²**dream** *verb* (**dreams, dreaming, dreamed** *or* **dreamt**) to have a dream

¹**dress** *verb* **1** to put clothes on; **2 dress up** to put on special clothes; **3** to clean and cover up a wound

²**dress** *noun* a piece of clothing for a woman or girl that has a top and skirt joined together

dressing table *noun* a piece of bedroom furniture with drawers and a mirror

drew *see* DRAW

drink *verb* (**drinks, drinking, drank, drunk**) to take liquid into the mouth and swallow it; **drink** *noun*

drip *verb* (**dripped**) to fall or let fall in drops; **drip** *noun*

¹**drive** *verb* (**drives, driving, drove, driven**) to make a vehicle or an animal move in the direction you want; **driver** *noun*

²**drive** *noun* **1** a journey in a vehicle; **2** a road to a house: *a* **driveway**

¹**drop** *noun* **1** a small amount of liquid; **2** a small round sweet; **3** a fall in prices, temperature, etc

²**drop** *verb* (**dropped**) **1** to fall suddenly or in drops; **2** to let fall or lower; **3 drop in** to visit

drove *see* DRIVE

drown *verb* **1** to die by being under water so that you are unable to breathe; **2** to kill by holding under water too long; **3** to make such a loud noise that another sound can no longer be heard

drowsy *adjective* sleepy

drug *noun* a medicine

drum kit

¹**drum** *noun* **1** a round musical instrument which you play by beating with your hand or a stick; **2** a large container shaped like a drum

²**drum** *verb* (**drummed**) **1** to beat or play a drum; **2** to make noises like those from a drum; **drummer** *noun*

¹**drunk** *adjective* having had too much alcohol

²**drunk** *see* DRINK

¹**dry** *adjective* **1** not wet; not containing water; **2** thirsty; **3** dull and not interesting; **dryly, drily** *adverb*; **dryness** *noun*

²**dry** *verb* **1** to make or become dry; **2** to preserve food by removing liquid

¹**duck** *noun* (*male* **drake**, *young* **duckling**) a common water bird with short legs and a short neck

²**duck** *verb* **1** to lower your head or body quickly, so as to avoid being hit; **2** to push someone under water

duckling *noun* a young duck

due (*say* **dyoo**) *adjective* **1** owing; to be paid; **2** expected; **3** because of; caused by ⚠ **dew**

dug *see* DIG

dull *adjective* **1** not bright, strong, or sharp; **2** cloudy; grey; **3** not interesting or exciting

dumb (*say* **dum**) *adjective* unable to speak

dumpling *noun* a ball of dough cooked with meat in a stew or filled with jam or fruit

during *preposition* all through, or at some point in the course of

dusk *noun* the time when daylight is fading

¹**dust** *noun* powder made up of very small pieces; **dusty** *adjective*

²**dust** *verb* **1** to clean the dust from something; **2** to cover with a fine powder

dustbin *noun* a container with a lid, for holding rubbish

duty *noun* **1** what you must do either because of your job or because you think it right; **2** a tax; **dutiful** *adjective*

duvet (*say* **du vay**) *noun* a large bag filled with soft warm material, such as feathers, to keep you warm in bed

dwarf *noun* **1** a person, animal, or plant of much less than the usual size; **2** a small imaginary person in fairy stories

each *adjective, pronoun, adverb* every one separately; for or to every one

eager *adjective* wanting to do something very much; keen; **eagerly** *adverb*; **eagerness** *noun*

eagle *noun* a very large strong bird that hunts other birds and animals

¹**ear** *noun* **1** the part of the body with which you hear: **earache 2 all ears** listening eagerly

²**ear** *noun* the seeds at the top of a stalk of corn, wheat, etc

early *adverb, adjective* **1** before the usual or right time; **2** near the beginning of the day or another period of time

earn *verb* **1** to get money by working; **2** to get something that you deserve; ⚠ **urn**

earring *noun* a piece of jewellery worn on the ear

earth *noun* **1 Earth** the planet on which we live; **2** soil; **3** the wire which connects a piece of electrical equipment to the ground; **4** the hole where certain wild animals live, such as foxes

earthquake *noun* a sudden shaking of the Earth's surface, that may cause great damage

earwig *noun* a thin brown insect

east *noun* one of the four main points of the compass; the direction in which the sun rises; **east** *adjective, adverb*; **easterly** *adjective*; **eastern** *adjective*

Easter *noun* the time when Christians remember the death of Jesus Christ and his coming back to life

easy *adjective* able to be done without much trouble; not difficult; **easily** *adverb*

eat *verb* **(eats, eating, ate, eaten)** to take food into the mouth and swallow it

in this solar eclipse the moon is passing between the Earth and the sun

eclipse *noun* the blocking off of the sun's light when the moon passes between it and the Earth, or of the moon's light when the Earth passes between it and the sun

ecology *noun* the way that the Earth, plants, animals, and people live together and can change one another

edge *noun* **1** the place or line where something begins or ends; **2** the thin sharp cutting part of a knife, saw, etc

educate *verb* to teach; to train the character or mind of something; **education** *noun*

eel *noun* a long slippery fish that looks like a snake

effect *noun* **1** a result; **2** a result produced on the mind or feelings; **effective** *adjective*

effort *noun* **1** a show of strength; **2** trying hard with body or mind

eg for example

egg *noun* **1** a round or oval object which comes out of the body of a female bird, fish, or reptile and contains new life; **2** a chicken's egg eaten for food; **3** the seed of life in a woman or female animal, which joins with the male seed to make a baby

eight *adjective, noun* the number 8; **eighth** *adjective, adverb*

eighteen *adjective, noun* the number 18; **eighteenth** *adjective, adverb*

eighty *adjective, noun* the number 80; **eightieth** *adjective, adverb*

either *adjective, pronoun* **1** one or the other of two; **2** one and the other of two; each

elastic *noun* a stretchy material which springs back into its original shape after being pulled; **elastic** *adjective*

elbow *noun* the joint where the arm bends

elder *adjective, noun* the older of two

eldest *adjective, noun* the oldest of three or more

electricity *noun* the power produced by a battery or sent along wires which gives us heat and light and makes machines work; **electric** or **electrical** *adjective;* **electrically** *adverb;* **electrician** *noun*

electronic *adjective* connected with anything that works by electronics

electronic mail *noun* see E-MAIL

electronics *noun* the science concerned with computers, radio and television

elephant *noun* a very large animal that has two long curved tusks and a long trunk with which it can pick things up

African elephant

eleven *adjective, noun* the number 11; **eleventh** *adjective, adverb*

else *adverb* **1** besides, as well, **2** different; other; **3 or else** or something different will happen

e-mail *noun* a system of computers by which people write messages to one another through their computers, either inside their company or round the world

embarrass *verb* to make somebody feel awkward or silly; **embarrassment** *noun*

embroidery *noun* patterns or pictures sewn on material; **embroider** *verb*

emerald *noun* **1** a bright green jewel; **2** bright green; **emerald** *adjective*

emergency *noun* something, usually something bad, that happens very suddenly and must be dealt with immediately

employ *verb* to give work to; **employee** *noun;* **employer** *noun;* **employment** *noun*

empty *adjective* containing nothing or nobody; **emptiness** *noun;* **empty** *verb*

encourage *verb* to give courage, praise, or hope to somebody so that he or she will do something; **encouragement** *noun*; **encouragingly** *adverb*

¹**end** *noun* **1** the furthest part of anything; the point where something stops; **2** the latest point; the time when something stops

²**end** *verb* to come to an end; to finish

enemy *noun* **1** a country against another country in a war; **2** a person who does not like another person and is not friendly to him or her

energy *noun* **1** the power to do things; being full of life and strength; **2** the power which does work and drives machines: **atomic/electrical energy**

engine *noun* **1** a machine that uses fuel, such as petrol or electricity, to make something move; **2** the front part of a train that pulls the carriages: **engine driver**

engineer *noun* a person who plans, makes, or looks after machines, roads, bridges, etc; **engineering** *noun*

enjoy *verb* to get happiness from; **enjoyable** *adjective*; **enjoyment** *noun*

enough *adjective, adverb* as much or as many as may be needed

enter *verb* to come or go in or into; **entry** *noun*

entertain *verb* **1** to have people as guests or give a party; **2** to make somebody amused or interested; **entertainment** *noun*

entire *adjective* whole, complete; **entirely** *adverb*

entrance *noun* a way into a place

envelope *noun* a paper cover for a letter

environment *noun* the air, water, and land in which people, plants, and animals live

equal *adjective* the same in number, size, etc; as good, big, many as; **equal** *noun*; **equal** *verb*; **equally** *adverb*

Equator *noun* an imaginary line drawn round the world halfway between its North and South Poles

George Stephenson's Rocket, an early steam engine

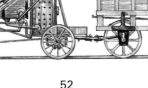

equipment *noun* the things that are necessary for doing something; **equip** *verb* (**equipped**)

escape *verb* to get free from something or somebody; **escape** *noun*

especially *adverb* **1** more than usual; particularly; **2** specially

etc also **et cetera** and other similar things; and so on

¹**even** *adjective* **1** smooth, flat, level; **2** equal; **3** **even number** a number that can be divided exactly by two; **evenly** *adverb*; **evenness** *noun*

²**even** *adverb* **1** used to show that something is more than you expect: *It's even colder than yesterday*; **2** **even if** whether something happens or not; **3** used when a statement is surprising: *Even I don't know the answer!*

evening *noun* the end of the day and early part of the night

event *noun* **1** a happening; **2** a race, competition, etc, arranged as part of a day's sports

ever *adverb* **1** at any time; **2** always; **3** **ever so/such** very

every *adjective* each one; all

everybody also **everyone** *pronoun* every person

everything *pronoun* all; the whole, made up of a number of things

everywhere *adverb* in or to all places

evil *adjective* very bad; wicked; **evil** *noun*

exact *adjective* completely correct; **exactly** *adverb*

exaggerate (*say* egzajerate) *verb* to say that something is bigger, better, worse, etc, than it really is; **exaggeration** *noun*

exam or **examination** *noun* a test in a school subject such as maths or history

examine *verb* **1** to look at closely, in order to find out something; **2** to ask somebody questions or to do something in order to test knowledge or skill; **examiner** *noun*

example *noun* **1** something taken from a number of things of the same kind, which shows a general rule or what the other things are like; **2** a person or action that you should try to copy

excellent *adjective* very good; **excellence** *noun*; **excellently** *adverb*

except *conjunction, preposition* apart from; leaving out

exciting *adjective* making you feel very lively and active and have strong pleasant feelings; **excite** *verb*; **excited** *adjective*; **excitement** *noun*

the exclamation mark on this road sign is a warning

exclamation mark *noun* a sign (!) used in writing to show surprise, shock, etc

¹**excuse** (*say* **ekskyoose**) *noun*
the reason given when asking to
be forgiven or not to be blamed

²**excuse** (*say* **ekskyooz**) *verb* **1**
to forgive somebody for a small
fault; to say that somebody is
not to blame; **2** to free
somebody from something he
or she should do

exercise *noun* **1** the use of your
body so as to strengthen it and
keep fit; **2** something, such as a
piece of schoolwork, that is
done for practice: **exercise
book**; **exercise** *verb*

exist *verb* to live or to be real

exit *noun* a way out of a place

expand *verb* to get or make
larger; **expansion** *noun*

expect *verb* **1** to think or believe
that something will happen; to
suppose; **2** to wait for

explain *verb* **1** to say what
something means; **2** to be the
reason for something;
explanation *noun*

explode *verb* to blow up or
burst with a loud noise;
explosion *noun*

¹**express** *noun* **1** also **express
train** a fast train that does
not stop at many stations;
2 a service given by the post
office, railways, etc, for carrying
things faster

²**express** *verb* to show a feeling,
opinion, or fact in words or in
some other way

expression *noun* **1** the look
on somebody's face;
2 a word or phrase that is
spoken

extend *verb* to make longer;
extension *noun*

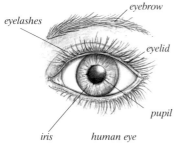

eyebrow
eyelashes
eyelid
pupil
iris   *human eye*

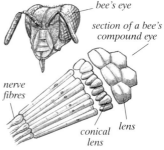

bee's eye
*section of a bee's
compound eye*
*nerve
fibres*
*conical
lens*
lens

expensive *adjective* costing a
lot of money

experience *noun* **1** knowledge
or skill which comes from
doing things rather than from
books; **2** something that
happens to you and has
an effect on your mind;
experience *verb*; **experienced**
adjective

eye *noun* **1** the part of the body
with which you see: **eyebrow,
eyelash, eyelid, eyesight**; **2** the
hole in a needle through which
the thread passes; **3** the dark
spot on a potato, from which a
new plant can grow; **4** the small
loop of metal or thread into
which a hook fits for fastening a
piece of clothing

Ff

¹**face** *noun* **1** the front part of the head from the chin to the hair; **2** a look or expression; **3** the front part of something

²**face** *verb* **1** to turn the face towards something; **2** to look at and not try to avoid

fact *noun* something that is known to be true; something that has actually happened

factory *noun* a building where things are made in large quantities, usually by machines

fade *verb* to lose colour through being in the light too long

Fahrenheit *noun* a scale of temperature in which water freezes at 32° and boils at 212°; compare CELSIUS

fail *verb* **1** not to succeed, or not to do what you wanted; **2** not to pass an exam; **failure** *noun*

¹**faint** *adjective* **1** not clear, loud, or strong enough to see, hear, or feel; **2** weak and about to lose your senses; **faintly** *adverb*

²**faint** *verb* to feel weak and lose your senses; **faint** *noun*

¹**fair** *adjective* **1** treating people equally, according to the rules, **2** good, but not very good; average; **3** light in colour; not dark; **fairly** *adverb*; ⚠ **fare**

²**fair** *noun* an outdoor show with rides, games, and other things to amuse you: **fairground**; ⚠ **fare**

fairy *noun* a small imaginary person with wings and magical powers

faith *noun* belief in something; **faithful** *adjective*; **faithfully** *adverb*

fall *verb* **(falls, falling, fell, fallen)** **1** to drop to a lower place; **2** to come down, like prices; **3** to become lower; **fall** *noun*

false *adjective* **1** not true or correct; **2** not faithful or loyal; **3** not real; **falsely** *adverb*

family *noun* a group made up of a parent or parents and their children; a group of people related by blood or marriage

famous *adjective* being well known and talked about; **fame** *noun*; **famed** *adjective*

¹**fan** *noun* an instrument used to make air move to cool you

lady's fan

²**fan** *verb* **(tanned)** to cause air to blow on something or somebody

³**fan** *noun* someone who admires a pop star, footballer, etc

¹**fancy** *adjective* more decorated, brightly coloured, or expensive than ordinary things; **fancily** *adverb*

²**fancy** *verb* **1** to have a liking for or wish for; **2** to believe without being certain; **3** to form a picture of; to imagine; **fancy** *noun*

far *adverb* (**farther** *or* **further**, **farthest** *or* **furthest**) **1** at or to a great distance; **2** very much

fare *noun* the price charged to carry a person on a bus, train, plane or taxi; ⚠ **fair**

farewell goodbye

farm *noun* land and buildings used for growing crops and/or keeping animals; **farm** *verb*; **farmer** *noun*

farther *see* FAR

fashion *noun* the way of dressing or behaving that is considered the best at a certain time; **fashionable** *adjective*

fast *adjective* **1** moving quickly; **2** showing a time that is later than the true time; **3** firmly fixed; **fast** *adverb*

fasten *verb* to make or become firmly fixed or closed; **fastener** *noun*; **fastening** *noun*

¹**fat** *adjective* (**fatter**) **1** having too much or a lot of fat; **2** thick and round; **fatness** *noun*

²**fat** *noun* **1** the material under the skin of people and animals which helps to keep them warm; **2** the white part of meat that can be used for cooking; **3** butter or oil, used in food; **fatty** *adjective*

fate *noun* the power which seems to cause everything to happen; **fateful** *adjective*; ⚠ **fête**

father *noun* a man who has children

fault *noun* **1** a mistake that someone can be blamed for; responsibility; **2** a bad point in your character; **3** a problem with a machine; **faulty** *adjective*

favour *noun* **1** something kind done for somebody; **2 in favour of** believing in or choosing; on the side of

favourite *noun* something that is liked more than others; **favourite** *adjective*

fax *noun* a letter that is sent from one machine using a phone line to another which prints it out; **fax** *verb*; **fax machine**

fear *noun* the feeling that you have when danger is near or when you are afraid; **fear** *verb*; **fearful** *adjective*; **fearless** *adjective*

feast *noun* **1** a specially good or grand meal; **2** a day kept in memory of some happy religious event

feat *noun* a clever action, showing strength, skill, or courage; ⚠ **feet**

feather *noun* one part of the soft, light covering of a bird's body; **feathery** *adjective*

February *noun* the second month of the year

feed *verb* (**feeds, feeding, fed**) to give food to

feel *verb* (**feels, feeling, felt**) **1** to touch; **2** to know through your senses; **3** to think; **feel** *noun*; **feeling** *noun*

feet *see* FOOT; ⚠ **feat**

fell *see* FALL

¹**felt** *see* FEEL

²**felt** *noun* thick firm cloth made of wool

felt-tip pen *noun* a pen with a soft tip made of felt

female *noun* a girl or a woman; any person or animal that gives birth to young

feminine *adjective* like girls or women

¹**fence** *noun* a wall made of wood or wire, round a garden, field, etc

²**fence** *verb* **1** to fight with a sword as a sport; **2** to put a fence round something

maidenhair fern

fern *noun* a plant with feathery leaves and no flowers

ferret *noun* a small animal used for catching rats and rabbits

ferry *noun* a boat for carrying people and things across a narrow stretch of water

fetch *verb* to go and get and bring back

fête (*say* fate) *noun* a large outdoor entertainment usually held to collect money for a special purpose, ⚠ **fate**

fever *noun* an illness in which you develop a very high temperature

few *adjective, pronoun, noun* **1** not many; not enough; **2** a small number

¹**field** *noun* **1** a piece of land on a farm usually surrounded by a fence or wall, and used for animals or crops; **2** any open area where games or sports are played, or a certain activity is done: **airfield, oilfield**

²**field** *verb* to catch or stop the ball in games like cricket

fierce *adjective* angry, wild, and cruel; **fiercely** *adverb*; **fierceness** *noun*

fifteen *adjective, noun* **1** the number 15; **2** a complete team of fifteen players in **rugby union** football; **fifteenth** *adjective, adverb*

fifty *adjective, noun* the number 50; **fiftieth** *adjective, adverb*

¹**fight** *verb* (**fights, fighting, fought**) **1** to use your body or weapons against somebody or something; **2** to argue against somebody, or what somebody wants to do

²**fight** *noun* an act of fighting; a battle or struggle

figure *noun* **1** the shape of a person's body; **2** a number or amount; **3** a drawing or diagram

file *noun* **1** an arrangement of drawers, shelves, boxes, or cases for storing papers in an office; **2** a collection of information used or stored in a computer; **3** a metal instrument with a rough edge for making things smooth; **nail file**; **4** a line of people one behind the other; **file** *verb*

fill *verb* **1** to make something full; to become full; **2** to block up a gap or a hole

¹**film** *noun* **1** a story shown in a cinema or on television; **2** the material in a camera on which you take photographs; **3** a thin layer of any material

²**film** *verb* to make a cinema picture

57

filthy *adjective* very dirty

fin *noun* a part of a fish that helps it to swim

final *adjective* last; coming at the end; **finally** *adverb*

find *verb* (**finds, finding, found**) **1** to discover something after you have been looking for it; **2 find out** to learn; **3** to discover somebody or something by chance

¹**fine** *adjective* **1** beautiful and good; **2** very thin; **3** in very small bits; **4** bright and sunny; not wet; **finely** *adverb*

²**fine** *noun* money paid as a punishment; **fine** *verb*

finger *noun* **1** one of the five movable parts at the end of your hand: **fingernail**; **2 keep your fingers crossed** to hope for the best

¹**finish** *verb* to bring something to an end; to stop

²**finish** *noun* the end or last part

fir also **fir tree** *noun* a straight tree that has leaves shaped like needles, and cones; ⚠ **fur**

¹**fire** *noun* **1** the heat and light given off by things that are burning: **fire engine, fire escape, fire alarm, firework**; **2** a heap of burning wood or coal for cooking, heating, etc: **fireplace, firelight**; **3** a small gas or electric heater; **4** shooting from guns: **gunfire**; **5 catch fire** to begin to burn; **6 set on fire** also **set fire to** to light something not really meant to burn

²**fire** *verb* to shoot a gun

¹**firm** *adjective* **1** strong; solid; hard; **2** steady and not easily moved; **firmly** *adverb*; **firmness** *noun*

²**firm** *noun* a business

first *adjective, noun, adverb* **1** before any others; **2** the person, thing, or group to do or be something first; **3** for the first time; **4 at first** at the beginning

¹**fish** *noun* (*plural* **fish** *or* **fishes**) a creature which lives in water and uses its fins and tail to swim

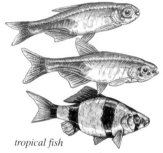

tropical fish

²**fish** *verb* to try to catch fish; to look for something; **fisherman** *noun*; **fishing** *noun*

fist *noun* the hand with the fingers closed in tightly when you are going to hit somebody

¹**fit** *verb* (**fitted**) to be the right size, shape, or kind

²**fit** *adjective* (**fitter**) **1** in good health; **2** suitable; good enough; **fitness** *noun*

³**fit** *noun* **1** a sudden short attack of an illness; **2** a strong feeling

five *adjective, noun* the number 5; **fifth** *adjective, adverb*

fix *verb* **1** to fasten firmly; **2** to arrange; **3** to cook or prepare; **4** to put in order or mend

Union Jack
(United Kingdom)   *Rising Sun (Japan)*   *Stars and Stripes (USA)*

flag *noun* a piece of cloth with a pattern or picture on it, used as the sign of a country, club, etc

flake *noun* a small thin piece

flame *noun* a bright red or yellow piece of burning gas

flan *noun* a round flat open pie

¹**flap** *noun* a wide flat thin part of anything that folds or hangs down over an opening

²**flap** *verb* **(flapped)** to wave slowly up and down or to and fro, making a noise

¹**flash** *verb* **1** to shine for a moment; **2** to move very fast

²**flash** *noun* a sudden quick bright light

¹**flat** *adjective* **(flatter) 1** smooth and level with no pieces sticking out; **2** below the true note (music); **3** not having enough air in it (tyre); **flatten** *verb*; **flatness** *noun*

²**flat** also **apartment** *noun* a set of rooms on one floor of a building

flavour *noun* a taste; **flavour** *verb*; **flavouring** *noun*; **flavourless** *adjective*

flaw *noun* a small mark or crack, that makes something not perfect; **flaw** *verb*; **flawless** *adjective*; ⚠ **floor**

flea *noun* a small jumping insect that bites people, dogs, etc; ⚠ **flee**

flee *verb* **(fleeing, fled)** to escape quickly; ⚠ **flea**

flesh *noun* **1** the soft substance, including fat and muscle, that covers the bones and lies under the skin; **2** the meat of animals used as food; **3** the soft part of a fruit or vegetable that can be eaten; **fleshy** *adjective*

flew *see* FLY; ⚠ **flue**

flex *noun* a length of wire for carrying electricity

flight *noun* **1** the act of flying; **2** a trip by plane; **3** a group of birds or aircraft flying together; **4** a set of stairs

float *verb* to stay at the top of liquid or to be held up in air without sinking

floe *noun* a large piece of ice floating in the sea: **an iceffoe** ⚠ **flow**

¹**flood** *noun* the covering with water of a place that is usually dry

²**flood** *verb* to fill or become covered with water

floor *noun* **1** the part of a room on which you stand; **2** one level of a building; ⚠ **flaw**

flour *noun* powder made from grain and used for making bread and cakes; **floury** *adjective*; ⚠ **flower**

59

flow *verb* to run or spread smoothly; to pour; **flow** *noun*; **flowing** *adjective*; ⚠ **floe**

flowchart also **flow diagram** *noun* a drawing in which lines and arrows are used to show the order of the actions needed to do something or to solve a problem

fold *verb* to turn or bend one part of something onto another part of it; **fold** *noun*

follow *verb* **1** to come or go after somebody or something; **2** to go in the same direction; **3** to understand; **follower** *noun*

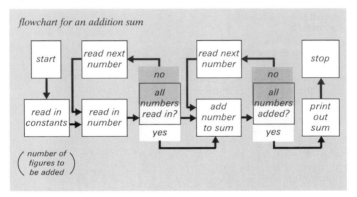

flowchart for an addition sum

start → read in constants → read in number → read next number

all numbers read in? — no / yes

add number to sum

all numbers added? — no / yes

read next number

print out sum → stop

(number of figures to be added)

¹**flower** *noun* the part of a plant which makes the seeds and is usually coloured; ⚠ **flour**

²**flower** *verb* to produce flowers; ⚠ **flour**

flown *see* FLY

flue *noun* a narrow passage up which smoke or heat passes; the inside of a chimney; ⚠ **flew**

flute *noun* a musical instrument which you blow

¹**fly** *verb* (**flies, flying, flew, flown**) **1** to move through the air using wings or in a machine; **2** to go quickly

²**fly** *noun* a small insect with wings

fog *noun* very thick mist; **foggy** *adjective*

fond *adjective* **1** loving; **2 to be fond of** to have a great liking or love for; **fondly** *adverb*

food *noun* something for eating

¹**fool** *noun* a silly person; **foolish** *adjective*; **foolishly** *adverb*

²**fool** *verb* **1** to deceive or trick; **2** to speak or behave in a silly way

foot *noun* (*plural* **feet**) **1** the part of the body at the end of the leg, on which a person or an animal stands: **footpath, footstep**; **2** the lowest or bottom part of anything; **3** a measure of length equal to 12 inches or 30.48 centimetres

football *noun* a game in which two teams kick a ball and try to score goals; **footballer** *noun*

for *preposition* **1** meant to belong to, be given to, or be used in this way; **2** in order to reach, get, or have; **3** as a sign of; instead of; **4** in support of; **5** because of; **6** at the price of; **7** the length or distance of; ⚠ **fore, four**

forbid *verb* (**forbids, forbidding, forbade** *or* **forbad, forbidden**) to tell somebody not to do something

force *noun* **1** strength or power; **2** a group of specially trained people; **force** *verb*

fore *adjective, adverb* front; in or near the front part; ⚠ **for, four**

forecast *verb* to say what you think will happen; **forecast** *noun*

forehead *noun* the part of the face above the eyes and below the hair

foreign *adjective* of or from another country; **foreigner** *noun*

forest *noun* a large area of land covered with trees and bushes

forever, also **for ever** *adverb* always; for all time

forget *verb* (**forgets, forgetting, forgot, forgotten**) not to remember; to no longer have the memory of something

forgive *verb* (**forgives, forgiving, forgave, forgiven**) to say or feel that you are no longer angry about something and will not punish somebody

fork *noun* **1** an instrument with a handle at one end and two or more points at the other; **2** a place where something divides, or one of the divided parts

¹**form** *noun* **1** shape or appearance; **2** a kind or sort; **3** a special paper on which certain things must be written

down; **4** a long wooden seat without a back; **5** a class in a school

²**form** *verb* **1** to take shape or appear; **2** to make; **3** to make up

fort *noun* a strong building which can protect people from attack; ⚠ **fought**

fortnight *noun* two weeks

fortune *noun* **1** a great amount of money; **2** whatever happens in the future to a person by good or bad luck; **fortunate** *adjective*; **fortunately** *adverb*

forty *adjective, noun* the number 40; **fortieth** *adjective, adverb*

¹**forward** also **forwards** *adverb* **1** towards the front in the direction you are facing; **2** to an earlier time; **3** look **forward to** to think something will be pleasant; **forward** *adjective*

²**forward** *verb* to send on letters or parcels to a new address

fought *see* FIGHT; ⚠ **fort**

found *see* FIND

fountain *noun* a stream of water that shoots straight up into the air from a pipe

a fountain in Florence, Italy

four *adjective, noun* the number 4; **fourth** *adjective, adverb*; ⚠ **for, fore**

fourteen *adjective, noun* the number 14; **fourteenth** *adjective, adverb*

fox *noun (female* **vixen***, young* **cub***)* a small wild animal like a dog, with a bushy tail and reddish fur

fraction *noun* a very small piece or amount; a part of a whole number ($\frac{2}{3}$, $\frac{7}{16}$, etc)

frame *noun* **1** the rods and bars which are fitted together to make something or round which something is built: **framework**; **2** the pieces of wood, plastic, or metal round a picture; **frame** *verb*

free *adjective* **1** able to do what you like; not tied up or in prison; **2** not costing any money; given away; **3** not busy; not being used; **free** *verb*; **freedom** *noun*

freeze *verb* (**freezes, freezing, froze, frozen**) **1** to harden or become solid as a result of great cold; **2 deep freeze** to keep and store food by freezing it

freezer also **deep freeze** *noun* a large refrigerator for frozen food

frequency *noun* **1** the number of times something happens or is repeated during a certain amount of time; **2** a particular number of radio waves per second at which a radio signal is broadcast

frequent *adjective* how often something happens

fresh *adjective* **1** new or different; **2** newly made; **3** newly picked, grown, or supplied; **4** not preserved in tins, bottles, etc; not frozen; **5** clean or pure; **6** not tired; healthy; **freshness** *noun*; **freshly** *adverb*

Friday *noun* the sixth day of the week

fridge a machine in which food and drinks can be kept cool

friend *noun* a person you like and enjoy talking to and going out with; somebody who is kind and helpful; **friendliness** *noun*; **friendly** *adjective*; **friendship** *noun*

frighten *verb* to make somebody afraid

fro *see* TO AND FRO

frog *noun* a small animal that can live in water and on land and has long back legs for swimming and jumping

South American poison arrow frog

from *preposition* **1** beginning at; **2** given or sent by; **3** out of; **4** using; **5** because of

front *noun* **1** the position directly before somebody or something; **2** the surface or part facing forwards, outwards, or upwards; **3** the most forward or important position; **4 in front of** in the position facing forward; whilst somebody is present; **front** *adjective*

frost _noun_ white powdery ice that forms on outside surfaces when the weather is very cold; **frosty** _adjective_

frown _verb_ to draw your eyebrows down and wrinkle your forehead when angry or worried; **frown** _noun_

froze _see_ FREEZE

frozen _see_ FREEZE

fruit _noun_ the part of a tree or bush that contains seeds and is often sweet and used for food

fry _verb_ to cook in hot fat or oil

fuel _noun_ material that is used for producing heat or power by burning

full _adjective_ holding as much or as many people, objects, liquids, etc, as possible; **fully** _adverb_

full stop _noun_ the sign (.) at the end of a sentence or a shortened form of a word

fun _noun_ amusement and enjoyment

funeral _noun_ the time when a dead person is buried

fungus _noun_ (_plural_ **fungi** _or_ **funguses**) a type of plant without flowers, leaves, or green colouring matter

_fly agaric toadstool –
a very poisonous fungus_

funny _adjective_ **1** amusing; **2** strange; unusual

fur _noun_ the soft hair that covers the body of animals such as bears, rabbits, cats, etc; **furry** _adjective_; ⚠ **fir**

a Tudor four poster bed

furniture _noun_ all the things used in a house or room such as beds, chairs, tables, etc

further _see_ FAR

furthest _see_ FAR

fuse _noun_ a short thin piece of wire placed in something electrical, which melts if too much power is used and prevents fires or other damage

¹**future** _noun_ **1** the time that will come; **2** things that will happen to somebody or something

²**future** _noun, adjective_ an action that will happen later: _the_ **future tense**

Gg

galaxy *noun* a very large group of stars

gale *noun* a strong wind

gallon *noun* a measure for liquids equal to eight pints or 4.546 litres

gallop *noun* the fastest movement of a horse; **gallop** *verb*

game *noun* **1** something you play, with rules which tell you what to do; **2** wild animals or birds which are hunted for food

gander *noun* a male goose

gang *noun* a group of people who go around together

gaol *see* JAIL; ⚠ **goal**

gap *noun* an empty space; a narrow opening

garage *noun* a place where cars are kept or repaired

garden *noun* a piece of land, near a house or in a public place, on which flowers, trees, and vegetables may be grown; **garden** *verb*; **gardener** *noun*; **gardening** *noun*

gas *noun* (*plural* **gases**) **1** a substance like air, which is not solid or liquid; **2** a substance like this which is used for heating and cooking

gate *noun* a sort of door which closes an opening in a fence or wall

gather *verb* to come or bring together; **gathering** *noun*

gauge (*say* **gage**) *noun* an instrument for measuring such things as the amount of rain or the width of wire

Geiger counter for measuring radioactivity

gave *see* GIVE

gaze *verb* to look steadily at something for a long time; **gaze** *noun*

gear *noun* **1** a set of toothed wheels in an engine or a machine, which helps to control the power, speed, or direction of movement; **2** clothes and things for doing an activity, such as swimming

geese *see* GOOSE

general *adjective* about, for, or by everybody or everything

generally *adverb* usually

generous *adjective* ready to give money or be helpful or kind; **generously** *adverb*

gentle *adjective* kind and friendly; soft and quiet; **gentleness** *noun*; **gently** *adverb*

gentleman *noun* a man who behaves well and can be trusted

geography *noun* the study of the world and its countries, seas, rivers, towns, etc; **geographer** *noun*; **geographical** *adjective*; **geographically** *adverb*

gerbil *noun* a small jumping animal like a large mouse, often kept as a pet

German measles *noun see*
RUBELLA

get *verb* (**gets, getting, got**) **1** to
have; to receive; **2** to obtain or
buy; to take; **3** to become;
4 to make happen; **5** to cause
somebody to do something;
6 to arrive; **7** to catch an
illness; **8** **have got to** must

ghost *noun* the spirit of a dead
person or animal which appears
again; **ghostly** *adjective*

giant *noun* a very big, strong
person who is written about in
fairy stories; **giant** *adjective*

gift *noun* something which is
given; a present

giraffe

giraffe *noun* an animal with a
very long neck and legs and a
yellowish coat with dark spots

girl *noun* a young female person

give *verb* (**gives, giving, gave,
given**) **1** to hand something
over to somebody; **2** to let
somebody have something;
3 to pay; **4** to cause to
experience; **5** to produce or
supply; **6** to show; to tell in
words; **7** to do: **give** *a speech*

glad *adjective* pleased and
happy; **gladly** *adverb*; **gladness**
noun

glance *verb* to look quickly;
glance *noun*

glass *noun* **1** a hard clear
material used for windows;
2 a drinking container made of
this material

glasses *noun* two pieces of
specially shaped glass held in a
frame and worn in front of the
eyes to help somebody to see
better

glider *noun* a plane that flies on
a current of air

glove *noun* a covering for the
hand

glow *verb* **1** to give out heat
and/or light without flames or
smoke; **2** to look or feel warm
or excited; **glow** *noun*

¹**glue** *noun* a sticky substance
used for joining things together

²**glue** *verb* (**glues, gluing** *or*
glueing, glued) to join with glue

gnaw (*say* **naw**) *verb* to keep
biting something until it is worn
away; ⚠ **nor**

go *verb* (**goes, going, went,
gone**) **1** to leave; **2** to travel or
move; **3** to reach; **4** to do or
start something: **go** *swimming*;
5 to have a usual or proper
place; **6** to work properly;
7 to become; **8** to wear out;
to disappear; to die

goal *noun* the place where the
ball must go for a point to be
won in football, hockey, etc:
goalkeeper; ⚠ **gaol**

goat *noun* (*female* nanny, *male*
billy, *young* kid) an animal like
a sheep, with horns and that
gives milk and a hairy sort
of wool

g

god *noun* **1** (feminine **goddess**) a being to whom people pray because they feel he or she has power over people and the world; **2 God** the being to whom Christians, Jews, and Muslims pray

goes *see* GO

going *see* GO

gold *noun* **1** a yellow metal that costs a lot of money and is used for making jewellery, coins, etc; **2** the colour of this metal; **gold, golden** *adjective*

goldfish *noun* a small fish that is often kept as a pet

golf *noun* a game in which a small hard ball is hit with special **golf clubs** into holes on a **golf course**; **golfer** *noun*

gone *see* GO

¹**good** *adjective* (**better, best**) **1** having the right qualities; **2** kind; helpful; **3** well-behaved; **4** useful or suitable; **5** enjoyable; **6** able to do something; **7** large in size, amount, etc; **8** used in greetings: **Good morning, Goodbye; goodness** *noun*

²**good** *noun* what is right or useful

goods *noun* things which are bought, sold, or owned

goose *noun* (*plural* **geese**) (*male* **gander**, *young* **gosling**) a large bird with webbed feet

gooseberry *noun* a small round green berry that grows on a bush

gorilla *noun* a large animal with human features, that is very strong, and lives in Africa; ⚠ **guerrilla**

gosling *noun* a young goose

got *see* GET

government *noun* the people who rule a country

grab *verb* (**grabbed**) to take hold of something with a sudden, rough movement; **grab** *noun*

gradual *adjective* happening slowly and little by little; **gradually** *adverb*

grain *noun* **1** a seed of rice, wheat, etc; **2** a small piece

gram *noun* a measure of weight equal to 0.035 ounces

grand *adjective* very large and fine

grandchild *noun* (*plural* **grandchildren**) the child of your child: **granddaughter, grandson**

grandparent *noun* the father or mother of your father or mother: **grandfather, grandmother**

grape *noun* a small round juicy fruit, usually green or dark purple, that grows in bunches and is used for making wine

grapefruit *noun* a large yellow fruit that is like an orange but is sour

grapefruit – a citrus fruit

graphics *noun* pictures in a computer program or game

grass *noun* a green plant that grows close to the ground and has thin leaves that cattle eat; **grassy** *adjective*

grasshopper *noun* a jumping insect which makes a sharp noise by rubbing parts of its body together

¹**grate** *verb* **1** to rub food on a hard rough surface so as to break it into small pieces; **2** to make a sharp unpleasant sound; **grater** *noun*; **grating** *noun*; ⚠ **great**

²**grate** *noun* the bars and frame which hold the wood, coal, etc, in a fireplace; ⚠ **great**

grateful *adjective* feeling or showing thanks to somebody; **gratefully** *adverb*

¹**grave** *noun* the place in the ground where a dead person is buried

²**grave** *adjective* serious; **gravely** *adverb*

gravity *noun* the natural force of the Earth which makes things fall to the ground

gravy *noun* a sauce made from the juice which comes out of meat as it cooks

grease *noun* oil or fat; **grease** *verb*; **greasy** *adjective*

great *adjective* **1** very large, important, etc; **2** very good, enjoyable, or pleasant; **3** unusually good at something; **greatly** *adverb*; ⚠ **grate**

great-grandchild *noun* the son or daughter of a grandchild: **great-granddaughter, great-grandson**

great-grandparent *noun* the father or mother of a grandparent: **great-grandfather, great-grandmother**

greed *noun* a wish to obtain more of something than you need, such as food or money; **greedy** *adjective*; **greedily** *adverb*

green *noun* **1** a colour between yellow and blue, which is that of leaves and grass; **2** a smooth piece of grass used for a special purpose; **green** *adjective*; **greenish** *adjective*

greengrocer *noun* a person who sells vegetables and fruit

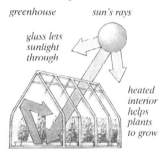

greenhouse   *sun's rays*

glass lets sunlight through

heated interior helps plants to grow

glass prevents warm air escaping

greenhouse *noun* a building made of glass or plastic used to protect growing plants

greet *verb* to welcome with words or actions; **greeting** *noun*

grew *see* GROW

grey *noun* a colour like black mixed with white which is that of ashes and of rain clouds; **grey** *adjective*; **greyish** *adjective*

grin *noun* a wide smile that shows your teeth; **grin** *verb*

grip *verb* **(gripped)** to take a very tight hold of something; **grip** *noun*

groan *verb* to make a deep low sound to show you are in pain or are very sad; **groan** *noun*

grocer *noun* a shop that sells foods, like flour, sugar, rice, and other things for the home, such as matches and soap

ground *noun* **1** the surface of the Earth; **2** soil; earth

group *noun* a number of people or things placed together; a set; **group** *verb*

grow *verb* (**grows, growing, grew, grown**) **1** to get bigger, taller, or longer; **2** to live and be able to develop; **3** to cause to or allow to grow; **4** to become; **growth** *noun*

grown-up *noun* a fully grown person; **grown-up** *adjective*

grubby *adjective* dirty

grunt *noun* a short deep rough sound like that of a pig; **grunt** *verb*

guarantee *noun* a promise to repair or replace something if it does not work; **guarantee** *verb*

¹guard *noun* **1** a person who guards; **2** somebody in charge of a train; **3** something which covers and protects: **fireguard, mudguard**

²guard *verb* to watch over and keep safe; **guardian** *noun*

guerrilla also **guerilla** *noun* a person who fights secretly against the government or against an army; ⚠ **gorilla**

guess *verb* to say something is correct or not correct without really knowing; **guess** *noun*

guest *noun* **1** a person you invite to stay in your home; **2** someone who stays at a hotel

guide *noun* something or somebody that shows the way or gives directions; **guide** *verb*; **guidance** *noun*

guilt *noun* knowing you have done wrong; **guiltily** *adverb*; **guiltless** *adjective*; **guilty** *adjective*

guinea pig *noun* **1** a small furry animal, often kept as a pet; **2** someone used as a test of something, such as a new drug or way of doing things

electric bass guitar

guitar *noun* a musical instrument with usually six strings, played by plucking

¹gum *noun* the part of the mouth in which your teeth are fixed

²gum *noun* **1** a substance used to stick things together; **2** a type of sweet

gun *noun* a weapon from which bullets are fired

gutter *noun* an open pipe at the edge of a roof or a channel at the side of the road to carry away water

gymnastics, gym *noun* the training of the body by exercises; **gymnasium** *noun*; **gymnast** *noun*

g

Hh

habit *noun* **1** something you always do; **2** a special kind of clothing, especially that worn by monks and nuns

¹hack *verb* to cut roughly; **hack** *noun*

²hack *noun* a ride on a horse; **hack** *verb*

hacker *noun* someone who breaks into a computer system; **hack** *verb*

had *see* HAVE

haddock *noun* a common sea fish that is eaten

hadn't *see* HAVE

hail *noun* little balls of ice that fall from the clouds; **hail** *verb*

hair *noun* the fine threads that grow from the skin of a person or animal: **hairbrush, haircut, hairdresser; hairy** *adjective;* **hairless** *adjective;* ⚠ **hare**

¹half *noun, pronoun (plural* **halves**) one of the two equal parts into which something is divided, ½, 50%, **half** *adjective,* **halfway** *adjective, adverb*

²half *adverb* **1** partly; not completely; **2 half past** thirty minutes after: **half past** *six*

hall *noun* **1** a large room in which meetings, dances, etc, can be held; **2** the space just inside the front door of a house, from which the rooms open; ⚠ **haul**

Hallowe'en also **Halloween** *noun* the night of 31st October

ham *noun* meat from a pig's leg

hammer *noun* a tool with a heavy metal head for hitting in nails, or for breaking things; **hammer** *verb*

¹hand *noun* **1** the movable part at the end of the arm, including the fingers, with which you hold things; **2** a pointer or needle on a clock or machine; **handful** *noun*

²hand *verb* to give from your own hand into somebody else's; **hand over**

handbag *noun* a small bag for money and personal things

handkerchief *noun (plural* **handkerchiefs** *or* **handkerchieves**) a piece of cloth or thin soft paper for drying the nose, eyes, etc

¹handle *noun* a part of something for holding it or for opening it: **handlebars**

²handle *verb* **1** to feel or move with your hands; **2** to deal with; to control

handsome *adjective* good-looking and attractive; **handsomely** *adverb*

¹hang *verb* (**hangs, hanging, hung**) **1** to fix something at the top so that the lower part is free; **2** to be in such a position

²hang *verb* (**hangs, hanging, hanged**) to kill or die, as a punishment for a crime, by dropping with a rope round the neck

pumpkin lantern for Hallowe'en

happen *verb* **1** to take place; to be; **2** to do by chance; **happening** *noun*

happy *adjective* feeling very pleased; giving pleasure; **happily** *adverb*; **happiness** *noun*

harass *verb* to annoy or trouble somebody; **harassment** *noun*

harbour *noun* an area of sheltered water where ships are safe from rough seas

a harbour wall keeps out rough seas so that boats can be moored safely

¹**hard** *adjective* **1** firm, solid, and not easily broken, pressed down, bent, etc; **2** difficult to do or understand; **harden** *verb*

²**hard** *adverb* **1** with great effort; **2** a lot; very much

hardly *adverb* almost not at all; only just

hardware *noun* **1** the machines that make up a computer; **2** goods for the home and garden, such as pans, tools, etc

hare *noun* (*young* **leveret**) an animal like a rabbit, with long ears and long back legs that make it able to run fast; ⚠ **hair**

harm *noun* damage; wrong; **harm** *verb*; **harmful** *adjective*; **harmfully** *adverb*; **harmfulness** *noun*

harp *noun* a large musical instrument with strings, played by stroking or plucking with the hands; **harpist** *noun*

harvest *noun* **1** the time of year when crops are picked; **2** the amount picked; **harvest** *verb*

has *see* HAVE

hasn't *see* HAVE

hat *noun* a covering placed on top of the head

hate *verb* to have a strong dislike for something or somebody; **hate** *noun*; **hateful** *adjective*; **hatred** *noun*

haul *verb* to pull hard; ⚠ **hall**

haunt *verb* to appear in a place as a ghost

have *verb* (**has, having, had, haven't, hasn't, hadn't**) **1** also **have got** to possess or own; **2** to receive or take; **3** to enjoy or experience; **4** to cause to be done; **5 had better** ought to; **6 have to** also **have got to** must

hay *noun* grass that has been cut and dried and is used as food for horses, sheep, and cows: **haystack, haymaking**

he *pronoun* (**him, himself**) that male person or animal

¹**head** *noun* **1** the part of the body which contains the eyes, ears, nose and mouth, and the brain – in people on top of the body, in other animals in front: **headache, headband, headfirst**; **2** the chief person; a ruler or leader; **3** the front side of a coin which often has a picture of the ruler's head: *heads or tails?*; **4** the top or front part of something; **5 head over heels** turning over in the air headfirst

²**head** *verb* **1** to be at the front or in charge of something; **2** to strike a ball with the head; **header** *noun*

headmaster (feminine **headmistress**) *noun* the teacher in charge of a school

headphones *noun* a piece of apparatus made to fit over the ears, for listening to a radio, cassette player, etc

headphones

heal *verb* to make or become better; ⚠ **heel**

health *noun* **1** the state of being well, without any illness; **2** the condition of the body; **healthily** *adverb*; **healthiness** *noun*; **healthy** *adjective*

heap *noun* a pile or mass of things one on top of another; **heap** *verb*

hear *verb* (**hears, hearing, heard**) **1** to receive and understand by using the ears; **2** to get news of; to be told; ⚠ **here**

heart *noun* **1** the organ inside the chest which pumps the blood round the body: **heartbeat, heart attack**; **2** the centre of your feelings; your true nature; **3** a playing card with one or more figures of this shape printed on it in red; **4** the centre or middle of something; **heartless** *adjective*; **hearty** *adjective*

¹**heat** *noun* **1** hotness; warmth; **2** a part of a race or competition to decide who will be in the final

²**heat** *verb* to make or become warm or hot; **heater** *noun*

heaven *noun* the place where God or the gods are said to live and where good people are believed to go after they die

heavy *adjective* **1** of great weight, and not easy to move or lift; **2** of unusual force or amount; **heavily** *adverb*; **heaviness** *noun*

hectare (*say* **hektair**) *noun* a measure of land equal to 10,000 square metres or 2.471 acres

hedge *noun* a row of bushes or small trees acting as a fence

hedgehog *noun* a small insect-eating animal which comes out only at night. It rolls itself into a ball and sticks up sharp spines when it is afraid

h

heel *noun* **1** the back part of the foot; **2** the part of a shoe, sock, etc, that covers this; the raised part of a shoe underneath the foot; ⚠ **heal**

height *noun* how tall or high something is

heir (*say* air) (feminine **heiress**) *noun* a person who gets money, property, or a title when somebody dies; ⚠ **air**

held *see* HOLD

passenger helicopter

helicopter *noun* a type of aircraft which is made to fly by a set of large fast-turning metal blades, and which can land in a small space, take off straight from the ground, and hover or hang in the air

hell *noun* the place where the Devil is said to live and where bad people are believed to go after they die

hello used as a greeting

helmet *noun* a hard covering to protect the head, worn by soldiers, policemen, etc

¹help *verb* **1** to do part of the work for somebody; **2** to be of use; **3 can't help** can't avoid or prevent; **helper** *noun*

²help *noun* **1** the act of helping; **2** something or somebody that helps; **helpful** *adjective*; **helpfully** *adverb*; **helpfulness** *noun*

hem *noun* the sewn bottom edge of a skirt, dress, etc; **hem** *verb*

hen *noun* (*male* **cock**; *young* **chick**) a female chicken often kept for its eggs on farms

¹her *adjective* belonging to her

²her *see* SHE

herd *noun* a group of animals of one kind that live and feed together; **herd** *verb*

here *adverb* **1** at, in, or to this place; **2** at this point of time; ⚠ **hear**

herring *noun* a fish which swims in large shoals in the sea and is eaten for food

hers *pronoun* that/those belonging to a female person

herself *see* SHE

hibernate *verb* to be in a state like a long sleep during the winter, as some animals do; **hibernation** *noun*

hide *verb* (**hides, hiding, hid, hidden**) to put or keep out of sight; to make or keep secret

hi-fi *noun* CD players, cassette recorders, and other equipment for reproducing sound very clearly

high *adjective, adverb* **1** at a point well above the ground; **2** important; chief; **3** near the top of the set of sounds that the ear can hear

high chair *noun* a chair with long legs and a tray in which a baby or small child can sit

hijack *verb* to force the driver of a plane, train, etc, to take you somewhere or give you something; **hijacker** *noun*

hill *noun* a raised piece of ground; a small mountain: **uphill, downhill; hilly** *adjective*

him *see* HE; ⚠ **hymn**

himself *see* HE

Hindu *noun* a person who follows **Hinduism**, the main religion of India

hip *noun* the fleshy part of either side of the human body above the legs

hippopotamus, hippo *noun* (*plural* **hippopotamuses** *or* **hippopotami, hippos**) a large animal with a thick skin, that lives near water

¹**his** *adjective* belonging to a male person

²**his** *pronoun* that/those belonging to a male person

history *noun* the study of past events; **historical** *adjective*; **historically** *adverb*

¹**hit** *verb* (**hits, hitting, hit**) to strike; to come against something with force

²**hit** *noun* **1** a blow; a stroke; **2** a successful song, film, play, etc

hive *also* **beehive** *noun* a place where bees live, like a small hut or box

hobby *noun* an enjoyable activity you do in your free time

hockey *noun* a game played by two teams of eleven players each, on a field with sticks and a ball

hog *noun* a male pig

hold *verb* (**holds, holding, held**) **1** to keep or support with the hands; **2** to contain; **3** to possess; **4** to arrange and give an event, such as a party; **hold** *noun*; **holder** *noun*

hole *noun* **1** an empty space or opening within something; **2** the home of a small animal; ⚠ **whole**

holiday *noun* **1** a time of rest from work or school; **2** going away to another country or place for a time to rest and enjoy yourself

hollow *adjective* having an empty space inside; not solid

holly *noun* a small tree with dark green prickly leaves and red berries

hologram, holograph *noun* a picture, that looks very real produced by lasers; **holograph** *verb*; **holography** *noun*

holy *adjective* of God and religion

home *noun* the house or place where somebody lives; **home** *adjective*; **homeless** *adjective*; **homelessness** *noun*

honest (**say onest**) *adjective* not telling lies or deceiving people; fair and true; **honestly** *adverb*; **honesty** *noun*

honey *noun* the sweet sticky material produced by bees

honeycomb with worker bee

honour (**say onor**) *noun* great respect; **honour** *verb*; **honourable** *adjective*

hood *noun* **1** a covering for the head and neck usually fastened to the back of a coat; **2** a folding cover over a car, pram, etc

hoof *noun* (*plural* **hoofs** or **hooves**) the hard foot of certain animals, such as horses and cows

¹**hook** *noun* a curved piece of metal, plastic, etc, for catching something on or hanging things on

²**hook** *verb* **1** to catch with a hook; **2** to hang on or fasten with a hook

hoop *noun* a round band of wood or metal; a ring

hop *verb* (**hopped**) **1** to jump on one leg; **2** to move along by jumping, like some birds and small creatures

hope *verb* to wish for and expect; **hope** *noun*; **hopeful** *adjective*; **hopefully** *adverb*; **hopeless** *adjective*; **hopelessly** *adverb*

horizon *noun* the place where the sky seems to meet the Earth or sea; **horizontal** *adjective*

horn *noun* **1** one of two hard pointed growths on the top of the heads of some animals such as cattle, sheep, and goats; **2** the material that these growths are made of; **3** a musical instrument that you blow; **4** an instrument in a car, bus, etc, that makes a noise to warn people; **horned** *adjective*; **hornless** *adjective*

horrendous *adjective* really terrible; causing great fear

horrible *adjective* very unkind, unpleasant, or ugly; **horribly** *adverb*

horror *noun* great shock, fear, and dislike; **horrid** *adjective*; **horridly** *adverb*; **horridness** *noun*

horse *noun* a large strong animal with a mane, tail, and hooves, that people ride and used for pulling and carrying heavy things in old times: **horseback, horsehair, horseshoe**

hose also **hosepipe** *noun* a piece of rubber or plastic tube that can direct water onto fires, a garden, etc

hospital *noun* a place where ill people stay and have treatment

host (feminine **hostess**) *noun* a person who receives and looks after guests

hot *adjective* (**hotter**) **1** having a lot of heat; **2** having a burning taste; **hotness** *noun*

hotel *noun* a building where people can stay if they pay

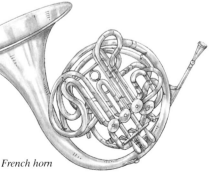

French horn

74

hour (*say* **our**) *noun* a measure of time; sixty minutes; **hourly** *adverb*; ⚠ **our**

house *noun* a building for people to live in: **household, housekeeper, housewife, housework**

House of Commons *noun* the lower, but more powerful, of the two parts of the British Parliament

House of Lords *noun* the upper, but less powerful, of the two parts of the British Parliament

hover *verb* to stay in the air in one place

hovercraft *noun* (*trademark*) a sort of boat that moves over land or water by means of a strong force of air underneath

how *adverb* **1** in what way or by what means; **2** in what condition of health or mind; **3** by what amount

howl *noun* a long loud cry like that made by wolves and dogs; **howl** *verb*

hug *verb* (**hugged**) to hold tightly in the arms; **hug** *noun*

huge *adjective* very big; **hugeness** *noun*

hum *verb* (**hummed**) **1** to make a buzzing sound like a bee; **2** to sing with the lips closed; **hum** *noun*

¹**human** *adjective* of or like a person

²**human** also **human being** *noun* a man, woman, or child, not an animal

humour *noun* the ability to laugh at things or make other people laugh; **humorous** *adjective*

this warning road sign shows a hump-back bridge ahead

hump *noun* a lump or round part which sticks out

hundred *adjective, noun* the number 100; **hundredth** *adjective, adverb*

hung *see* HANG

hunger *noun* the wish or need for food; **hungrily** *adverb*; **hungry** *adjective*

hunt *verb* **1** to chase and kill animals and birds either for food or sport; **2** to search for; **hunt** *noun*; **hunter** *noun*

hurricane *noun* a violent wind storm

hurry *verb* to move or do something quickly; **hurry** *noun*

hurt *verb* (**hurts, hurting, hurt**) to cause pain and/or injury; to damage; **hurt** *noun*; **hurtful** *adjective*

husband *noun* the man to whom a woman is married

hut *noun* a small building, often made of wood

hutch *noun* a small box or cage for keeping rabbits in

hydrogen *noun* a colourless gas that is lighter than air and burns very easily

hyena *noun* a wild animal like a dog, that has a cry like a laugh

hymn *noun* a song to or about God; ⚠ **him**

hyphen *noun* a short line (-) that joins words or parts of words

Ii

I *pronoun* **(me, myself)** the person speaking

ice *noun* water which has frozen to a solid; **icy** *adjective*

ice cream *noun* a sweet frozen mixture, usually containing milk products

icicle *noun* a pointed stick of ice formed when running water freezes

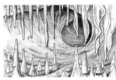

stalactites

stalagmites

stalactites and stalagmites look like stone icicles – they form in caves from the constant dripping of water

icing *noun* a sweet and either creamy or hard covering for cakes, biscuits, etc

idea *noun* a picture in the mind; a thought of something new to do

ideal *adjective* perfect; the best possible

identical *adjective* exactly the same

identify *verb* to say who somebody is or what something is; **identification** *noun*; **identity** *noun*

idle *adjective* **1** not working; not doing anything; **2** lazy; **idleness** *noun*; **idly** *adverb*; ⚠ **idol**

idol *noun* **1** a statue worshipped as a god; **2** somebody who is greatly loved or admired; ⚠ **idle**

i e that is to say

if *conjunction* on condition that; whether

ignorant *adjective* not knowing much; not having been taught; **ignorance** *noun*

ignore *verb* to take no notice of somebody or something

¹**ill** *adjective* not well

²**ill** *adverb* **(worse, worst)** badly, cruelly, or unpleasantly: *The child has been **ill**-treated*

illness *noun* a disease; sickness

illustration *noun* a picture to go with the words of a book, a speaker, etc; **illustrate** *verb*

imagine *verb* **1** to form a picture of something in the mind; **2** to suppose or have an idea about; **imaginary** *adjective*; **imagination** *noun*; **imaginative** *adjective*

immediate *adjective* done or needed at once; **immediately** *adverb*

impatient *adjective* not able to wait for something to happen; **impatience** *noun*; **impatiently** *adverb*

important *adjective* powerful; having a big effect; **importance** *noun*; **importantly** *adverb*

impossible *adjective* not possible; not able to be done; **impossibility** *noun*; **impossibly** *adverb*

impress *verb* to cause admiration; to have a strong effect on the mind; **impression** *noun*; **impressive** *adjective*; **impressively** *adverb*

improve *verb* to make or get better; **improvement** *noun*

in *preposition, adverb* **1** contained or surrounded by something; within; inside; **2** during; at the time of; ⚠ **inn**

inch *noun* a measure of length equal to $\frac{1}{12}$ of a foot or 2.54 centimetres

include *verb* to have or put in as a part; to contain

increase *verb* to make or become larger in amount or number; **increase** *noun*; **increasingly** *adverb*

incredible *adjective* too strange or good to be believed; **incredibly** *adverb*

indeed *adverb* really; certainly

independent *adjective* not needing other things or people; **independence** *noun*; **independently** *adverb*

indigestion *noun* illness or pain caused by the stomach not being able to deal with the food which has been eaten

indigo *noun* a dark purple-blue colour

indoor *adjective* done, used, etc, indoors

indoors *adverb* to, in, or into the inside of a building

industry *noun* the making of machines, getting oil out of the ground, or other activities when employing lots of people: *the computer industry*, **industrial** *adjective*

infant *noun* a very young child

infect *verb* to put disease into a person's body; **infection** *noun*; **infectious** *adjective*

influence *verb* to have an effect on; **influence** *noun*

inform *verb* to tell

information *noun* **1** facts or other things that people know; **2** these things stored in a computer

initial *noun* a large letter at the beginning of a name, used to stand for the name

inject *verb* to give medicine through the skin, with a needle; **injection** *noun*

injure *verb* to hurt; **injury** *noun*

ink *noun* coloured liquid used for writing or drawing; **inky** *adjective*

in-laws *noun* the father and mother, and sometimes other relatives, of the person somebody has married

inn *noun* a pub or small hotel; ⚠ **in**

inner *adjective* inside; closest to the centre

input *verb* to put data into a computer; **input** *noun*

insect *noun* a small creature with six legs and a body divided into three parts, such as an ant or fly

stick insect

¹**inside** *noun* the area within something else; that part that is nearest to the centre, or that faces away from other people or from the open air

²**inside** *preposition, adjective, adverb* in; on or to the inside of something

instead *adverb* in place of somebody or something

instruct *verb* **1** to teach; **2** to order; **instruction** *noun*

instrument *noun* **1** a tool; **2** an object such as a piano, horn, etc, played to give music

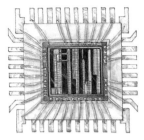

an integrated circuit as on a microchip

integrated circuit *noun* a tiny electronic circuit on a single computer chip

intelligence *noun* the ability to learn and understand; **intelligent** *adjective*

intend *verb* to plan to do something; **intention** *noun*

interest *noun* wanting to know more about something; getting pleasure from studying something; **interest** *verb*; **interesting** *adjective*; **interestingly** *adverb*

interfere *verb* to get in the way; to prevent somebody from doing something; **interference** *noun*; **interfering** *adjective*

internet *noun* a system of computers that allows people to write to one another through their own computers round the world

interrupt *verb* to stop something continuing; to break in on somebody who is already speaking; **interruption** *noun*

into *preposition* to the inside of; in

introduce *verb* **1** to make two people known for the first time to each other; **2** to bring in a new thing; **introduction** *noun*

invent *verb* to make up or produce something new; **invention** *noun*; **inventor** *noun*

invisible *adjective* not able to be seen

invite *verb* to ask somebody to do something or go somewhere, such as to a party; **invitation** *noun*

inwards *adverb* towards the inside

¹**iron** *noun* **1** a useful grey-white metal; **2** a heavy metal object with a handle, pointed at the front and flat underneath, used for making clothes smooth: **ironing board**

²**iron** *verb* to make smooth with an iron

irritate *verb* **1** to annoy; **2** to make sore; **irritation** *noun*

is *see* BE

island *noun* a piece of land surrounded by water

isn't *see* BE

it *pronoun* (**itself**) **1** that thing already mentioned; **2** that person or animal whose sex is not known or not thought important

itch *verb* to feel or cause a soreness which you want to scratch; **itch** *noun*; **itchy** *adjective*; **itchiness** *noun*

its *adjective* belonging to it; ⚠ **it's**

it's it is; it has; ⚠ **its**

itself *see* IT

ivory *noun* **1** a hard white substance of which elephants' tusks are made; **2** the creamy colour of ivory

ivy *noun* a plant which climbs up walls and has shiny leaves

Jj

jack *noun* **1** an apparatus for lifting something heavy, such as a car, off the ground; **2** also **knave** any of the four playing cards with a picture of a man, that comes between the 10 and the queen

car jack

jackal *noun* a wild animal like a dog

jacket *noun* a short coat

jail also **gaol** *verb* to put in prison; **jail** *noun*

¹jam *noun* sweet food made of fruit boiled in sugar, for spreading on bread

²jam *noun* a mass of people or things: *a traffic* **jam**

³jam *verb* (**jammed**) **1** to pack tightly into a small space; to push or press together; **2** to get stuck

January *noun* the first month of the year

jar *noun* a container like a bottle with a short neck and wide mouth

javelin *noun* a light throwing spear used in sport

jaw *noun* either of the two face bones which hold the teeth

jazz *noun* a type of music with a strong beat

jealous *adjective* **1** wanting to get what somebody else has; **2** being afraid of losing what you have; **jealously** *adverb*; **jealousy** *noun*

jeans *noun* strong cotton trousers that are often blue

jelly *noun* a soft food that shakes when moved

jersey *noun* a sweater

jet *noun* **1** a type of aircraft that has a **jet engine**; **2** a narrow stream of liquid, gas, etc, forced through a small hole

Jew *noun* a person belonging to the worldwide group descended from the people of ancient Israel and practising their religion; **Jewish** *adjective*

jewel *noun* a precious stone, used as an ornament

jewellery or **jewelry** *noun* ornaments with jewels

jigsaw puzzle or **jigsaw** *noun* a picture made up of pieces which have to be fitted together

job *noun* **1** a piece of work; **2** regular work for which you are paid

jockey *noun* a person who rides in horse races

jog *verb* (**jogged**) **1** to run slowly and steadily; to run like this to keep fit; **2** to shake or push slightly; **jog** *noun*; **jogger** *noun*; **jogging** *noun*

join *verb* **1** to fasten together; to connect; **2** to become a member of a group; **join** *noun*

juggler

j

joint *noun* **1** a join; a thing used for making a join; **2** a place where two or more bones fit together; **3** a large piece of meat

joke *noun* anything said or done to cause amusement; **joke** *verb*; **jokingly** *adverb*

journey *noun* (*plural* **journeys**) a trip of some distance

joy *noun* great happiness

joystick *noun* a lever in a control box that is connected to a computer to move figures, pictures, etc, about on a computer screen, especially in computer games

¹judge *verb* **1** to act as a judge; **2** to give a decision about somebody or something; **3** to give an opinion about

²judge *noun* **1** the person who has the power to decide questions brought before a court of law; **2** a person who decides who has won a competition; **judgement, judgment** *noun*

jug *noun* a pot for liquids, with a handle and a lip for pouring

juggle *verb* to keep several things in the air at the same time, throwing them up and catching them; **juggler** *noun*

juice *noun* the liquid part of fruit, vegetables, and meat; **juiciness** *noun*; **juicy** *adjective*

July *noun* the seventh month of the year

¹jump *verb* **1** to move your body suddenly and quickly off the ground, into the air, or over something; **2** to make a quick sudden movement

²jump *noun* **1** an act of jumping; **2** something you jump over, in a race

June *noun* the sixth month of the year

junior *adjective* **1** younger; **2** of lower importance or position; **junior** *noun*

the planet Jupiter –
the big red spot is a violent storm

Jupiter *noun* the largest planet of the solar system

¹just *adverb* **1** exactly; **2 just now**: very near the present time; **3** hardly; almost not; **4** only

²just *adjective* fair and honest; **justice** *noun*; **justly** *adverb*

kaleidoscope *noun* a tube fitted with mirrors and pieces of coloured glass which shows coloured patterns when turned

kangaroo *noun* (*young* **joey**) an animal which jumps along on large back legs and carries its young in a special pocket

red kangaroo with a joey in its pouch

keen *adjective* eager to do something; liking to do something; **keenly** *adverb*; **keenness** *noun*

keep *verb* (**keeps, keeping, kept**) **1** to have without giving back; **2 keep on** to do again and again; **3** to have or hold for some time; **4** to take care of; **5** to own; to have the use of; **6** to cause to continue, to stay, or to remain

kennel *noun* a small house for a dog

kerb *noun* a line of raised stones separating the footpath from the road

ketchup *noun* a sauce, made usually of tomatoes, for flavouring food

kettle *noun* a pot with a lid, handle, and spout for heating water to make tea, coffee, etc

key *noun* **1** a metal instrument for locking or unlocking a door, winding a clock, etc: **keyhole, key ring; 2** a part of a piano, computer, etc, that is pressed with the finger: **keyboard; 3** something that explains or helps you to understand, such as the list of symbols or abbreviations on a map; **4** a set of musical notes with a certain starting note

kick *verb* **1** to hit with the foot; **2** to move the feet backwards and forwards; **kick** *noun*; **kicker** *noun*

kid *noun* **1** a child or young person; **2** a young goat

kidnap *verb* to take somebody away and ask for money in return for bringing him or her back safely; **kidnapper** *noun*

kill *verb* to cause somebody or something to die; **killer** *noun*

kilogram also **kilo** *noun* a measure of weight equal to 1000 grams or 2.21 pounds

kilometre *noun* a measure of length equal to 1000 metres or 0.62 miles

¹**kind** (*say* **kynd**) *noun* a group that are alike; type; sort

²**kind** *adjective* helpful; gentle and wanting to do good; **kindness** *noun*

k

king *noun* **1** the male ruler of a country: **kingdom**; **2** any of the four playing cards with a picture of a king

kipper *noun* a smoked salted herring used for food

kiss *verb* to touch with the lips as a greeting or sign of love; **kiss** *noun*

kitchen *noun* a room used for cooking

kite *noun* a very light frame covered with paper or cloth for flying at the end of a long string

kitten *noun* a young cat

knee *noun* the middle joint of the leg

kneel *verb* (**kneels, kneeling, knelt**) to go down on the knees

knew *see* KNOW; ⚠ **new**

knife *noun* (*plural* **knives**) a blade fixed in a handle for cutting

knight – a chess piece: the horse's head symbolises a soldier on horseback

knight *noun* **1** a man given the title 'Sir' by the king or queen of Great Britain; **2** a soldier on horseback serving a ruler; ⚠ **night**

knit *verb* (**knits, knitting, knitted or knit**) **1** to make a sort of cloth or a piece of clothing by joining threads using long **knitting needles**; **2** to join together closely; **knitter** *noun*; **knitting** *noun*

knob *noun* a round lump, handle, or control button; **knobbly** *adjective*

¹**knock** *verb* **1** to strike something so that it makes a noise; **2** to hit hard

²**knock** *noun* **1** a sound caused by knocking; **2** a hit

figure of eight knot

knot *noun* **1** a fastening formed by tying two ends of something together; **2** a hard mass in wood where a branch has come off a tree; **3** a measure of the speed of a ship, 1852 metres or 6076.12 feet per hour; **knot** *verb*; ⚠ **not**

know *verb* (**knows, knowing, knew, known**) **1** to have in the mind; **2** to have learnt; **3** to have seen, heard, etc, before; to recognise somebody or something; **knowledge** *noun*; ⚠ **no**

knuckle *noun* a finger joint

label *noun* a piece of paper fixed to something, on which is written what it is, where it is to go, etc; **label** *verb*

lace *noun* **1** a string for fastening the edges of something together: **shoelaces**; **2** pretty cloth with a pattern of holes in it

ladder *noun* a frame of two bars or ropes of equal length joined by shorter bars that form steps for climbing

lady *noun* **1** a polite way of saying woman; **2 Lady** the wife of a Lord or knight; the daughter of an earl, duke, etc

ladybird *noun* a small round beetle, usually red with black spots

laid *see* LAY

lain *see* LIE; ⚠ **lane**

lake *noun* a large mass of water surrounded by land

lamb (*say* **lam**) *noun* **1** a young sheep; **2** the meat of sheep

lamp *noun* an object for giving light: **table lamp**; **street lamp**

¹**land** *noun* **1** the solid dry part of the Earth's surface; **2** a country

²**land** *verb* to come to, bring to, or put on land

landing *noun* the level space or passage at the top of stairs

lane *noun* **1** a narrow, often winding, road; **2** any of the parallel parts into which wide roads are divided; ⚠ **lain**

language *noun* **1** the words people use in speaking or writing; **2** a system of signs for use in a computer

laptop *noun* a small computer that you can carry round with you

laptop computer

large *adjective* more than usual in size, number, or amount; big; **largely** *adverb*

lark *noun* a small light brown bird with long pointed wings

argon laser beam – for measuring distances to objects in space

laser *noun* a machine with a very strong, very narrow beam of light used to cut materials, send messages, etc

¹**last** *adjective, adverb, pronoun* **1** after all others; **2** the one before now; most recent

²**last** *verb* to continue

late *adjective, adverb* arriving, developing, happening, etc, after the expected time; **lateness** *noun*

lately *adverb* recently

laugh *verb* to make a sound to show that you are pleased, happy, amused, etc; **laugh** *noun*; **laughter** *noun*

launching the American space shuttle

launch *verb* **1** to set a boat into the water; **2** to send a rocket into space: **launch pad, launching site**

launderette *noun* a place where the public can wash clothes in machines that work when coins are put into them

laundry *noun* **1** a place where clothes are washed and ironed; **2** clothes, sheets, etc, that need washing or have just been washed

lava *noun* very hot liquid rock that comes out of a volcano

lavatory *noun* **1** a large seatlike bowl connected to a drain, used for passing body waste; **2** a room or building containing this

law *noun* a rule made by the government that everybody must follow; **lawful** *adjective*; **lawyer** *noun*

lawn *noun* a stretch of smooth ground covered with short grass: **lawn mower**

¹**lay** *verb* (**lays, laying, laid**) **1** to place or set; to put in a certain position; **2** to produce an egg or eggs

²**lay** *see* LIE

layer *noun* a thickness of some material laid over something or put between two things

lazy *adjective* not wanting to work; **lazily** *adverb*; **laziness** *noun*

¹**lead** (*say like* need) *verb* (**leads, leading, led**) **1** to show somebody the way; to guide; **2** to be the chief person in doing something; to be first, especially in a race or competition; **leader** *noun*

²**lead** (*say like* need) *noun* **1** the first or front place; a guiding example; **2** the chief acting part in a play or film; **3** also **leash** a length of leather, chain, etc, tied to a dog to control it; **4** a wire that carries electrical power

³**lead** (*say like* dead) *noun* **1** a soft heavy metal, sometimes used as a covering for roofs; **2** the black substance in the middle of pencils; ⚠ **led**

leaf *noun* (*plural* **leaves**) one of the flat parts of a plant that grow from a stem or branch

leak *noun* a hole or crack through which a liquid or gas may pass in or out; **leak** *verb*; **leaky** *adjective*; ⚠ **leek**

¹**lean** *verb* (**leans, leaning, leant** *or* **leaned**) **1** to bend forwards, backwards, sideways, or towards; **2** to rest something against or on another

²**lean** *adjective* without much fat; thin; **leanness** *noun*

84

leap *verb* **(leaps, leaping, leapt** *or* **leaped)** to jump; **leap** *noun*

learn *verb* **(learns, learning, learned** *or* **learnt) 1** to get knowledge or skill; **2** to find out; **learner** *noun*; **learning** *noun*

least *noun, adjective, adverb* **1** the smallest thing, amount, etc; **2** *see* LITTLE

leather *noun* animal skin treated for use in shoes, jackets, etc

¹**leave** *verb* **(leaves, leaving, left) 1** to go away from; **2** to allow something to stay somewhere; **3** to let things stay as they are

²**leave** *noun* a short time away from work

leaves *see* LEAF

led *see* ¹LEAD; ⚠ ³**lead**

leek *noun* a vegetable like an onion, with a long white fleshy stem; ⚠ **leak**

¹**left** *noun, adjective* the side or direction opposite to right

²**left** *see* LEAVE

leg *noun* **1** the part of the body on which an animal walks and which supports its body; **2** the part of a piece of clothing that covers the leg; **3** one of the pieces of wood, metal, or plastic on which a table, chair, etc, stands

legal *adjective* allowed by the law; **legally** *adverb*

lemon *noun* **1** a type of fruit like an orange but with a light yellow skin and sour juice; **2** a light bright yellow colour; **lemon** *adjective*

lemonade *noun* a drink tasting of lemons and usually containing bubbles of gas

lend *verb* **(lends, lending, lent)** to give somebody the use of something, such as money or a book for a short time, after which he or she must give it back; **lender** *noun*

length *noun* the measurement from one end of something to the other; **lengthen** *verb*; **lengthy** *adjective*

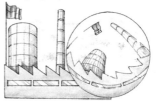

a fisheye lens creates a curved, slightly distorted picture

lens *noun* (*plural* **lenses**) a piece of glass or plastic with curved surfaces, used in cameras, telescopes, microscopes, glasses, etc, for seeing things clearly

lent *see* LEND

Lent *noun* the forty days before Easter, during which many Christians give up some of their usual pleasures

leopard *noun* (*female* **leopardess**) a large meat-eating wild animal of the cat family, that is yellowish with black spots

leotard *noun* a piece of clothing that fits tightly, worn when doing exercise, etc

less *noun, adjective, adverb* **1** a smaller amount; not so much; **2** *see* LITTLE

lesson *noun* **1** part of a school day, when a pupil or class studies a subject; **2** something that we must learn

let *verb* (**lets, letting, let**) **1** to allow to do or happen; **2** to give the use of a room, a building, land, etc, in return for money; **3 let's** let us; used when you ask somebody to do something with you

letter *noun* **1** a written or printed message sent to somebody, usually in an envelope; **2** one of the signs we use in writing

lettuce *noun* a garden plant with large pale green leaves which are used in salads

¹level *adjective* **1** having a surface which is the same height above the ground all over; **2** flat; smooth; **3** equal

²level *verb* (**levelled**) to make or become flat

a carpenter's spirit level

lever *noun* a long bar used for lifting or moving something heavy

leveret *noun* a young hare

library *noun* **1** a room or a building that contains books that may be looked at or borrowed: **public library**; **2** someone's collection of books

licence *noun* a written or printed paper which allows you to do something: **driving licence**; △ **license**

license *verb* to give or get permission to do something; △ **licence**

lick *verb* to move the tongue across something in order to taste, clean, make wet, etc; **lick** *noun*

lid *noun* **1** the top of a box or other hollow container, that can be taken off; **2** an eyelid

¹lie *verb* (**lies, lying, lay, lain**) **1** to have your body in a flat resting position on something such as the ground or a bed; **2** to be or stay in a certain place

²lie *noun* something said which is not true; **lie** *verb*

life *noun* (*plural* **lives**) **1** the active force that makes humans, animals, and plants able to grow and produce young ones, and that makes them different from stones, machines, objects, etc; **2** the time that humans, animals, and plants are alive; **3** the way somebody lives or spends their time; **4** activity; strength; cheerfulness

¹lift *verb* to pick up; to pick up and put in a higher place; to raise

²lift *noun* **1** a machine in a building for taking people and goods from one floor to another; **2** a free ride in a vehicle

lift-off *noun* the start of the flight of a spacecraft

¹light *noun* **1** that which makes you able to see things; **2** something that gives out light such as a lamp or torch; **3** something that will make something else start burning

²light *adjective* **1** having light; not dark; bright; **2** not deep or dark in colour; pale

³light *verb* (**lights, lighting, lit** *or* **lighted**) **1** to make a fire, match, etc, start to burn; **2** to give light to something

⁴light *adjective* of little weight; not heavy; **lightly** *adverb*; **lightness** *noun*

lighten *verb* to make or become brighter or less dark; **lightening** *noun*; ⚠ **lightning**

lighthouse *noun* a tower with a powerful flashing light that guides ships or warns them of dangerous rocks

forked lightning

lightning *noun* a powerful flash of light in the sky, usually followed by thunder; ⚠ **lightening**

light year *noun* a unit of length in astronomy equal to the distance that light travels in one year in a vacuum: 9460 thousand million kilometres (5878 thousand million miles)

¹**like** *verb* **1** to be fond of; to find pleasant; **2** to wish; **liking** *noun*

²**like** *adjective, preposition* **1** in the same way as; of the same kind; **2** for example; **likeness** *noun*; **likewise** *adverb*

likely *adjective* **1** expected; **2** suitable

lilac *noun* a tree with pinkish purple or white flowers giving a sweet smell

lily *noun* a plant with large white flowers

limb (*say* **lim**) *noun* a part of the body, such as an arm or a leg

lime *noun* a fruit like a small green lemon

¹**limp** *verb* to walk as if your leg or foot has been hurt; **limp** *noun*

²**limp** *adjective* not stiff or firm

line *noun* **1** a long very thin mark which can be drawn on a surface; **2** a piece of string, wire, or thin cord: **fishing line**; **3** a set of people or things one after the other or beside each other; a row

lion *noun* (*female* **lioness**, *young* **cub**) a large wild animal of the cat family. The male has a thick mane over the head and shoulders

lion cub

lip *noun* **1** one of the two soft pink edges of the mouth: **lipstick**; **2** the edge of something such as a cup

liquid *noun* a substance, like water, that is not solid or gas, that flows and has no fixed shape

list *noun* a set of names of things written one after the other, so as to remember them

listen *verb* to try to hear; to pay attention to what someone is saying; **listener** *noun*

lit *see* LIGHT

litre *noun* a measure of liquid equal to 1.759 pints

litter *noun* **1** waste paper and other things thrown away; **2** a group of young animals born at the same time

¹**little** *adjective* small; not big; young

²**little** *adjective, adverb, noun* (**less, least**) **1** a small amount, but at least some; **2** not much; not enough

¹**live** (*say* **liv**) *verb* **1** to be alive; to have life; **2** to have your home somewhere; to stay in a place or at a house; **3** to keep yourself alive by eating food or by working

²**live** (*say like* **dive**) *adjective* **1** having life; not dead; **2** seen and/or heard as it happens; not recorded: *a* **live** *television programme*; **3** carrying electricity which can kill anyone who touches it

lives (*say like* **dives**) *see* LIFE

lizard *noun* a reptile with a rough skin, four legs, and a long tail

cave lizard from Chile, South America

¹**load** *verb* **1** to put a full load on or in something; **2** to put bullets into a gun or film into a camera; **3** to put a program onto a computer

²**load** *noun* things that are carried by train, ship, or lorry

loaf *noun* (*plural* **loaves**) bread shaped and baked in one large piece

lobster *noun* a sea animal with a shell, eight legs, and a pair of powerful claws, eaten as food

local *adjective* in a certain place that is near the place or area in which you live

lock *noun* a thing for closing and fastening something by means of a key or special number; **lock** *verb*

log *noun* a thick piece of wood from a tree

lollipop *noun* a sweet on a stick

lonely *adjective* unhappy because of being on your own or without friends; **loneliness** *noun*

¹**long** *adjective* **1** measuring a great distance or time from one end to the other; **2** covering a certain distance or time

²**long** *adverb* for a long time

³**long** *verb* to want very much; **longing** *noun, adjective*; **longingly** *adverb*

long wave *noun* radio broadcasting on waves of 1000 metres or more in length

look *verb* **1** to try to see; to use your eyes; **2** to seem to be; **look** *noun*

loop *noun* a ring made by a piece of rope, string, etc, crossing itself

loose *adjective* **1** not tied up, shut up, etc; **2** not firmly fixed; not tight; **loosely** *adverb*; **loosen** *verb*; **looseness** *noun*; ⚠ **lose**

lord *noun* **1** a man who rules people; a master; **2 Lord** a title for a man of high position

lorry also **truck** *noun* a large motor vehicle for carrying goods

car transporter

low *adjective* **1** near the ground; not high; **2** not loud; soft; not high in sound; **lower** *verb*; **lowness** *noun*

loyal *adjective* true to our friends, country, etc; faithful; **loyally** *adverb*; **loyalty** *noun*

luck *noun* good or bad things which happen to you by chance; fate; **luckily** *adverb*; **lucky** *adjective*

lose *verb* (**loses, losing, lost**) **1** not to keep; not to have something any more; not to find; not to win; not to do well; ⚠ **loose**

lost *adjective* not able to find your way

lot *noun* **a lot** a large number or amount; much

loud *adjective* being or producing much sound; not quiet; noisy; **loudly** *adverb*; **loudness** *noun*

loudspeaker also **speaker** *noun* an apparatus that turns electrical current into sound

love *noun* **1** a strong warm feeling of liking somebody or something very much; **2** a person who is loved; **lovable** *adjective*; **love** *verb*; **loving** *adjective*; **lovingly** *adjective*

lovely *adjective* **1** beautiful, attractive, etc; **2** very pleasant; **loveliness** *noun*

luggage *noun* the cases and bags that you take with you when you travel

lukewarm *adjective* not much hotter than cool

lump *noun* **1** a mass of something solid without a special size or shape; **2** a hard swelling on the body

lunar *adjective* of the moon; made for use on or around the moon: **lunar module**

lunch *noun* a meal eaten in the middle of the day

lung *noun* either of the two organs for breathing in the chest of humans and certain other creatures

luxury *noun* **1** great comfort; **2** something not necessary and not often had or done but which is very pleasant

lying *see* LIE

Mm

macaroni *noun* a food made of thin tubes of pasta

machine *noun* an instrument or apparatus that uses power (such as electricity) to do work; **machinery** *noun*

mackerel *noun* a sea fish with green and dark blue stripes on its back

mad *adjective* (**madder**) **1** having a sick mind; **2** very foolish; **3** angry

made *see* MAKE; ⚠ **maid**

magazine *noun* a thin book with a paper cover which contains articles or stories, pictures, and advertisements, and which is sold usually every week or month

magic *noun* **1** the use of spells, spirits, secret forces, etc, to try to control events; **2** the skill used by a conjuror who produces unexpected results by tricks; **magical** *adjective*; **magician** *noun*

magnet *noun* an object, such as a piece of iron, steel, etc, that can draw iron towards it; **magnetic** *adjective*; **magnetism** *noun*

magpie *noun* a noisy black and white bird which often takes small bright objects

maid *noun* a female servant; ⚠ **made**

[1]**mail** *noun* letters and anything else sent or received by post; ⚠ **male**

[2]**mail** *noun* armour made of pieces or rings of metal; ⚠ **male**

main *adjective* chief; first in importance or size: **main road**; **mainly** *adverb*; ⚠ **mane**

maintain *verb* to keep in good condition; **maintenance** *noun*

[1]**make** *verb* (**makes, making, made**) **1** to produce or form something, especially by work or action; **2** to earn, get, or win; **3** to force or cause a person to do something or a thing to happen; **maker** *noun*

[2]**make** *noun* the type to which a set of man-made objects belongs, especially the name of the makers: *a foreign* **make** *of car*

male *noun* a boy or a man; any person or animal of the sex that does not give birth to young; **male** *adjective*; ⚠ **mail**

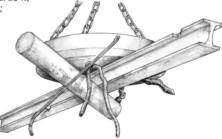

electro-magnet used in a scrapyard

mammal *noun* an animal that feeds its young on milk from the mother's body

map of the moon

Copernicus crater

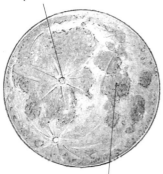

Sea of Tranquillity

¹**man** *noun* (*plural* **men**) **1** a fully grown human male; **2** a human being; **3** also **mankind** the human race

²**man** *verb* (**manned**) to provide with people for an activity

manage *verb* **1** to succeed in dealing with something; **2** to control or be in charge of something or somebody; **management** *noun*; **manager** *noun*

mane *noun* the long hair on the back of a horse's neck, or around a lion's face; ⚠ **main**

man-made *adjective* made by people; not growing or produced by nature

manner *noun* the way in which anything is done or happens

manners *noun* the way you behave, especially the correct way to behave when you are with other people

many *adjective, pronoun, noun* (**more, most**) a great number

map *noun* **1** a drawing of the Earth's surface or of a part of it, showing the shape of countries, the position of towns, the height of land, etc; **2** a plan of the stars in the sky or of the surface of the moon or a planet

marble *noun* **1** a hard stone that can be polished to make it smooth that is used for building; **2** a small hard glass ball used in the game of **marbles**

¹**march** *verb* to walk with a regular step like a soldier

²**march** *noun* **1** the act of marching; **2** a piece of music that can be marched to

March *noun* the third month of the year

¹**mark** *noun* **1** a spot or line on something by which it can be recognised; **2** something like this which spoils it or makes it dirty; **3** a number, sign or letter that shows something, such as how well somebody has done a piece of work

²**mark** *verb* **1** to make or put a mark on something, especially one that spoils the appearance; **2** to give a mark to a person, piece of work, etc

market *noun* a place where people bring goods to sell

marmalade *noun* a type of jam made from eg oranges

marry *verb* **1** to become the husband or wife of somebody; **2** to join two people as husband and wife; **marriage** *noun*

Mars *noun* the planet that is fourth in order from the sun

m

91

martyr *noun* a person who dies for what he or she believes in, especially a religion

marvellous *adjective* wonderful

masculine *adjective* concerning boys or men

mask *noun* a covering for the face which hides, protects it, etc; **masked** *adjective*

Aztec mask

m

mass *noun* **1** a quantity or heap of something; **2** a large number of people or things

master *noun* a person in control of people, animals, or things; the chief person

mat *noun* a small piece of material for covering part of a floor or for putting under an object such as a plate

¹**match** *noun* a short thin stick with one end covered by chemicals that catch fire when rubbed or struck against a rough surface

²**match** *verb* to be like or suitable for use with something else

³**match** *noun* **1** something that is like or that is suitable to be used with something else; **2** a game or sports event between two teams or people

¹**mate** *noun* **1** a friend; **2** one of a male-female pair of animals

²**mate** *verb* to join together as a pair to have young

material *noun* **1** anything from which something can be made; **2** cloth from which clothes, curtains, etc, can be made

mathematics also **maths** *noun* the study or science of numbers; **mathematical** *adjective*; **mathematically** *adverb*; **mathematician** *noun*

¹**matter** *noun* **1 What's the matter?** What is wrong? **2** a subject to which you give attention; **3** the material that makes up the world and everything which can be seen or touched

²**matter** *verb* to be important

mattress *noun* a large bag filled with soft material, on which you sleep

may *verb* **(might) 1** to be possible or likely to: *She **may** come, or she **may** not*; **2** to have permission to do something: ***May** I come in?* **3** used to show a hope that something will happen: ***May** the best team win!* ⚠ **might** Used correctly, ***may*** and ***might*** have mean different things. Compare: *he **may** have been* (=perhaps he was) *drowned/he **might** have been* (=but he was not) *drowned*

May *noun* the fifth month of the year

maybe *adverb* perhaps

mayor *noun* the chief person of a city or town

me *see* I

meal *noun* an amount of food eaten at one time

¹**mean** *adjective* **1** not generous; not willing to give or help; **2** nasty; spiteful; **meanly** *adverb*; **meanness** *noun*

²**mean** *verb* **(means, meaning, meant) 1** to be the same as; to have as a meaning; **2** to plan or want to do or say something

meaning *noun* the idea that is intended to be understood

measles *noun* an infectious disease that causes a temperature and small red spots on the face and body

¹**measure** *noun* **1** a unit used for calculating amount, size, weight, etc; **2** an instrument used for measuring: **tape measure**

²**measure** *verb* **1** to find the size, weight, amount, etc, of something; **2** to be of a certain size; **measurement** *noun*

meat *noun* the parts of an animal's body that are eaten; ⚠ **meet**

medal *noun* a piece of metal in the shape of a coin, cross, etc, given to somebody for something he or she has done,

such as a brave action or for winning a race; ⚠ **meddle**

meddle *verb* to interest yourself in something that is nothing to do with you; to interfere; **meddler** *noun*; **meddling** *adjective*; ⚠ **medal**

media *noun* the newspapers, television, and radio

medicine *noun* **1** a substance used for treating disease; **2** the science of treating and understanding diseases; **medical** *adjective*; **medically** *adverb*

medium *adjective* of middle size, amount, etc

medium wave *noun* radio broadcasting on waves of about 200 to 700 metres in length

meet *verb* **(meets, meeting, met) 1** to get to know or be introduced to somebody for the first time; **2** to come together; **meeting** *noun*; ⚠ **meat**

melon *noun* a large very juicy round or oval fruit with a thick skin

melt *verb* to become or cause to become liquid

member *noun* a person who belongs to a club, group, etc: **Member of Parliament**

memorise *verb* to learn by heart

memory *noun* **1** the ability to remember things; **2** something remembered; **3** the part of a computer in which information is stored

men *see* MAN

mend *verb* to put something back into its proper condition

Olympic medal

menu *noun* **1** a list of the foods that are available in a restaurant or at a meal; **2** a list of the choices that are available in a computer program

mercury *noun* a silver-white metal that is liquid at ordinary temperatures and is used in thermometers

Mercury *noun* the planet that is nearest to the sun

mercy *noun* kindness shown by somebody who has the power to hurt or punish; **merciful** *adjective*; **merciless** *adjective*

mermaid *noun* an imaginary creature with the head and body of a woman and a fish's tail instead of legs

merry *adjective* full of laughter; cheerful; happy; **merrily** *adverb*; **merriness** *noun*

mess *noun* a dirty or untidy state; **messy** *adjective*

message *noun* a spoken or written piece of information passed from one person to another

messenger *noun* a person who brings a message

mess up *verb* **1** to make something dirty or untidy; **2** to do something badly

met *see* MEET

metal *noun* one of a group of usually solid shiny substances such as tin, gold, silver, and iron

meteor *noun* a small piece of matter in space that glows as it falls into the Earth's atmosphere

meteorite *noun* a meteor that has fallen onto the Earth

metre *noun* a measure of length equal to 3.28 ft; **metric** *adjective*

metric system *noun* a system of measurement that uses the metre for measuring length and the kilogram for measuring weight

mice *see* MOUSE

microphone or **mike** *noun* an instrument for recording sounds or carrying them over a distance, or for making sounds louder

microprocessor *noun* a CHIP in a computer

microscope *noun* an instrument that makes very small close objects look larger

muscle fibres as seen under a microscope

microwave also **microwave oven** *noun* an oven in which food is cooked very quickly by radio waves of very short length entering the food

microwave oven

midday *noun* the middle of the day; 12 o'clock in the day

middle *noun* the part, point, or position which is an equal distance from the two ends or sides of something; **middle** *adjective*

middle-aged *adjective* neither old nor young

midnight *noun* 12 o'clock at night

¹**might** 1 see MAY; **2** to be possible or likely to: *Jane might come later, but I don't think she will;* △ **may**

²**might** *noun* power; strength; force

mile *noun* a measure of length or distance equal to 1760 yards or 1609 kilometres

¹**milk** *noun* a white liquid produced by female mammals for feeding their young, especially cow's milk

²**milk** *verb* to take milk from a cow, goat, or other animal

milkman *noun* (*plural* **milkmen**) someone who delivers milk to people's houses

Milky Way *noun* the galaxy to which the sun and solar system belong

mill *noun* **1** a place where grain is made into flour; **2** a place, such as a factory, where something is produced or made; *a steel mill;* **3** a small machine in which something, such as coffee, can be ground into smaller pieces

million *adjective, noun* the number 1,000,000; a thousand thousand; **millionth** *adjective*

¹**mince** *verb* to cut food, especially meat, into very small pieces; **mincer** *noun*

²**mince** *noun* minced meat

mincemeat *noun* a mixture of spices and dried fruits such as raisins and currants that is used as a filling for **mince pies**

¹**mind** *noun* **1** thoughts; a person's way of thinking or feeling; **2 make up your mind** to reach a decision

²**mind** *verb* **1** to be careful of; to take notice of; **2** to dislike or to have a reason against something; **3** to take care or charge of; look after

¹**mine** *pronoun* that or those belonging to me

²**mine** *noun* a hole, usually under the ground, from which coal, gold, tin, etc, are dug; **mine** *verb*; **miner** *noun*

mineral *noun* any of various usually solid substances that are formed naturally in the ground, such as stone, coal, and salt

mineral water *noun* **1** water that comes from a natural spring and contains minerals, often drunk for health reasons; **2** a drink with a sweet taste and bubbles in it

minibus *noun* a small bus

¹**minute** (*say* **min-it**) *noun* one of the sixty parts into which an hour is divided

²**minute** (*say* **my-newt**) *adjective* very small; tiny

mirror *noun* a piece of glass with a silvery back in which you can see things reflected

mischief *noun* naughty behaviour, such as playing tricks on people; **mischievous** *adjective* (*say* **mis-chuvus**)

miss *verb* **1** to fail to hit, catch, find, meet, see, etc; **2** to feel sorry or unhappy because somebody or something is not there; **3** to discover that somebody or something is lost or is not there

Miss *noun* a title placed before the name of a girl or a woman who is not married

mist *noun* thin cloud near the ground; thin fog; **mist** *verb*; **misty** *adjective*

¹**mistake** *noun* a wrong thought, act, etc; something done, said, believed, etc, as a result of wrong thinking or understanding

²**mistake** *verb* (**mistakes, mistaking, mistook, mistaken**) to have a wrong idea about somebody or something; to understand wrongly

mitt *noun* a glove that leaves the ends of the fingers bare

mitten

mitt

mitten *noun* a type of glove having one part for all of the fingers and one part for the thumb

mix *verb* **1** to put different things together so that the separate parts no longer have a separate shape, appearance, etc, or cannot easily be separated; **2 mix up** to mistake one thing for another; to confuse in your mind; **mixer** *noun*; **mixture** *noun*

moan *verb* **1** to make a low sound of pain; **2** to complain; **moan** *noun*

moat *noun* a deep ditch, often filled with water, surrounding a castle

mode *noun* **1** a way of doing something; **2** the way a computer works: *in print* **mode**

model *noun* **1** a small copy of something or a small object, such as a building, which is to be made in a large size; **2** a person whose job is to wear clothes and to show them to possible buyers; **3** a person who is painted by an artist or photographed by a photographer; **4** an object, such as a car, which is one of a number of objects of a standard pattern; **model** *verb*

m

modem *noun* a small machine that sends information from one computer to another one far away through a phone line

modern *adjective* of the present time; not old

module *noun* **1** a part of a space vehicle that can be used on its own without the rest of the vehicle: **command module, lunar module**; **2** a part of a school course, treating a particular subject

monk *noun* one of a group of men who live together and have given their lives to a religion

monkey *noun* any of several types of long-tailed active tree-climbing animals, belonging to that class most like humans

monster *noun* a creature that is unusual in shape or qualities, and that is often very large and ugly

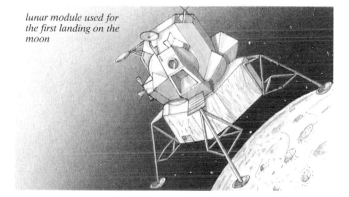

lunar module used for the first landing on the moon

¹**mole** *noun* a small animal with soft fur, that digs holes in the ground

²**mole** *noun* a small dark spot on the skin

³**mole** *noun* a spy

moment *noun* **1** a short period of time; **2** the time for doing something

Monday *noun* the second day of the week

money *noun* metal coins or paper notes with their value printed on them, used in buying and selling

month *noun* one of the twelve parts into which the year is divided; about four weeks

moon *noun* a body that moves round a planet, especially the body that moves round the Earth once every 28 days, and can be seen in the sky at night: **moonlight**

¹**moor** *noun* a wide open area covered with rough grass or bushes; ⚠ **more**

²**moor** *verb* to fasten (a boat, an airship, etc) to land, the sea bed, etc, by means of ropes, an anchor, etc; ⚠ **more**

mop *noun* a long stick with threads of thick string or a sponge on one end for washing floors or dishes

more *adjective, pronoun, adverb* **1** *see* MANY, MUCH; **2 more or less** nearly; about; ⚠ **moor**

morning *noun* **1** the first part of the day from sunrise until midday; **2** the part of the day from midnight until midday; ⚠ **mourning**

mosquito *noun* (*plural* **mosquitoes**) a small fly that pricks the skin and then drinks blood

moss *noun* a small flat green or yellow plant that grows in a thick furry mass on damp surfaces; **mossy** *adjective*

most *see* MANY, MUCH

moth *noun* an insect like a butterfly but not usually so brightly coloured, that flies mainly at night and is attracted by lights

mother *noun* **1** a woman who has children; **2** a female animal that has young

¹**motor** *noun* a machine that changes power, especially electrical power, into movement and makes cars go and other machines work

²**motor** *adjective* driven by an engine: **motorboat, motorbike, motorcycle**

motorist *noun* a person who drives a car

motorway *noun* a very wide road for fast long-distance vehicles

mountain *noun* a very high hill

mourn *verb* to be very sad when somebody dies; **mourning** *noun*; ⚠ **morning**

mouse *noun* **1** (*plural* **mice**) a small furry animal with a long tail; **2** a small electronic machine that you move with your hand to move something on a computer screen

mouth *noun* **1** the opening in the face through which an animal or person eats and makes sounds; **2** an opening: *the **mouth** of the cave*

move *verb* **1** to go from one place to another; **2** to change the position of something; to put something in a different place; **3** to cause a person to have certain feelings, such as sadness; **movable, moveable** *adjective*; **move** *noun*; **movement** *noun*

mow *verb* (**mows, mowing, mowed, mown** *or* **mowed**) to cut grass; **mower** *noun*

Mr *noun* a title placed before the name of a man

Mrs *noun* a title placed before the name of a married woman

Ms *noun* a title placed before the name of a woman instead of Mrs or Miss

much *adjective, noun, adverb* (**more, most**) **1** a large quantity or amount; **2** often

mud *noun* very wet sticky earth or soil; **muddy** *adjective*

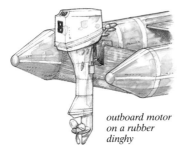

outboard motor on a rubber dinghy

m

muddle *noun* a confused, untidy, or mixed-up state; **muddle** *verb*

¹**mug** *noun* a big cup usually with straight sides and a handle, that is not normally used with a saucer

²**mug** *verb* (**mugged**) to attack and rob somebody, as in a dark street; **mugger** *noun*; **mugging** *noun*

mule *noun* an animal that is a cross between a horse and a donkey

mule

multimedia *noun* computer programs using sound, pictures and words to give information; **multimedia** *adjective*

multiply *verb* **1** to increase a number by a certain number of times; **2** to increase; to make more; **multiplication** *noun*

mumble *verb* to speak in a way that is hard to hear

mumps *noun* an infectious disease which causes swelling of the face and neck

murder *verb* to kill somebody on purpose; **murder** *noun*; **murderer** *noun*

muscle *noun* one of the pieces of elastic material in the body that tighten to produce movement; ⚠ **mussel**

museum *noun* a building where interesting objects are kept and shown to the public

mushroom *noun* a fungus that can be eaten

musical symbols

music *noun* **1** sounds arranged in pleasant patterns and tunes produced by singing or playing instruments; **2** a written set of musical notes; **musical** *adjective*

musician *noun* somebody who plays a musical instrument

Muslim also **Moslem** *noun* a person of the religion started by Mohammed

mussel *noun* a type of shellfish; ⚠ **muscle**

must *verb* (**mustn't**) **1** to have to because it is necessary; **2** to be sure or likely to

mustard *noun* a hot-tasting yellow powder used in cooking, or a thick mixture of this powder with water, eaten with food

mutton *noun* the meat from quite an old sheep

my *adjective* belonging to me

myself *see* I

mystery *noun* something strange that cannot be easily explained; **mysterious** *adjective*; **mysteriously** *adverb*

m

Nn

nail *noun* **1** a thin piece of metal with a point at one end and a flat head at the other for hammering into a piece of wood or other material; **2** a fingernail or toenail; **nail** *verb*

naked *adjective* **1** not wearing any clothes; **2** not covered: *a **naked** flame*

name *noun* the word or words that somebody or something is called by; **name** *verb*

narrow *adjective* **1** small from one side to the other; not wide; **2** almost not enough or only just successful: *a **narrow** escape*; **narrowness** *noun*

nasty *adjective* unpleasant; unkind; ugly; **nastily** *adverb*; **nastiness** *noun*

natural *adjective* **1** to do with nature; not made by people; **2** usual; normal; **naturally** *adverb*

nature *noun* **1** the qualities which make somebody or something different from others; the character of somebody or something; **2** the whole world and everything in it that is not made or changed by people, such as the mountains, sea, sky, animals, and plants

naughty *adjective* badly behaved; not obeying a parent, teacher, set of rules, etc; **naughtily** *adverb*; **naughtiness** *noun*

navy *noun* **1** the ships, people, etc, which make up the power of a country for war at sea; **2** a dark blue colour

near *adjective, adverb, preposition* not far from in distance, time, etc; close

nearly *adverb* almost but not quite

neat *adjective* showing care in appearance; liking order; clean and tidy; **neatly** *adverb*; **neatness** *noun*

nebula *noun* a large cloud of gas and dust in space

the Rosette nebula

necessary *adjective* something that must be had or done; **necessarily** *adverb*; **necessity** *noun*

neck *noun* **1** the part of the body between the head and shoulders; **2** the narrow part of something that is shaped like this: *the **neck** of a bottle*

necklace *noun* a string of jewels or beads worn round the neck

need *verb* **(needn't) 1** to want or not have something necessary or very useful; **2** need to to have to; **need** *noun*

needle *noun* **1** a long thin pointed piece of metal with a hole in one end, for carrying thread through material in sewing; **2** a thin pointed object: *a pine **needle***; **3** any of various thin rods with points or hooks used in working with wool, cloth, etc: *knitting **needles***; **4** the small pointed marker that moves along a row of marks to show how fast a car is going, how much petrol there is, etc

neighbour *noun* somebody who lives very near you

neither *adjective, pronoun, adverb* **1** not one and not the other of two; **2** also not

nephew *noun* the son of your brother or sister

Neptune *noun* the planet eighth in order from the sun

nerve *noun* any of the threadlike parts of the body that form a system to carry feelings and messages to and from the brain

nervous *adjective* slightly afraid; anxious; worried; **nervously** *adverb*; **nervousness** *noun*

nest *noun* **1** a hollow place built or found by a bird as a home; **2** the home of certain animals or insects; **nest** *verb*

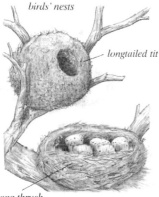

birds' nests

longtailed tit

song thrush

net *noun* **1** a material of strings, wires, threads, etc, twisted, tied, or woven together with regular equal spaces between them; **2** any of various objects made from this, such as a fishing net or the goal in football

netball *noun* a game in which two teams of seven people try to score goals by throwing a large ball through a ring on a high post

nettle *noun* a wild plant covered with stinging hairs

network *noun* **1** a set of lines, wires, or roads that are linked and work together; **2** all the parts of a TV channel; **3** a set of computers that are linked

neutral *adjective* **1** neither for nor against something; not taking sides; **2** in a position between opposites; not one thing or the other; **3** not electrically live; being the wire in a plug which is neither live nor earth

never *adverb* **1** not ever; not at any time; **2 never mind** do not worry, it does not matter

new *adjective* **1** not used by anyone before; **2** different from the earlier thing or things; not seen or known before; **newly** *adverb*; **newness** *noun*; ⚠ **knew**

news *noun* **1** new information; **2** any of the regular reports of recent events broadcast on radio and television

newsagent *noun* a person in charge of a shop selling newspapers and magazines

newspaper or **paper** *noun* a paper printed usually daily or weekly, with news, notices, etc

newt *noun* a small animal that can live both on land and in water

next *adjective, adverb* **1** without anything coming between; **2** following nearest in time

nibble *verb* to eat with small bites; **nibble** *noun*

nice *adjective* good; kind; pleasant; **nicely** *adverb*

n

niece *noun* the daughter of your brother or sister

night *noun* the dark part of each day: **nighttime**; ⚠ **knight**

nightingale *noun* a bird with a beautiful song

nightmare *noun* an unpleasant and frightening dream

nine *adjective, noun* the number 9; **ninth** *adjective, adverb*

nineteen *adjective, noun* the number 19; **nineteenth** *adjective, adverb*

ninety *adjective, noun* the number 90; **ninetieth** *adjective*

no *adverb, adjective* **1** a word used in an answer to show that you refuse or do not agree with something; **2** not one; not any; ⚠ **know**

noble *adjective* **1** brave and not selfish; **2** belonging to the group of people who have titles, such as Lord and Lady: **nobleman**

nobody also **no one** *pronoun* not anybody; no person

nod *verb* **(nodded)** to bend the head forwards and down, especially to show agreement or give a greeting or sign; **nod** *noun*

noise *noun* a loud sound that is often unpleasant; **noisily** *adverb*; **noisy** *adjective*

none *pronoun* not one; not any; ⚠ **nun**

nonsense *noun* something that is said that is not sensible

no one *see* NOBODY

nor *conjunction* used between the two or more choices after *neither* or *not*: *just warm, neither cold nor hot*; ⚠ **gnaw**

normal *adjective* usual; expected; ordinary; **normally** *adverb*; **normality** *noun*

north *noun* one of the four main points of the compass; the direction which is on the left of a person facing the rising sun; **north** *adjective, adverb*; **northerly** *adjective*; **northern** *adjective*

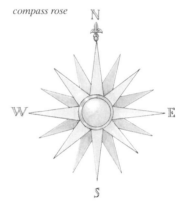

compass rose

northeast *noun* the direction of the point of the compass which is halfway between north and east

northwest *noun* the direction of the point of the compass which is halfway between north and west

nose *noun* **1** the part of the face above the mouth through which we breathe and with which we smell things; **2 turn your nose up at** to consider something not good enough to eat, take part in, etc

not *adverb* used for changing a word or sentence to one with the opposite meaning; ⚠ **knot**

¹**note** *verb* to look or listen carefully and remember

²**note** *noun* **1** a single particular musical sound; **2** a reminder of something in writing: **notebook**; **3** a short letter or written message; **4** a piece of paper money

a Jamaican bank note

nothing *pronoun* no thing; not any thing

¹**notice** *verb* to see, feel, hear, etc, something; **noticeable** *adjective*

²**notice** *noun* **1** a written message in a public place for people to see; **2** warning or information about something that is going to happen

nought *noun* the figure 0; zero

noun *noun* a word that is the name of a person, place, animal, or thing

nova *noun* a star that suddenly becomes very bright

November *noun* the eleventh month of the year

now *adverb* at this time; at present

nowhere *adverb* not anywhere; in, at, or to no place

nuclear *adjective* using or to do with the energy that comes from splitting atoms or joining

them together: **nuclear weapon, nuclear power**

number *noun* **1** a member of the system used in counting and measuring; a word or figure for one of these; **2** a quantity or amount; **number** *verb*

nun *noun* one of a group of women who live together and have given their lives to God; ⚠ **none**

nurse *noun* a person who cares for the sick, hurt, old, or very young people; **nurse** *verb*

nursery *noun* **1** a place where small children are looked after for a short time; **2** a place where young plants and trees are grown for sale

nut *noun* **1** a dry fruit or seed with a hard shell; **2** a block, usually of metal, with a hole in the centre for screwing onto a bolt

nuts

Brazil nut

hazelnut

pistachio

almond

nylon *noun* a strong man-made material, often made into cloth or thread

oak *noun* a large tree with hard wood

oar *noun* a pole with a wide flat blade, used for rowing a boat

oats *noun* a plant which produces grain that can be eaten

obey *verb* to do what somebody tells you; **obedient** *adjective*; **obedience** *noun*

¹**object** (*say* ob-*ject*) *noun* **1** a thing; **2** an aim or purpose

²**object** (*say* ob-ject) *verb* to be against something or somebody; **objection** *noun*

oblong *noun* a shape with four straight sides that is longer than it is wide

oboe *noun* a musical instrument that you blow

observatory *noun* a place from which the stars can be watched using a telescope

Mauna Kea observatory, Hawaii

observe *verb* to watch; to see; **observation** *noun*; **observer** *noun*

obtain *verb* to get

occasion *noun* a particular or special time; a time when something happens; **occasional** *adjective*; **occasionally** *adverb*

occur *verb* (**occurred**) to happen; **occurrence** *noun*

ocean *noun* a very large sea

o'clock *adverb* used in telling the time to say what hour it is

October *noun* the tenth month of the year

odd *adjective* **1** strange; unusual; **2** not matching; not part of a set; left over; **3** not regular or planned: *odd jobs*; **4 odd number** a number that cannot be divided by two; **oddly** *adverb*

of *preposition* **1** belonging to; **2** made from; **3** containing; **4** that is one or some from the whole or all; **5** connected or concerned with; to do with; ⚠ **off**

off *adverb, preposition, adjective* **1** away; from a place or position; **2** not to be working or in use; **3** to or at a distance away; **4** no longer keen on or fond of: *He's **off** his food*; **5** no longer good to eat or drink; not fresh; **6** not going to happen after having been arranged; ⚠ **of**

offend *verb* **1** to do wrong; **2** to cause somebody to feel annoyed or unhappy; **offence** *noun*; **offender** *noun*; **offensive** *adjective*

offer *verb* to say or show that you are ready to give or do something; **offer** *noun*

office *noun* **1** a place where business, or written work connected with a business, is done; **2** a part of the government: *the Foreign* ***Office***

officer *noun* **1** a person who gives orders to others in the army, navy, etc; **2** a police officer

often *adverb* many times

oil *noun* any of several types of liquid used for burning, for making machines run easily, or for cooking; **oily** *adjective*

ointment *noun* a sticky substance that is rubbed on the skin to heal wounds

old *adjective* **1** used when asking or showing the age of somebody or something; **2** having lived, been in use, or continued for a long time; not young or new

on *preposition, adverb, adjective* **1** to be above or supported from below; at or covering the top; **2** attached to or touching; **3** towards; by; near to; **4** about; to do with; **5** at the time of; **6** by means of; using; **7** further; forwards; **8** in use; working; **9** happening or about to happen

once *adverb* **1** one time; **2** some time ago; **3 all at once** suddenly; **4 at once** immediately; at the same time

¹**one** *adjective, noun* the number 1; ⚠ **won**

²**one** *pronoun* a single thing or person; any person; ⚠ **won**

onion *noun* a round white vegetable with a strong smell, that is much used in cooking

only *adjective, adverb* **1** having no others in the same group; **2** and nothing more; and no one else: ***Only*** *the goalkeeper can handle the ball*

onto *preposition* to a position or point on

¹**open** *adjective* **1** not shut; **2** ready for business: *The bank is* ***open***; **3** not covered; not fastened; **4** not surrounded by other things

²**open** *verb* **1** to make or become open; **2** to start or cause to start

operation *noun* **1** a state of working; the way a thing works; **2** a carefully planned action or activity; **3** an act of using instruments on a person's body in order to set right or cut out a diseased part; **operate** *verb*

opinion *noun* what a person thinks about something

opponent *noun* somebody who is on the opposite side in a fight, game, argument, etc

opportunity *noun* a chance or time to do something

¹**opposite** *noun* a person or thing that is as different as possible from another

²**opposite** *adjective* **1** as different as possible; **2** facing

or *conjunction* **1** and not; **2** used to show that there is a choice

orange *noun* **1** a round sweet juicy fruit with a reddish yellow peel; **2** a colour between red and yellow; **orange** *adjective*

o

moon orbiting Earth

orbit *noun* the path of one thing, such as a planet, moon, or satellite, round another in space; **orbit** *verb*; **orbital** *adjective*

orbital *noun* a big road that goes round a town to take the traffic away from the centre

orchard *noun* a place where fruit trees are grown

orchestra *noun* a large group of people who play music together on different instruments; **orchestral** *adjective*

order *noun* **1** neatness; tidiness; **2** fitness for working or use; **3** a special way in which a group of people, objects, etc, are arranged: *alphabetical order;* **4** the condition in which laws and rules are obeyed; **5** a command to do something; **6** a request to supply something; **7 in order that** so that; **8 in order to** with the purpose of; so as to; **9 out of order** *not working;* **order** *verb*

ordinary *adjective* not unusual; common; **ordinarily** *adverb*; **ordinariness** *noun*

organ *noun* **1** a part of an animal or plant that has a special purpose, especially the heart, liver, etc; **2** a musical instrument consisting of pipes through which air is forced to make the sounds

origin *noun* a place or time at which something begins; a starting point

original *adjective* **1** earliest; first; **2** new; different from others; not copied; **originally** *adverb*

ornament *noun* an object that we have for its beauty; **ornamental** *adjective*

ostrich *noun* a very large bird with long legs and a long neck, that runs very quickly but cannot fly

other *adjective, pronoun* the remaining one or ones of a set; a different one from that spoken of

otherwise *adverb* **1** if not; **2** apart from that

otter *noun* an animal with dark brown fur that swims well and eats fish

ought *verb* **1** should; **2** will probably

ounce *noun* a measure of weight equal to 1/16 of a pound or 28.35 grams

our *adjective* belonging to us; ⚠ **hour**

ours *pronoun* that or those belonging to us

ourselves *see* WE

out *adverb* **1** in or to the open air, the outside, etc; away from the inside or centre; **2** not at home; **3** no longer in a game; **4** no longer lit or shining

outdoor *adjective* existing, happening, done, or used not in a building

outdoors *adverb* in the open air; not in a building

outer space *noun* space beyond the Earth's atmosphere; space between the stars

outing *noun* a pleasure trip

output *noun* something that is produced; the quantity of things produced

¹**outside** *noun* the part furthest from the centre

²**outside** *adverb, preposition, adjective* **1** in, on, or to the outside; out; **2** not in a building; in the open air

outwards *adverb* towards the outside

oval *adjective* shaped like an egg or flattened circle; **oval** *noun*

oven *noun* a machine that can be made hot to cook food in

over *adverb, preposition* **1** directly above; **2** completely or partly covering; **3** to or on the other side of; across; **4** downwards from an upright position; **5** right through; from the beginning to the end; **6** more; more than; **7** remaining; more than; at an end

overalls *noun* loose clothes worn over other clothes to keep them clean

overflow *verb* to be so full that the contents flow over the edges; **overflow** *noun*

owe *verb* **1** to have to pay; **2** to feel grateful to somebody for what he or she has done for us or given to us

owing to *preposition* because of

owl *noun* a bird with large eyes that flies at night

¹**own** *adjective, pronoun* **1** belonging to the particular person spoken of and to nobody else; **2 on your own** alone or without help

²**own** *verb* to have; to possess; **owner** *noun*

oxygen *noun* a colourless gas that is present in the air and is needed by plants and animals in order to live

oyster *noun* a shellfish that is used for food and whose shell sometimes contains a pearl

ozone layer *noun* a layer of gas in the sky that protects the Earth from the harmful rays of the sun

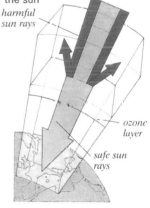

harmful sun rays

ozone layer

safe sun rays

cross section of Earth's atmosphere showing the protective ozone layer which absorbs harmful rays from the sun

o

Pp

¹**pack** *noun* **1** a number of things put together; **2** a group of animals, such as wolves, that hunt together

²**pack** *verb* **1** to put things into containers; **2** to crush or crowd together into a space

package *noun* a parcel

packet *noun* a small parcel or container

pad *noun* **1** a mass of soft material used to protect something or make it more comfortable, or to fill out a shape; **2** a number of sheets of paper fastened together along one edge

¹**paddle** *noun* a short pole with a wide flat end used for pushing and guiding a small boat, such as a canoe

²**paddle** *verb* **1** to move a boat through water using a paddle; **2** to walk about in shallow water; **3** to swim about in water as a dog or duck does

¹**page** *noun* one side of a sheet of paper in a book, newspaper, etc

²**page** *noun* a boy servant

paid *see* PAY

pail *noun* a bucket; ⚠ **pale**

pain *noun* a feeling of hurt or suffering; **painful** *adjective*; **painfully** *adverb*; ⚠ **pane**

¹**paint** *verb* **1** to put on a surface, such as a wall; **2** to make a picture using paint; **painter** *noun*

²**paint** *noun* liquid colouring matter for putting or spreading on a surface

painting *noun* a painted picture

pair *noun* **1** two things that are alike or of the same kind, and are used or thought of together; **2** something made up of two parts that are alike and which are joined and used together: *a **pair** of trousers*; ⚠ **pear**

palace *noun* a very large grand house in which an important person, such as a king or queen, lives

pale *adjective* **1** light in colour; not bright; **2** with a white face through feeling ill; **paleness** *noun*; ⚠ **pail**

¹**palm** *noun* the inside part of a hand between the fingers and the wrist

²**palm** *noun* usually a very tall tree with large leaves at the top and no branches

palm trees in a desert oasis

pan *noun* a round metal container with a handle, used in cooking food: **saucepan**

pancake *noun* a very thin cake made from batter and cooked in a frying pan

pane *noun* a flat piece of glass in a window; ⚠ **pain**

pansy *noun* a small plant with wide flat flowers

pant *verb* to breathe quickly, taking short breaths, especially after exercise or in great heat

pantomime *noun* a play, usually telling an old story, which includes singing and dancing

pants *noun* underpants or trousers

paper *noun* **1** material made in the form of sheets from very thin threads of wood or cloth, used for writing or printing on, covering parcels or walls, etc; **2** a newspaper

parachute *noun* a large piece of material which is fastened to people or objects dropped from aircraft in order to make them fall slowly

parachute

parallel *adjective* running side by side but staying the same distance apart: ***parallel*** lines

parcel *noun* a thing or things wrapped in paper and tied or fastened for posting or carrying

parent *noun* a father or mother

¹**park** *noun* **1** a large garden or grass place in a town, used by the public; **2** a piece of land with grass and trees round a large country house

²**park** *verb* to stop or leave a vehicle for a time; **parking** *noun*

parliament *noun* the group of people who make the laws of a country: **Member of Parliament (MP)**

parrot *noun* a brightly coloured tropical bird that has a curved beak and can be taught to copy human speech

¹**part** *noun* **1** any of the pieces that make up a whole; some of a thing; **2** a share in some activity: *take **part** in*; **3** a character acted by an actor in a play or film; the words and actions of an actor in a play or film

²**part** *verb* to separate or no longer be together

participle *noun* one of two forms of a verb which may be used with other parts of a verb or as adjectives: **present participle** *opening*; **past participle** *opened*

particular *adjective* separate or different from others; special; **particularly** *adverb*

parting *noun* the line on the head where the hair is parted

partly *adverb* in some way but not completely

partner *noun* one or two, or sometimes more, people who share in the same activity; **partnership** *noun*

party *noun* **1** a meeting of people, usually by invitation, to eat, drink, and enjoy themselves; **2** a group of people doing something together; **3** a group of people having the same political opinions

p

¹**pass** *verb* **1** to reach and move beyond; **2** to go forward, through, across, over, or between; **3** to give: *Please **pass** the bread*; **4** to succeed in an examination or test; **5** to go by: *several years **passed***; ⚠ **past**

²**pass** *noun* **1** an act of passing something, such as the ball in various sports; **2** a way by which one may pass, especially through mountains; **3** a printed piece of paper, which shows that one is permitted to do a certain thing; **4** a successful result in an examination

passage *noun* **1** a narrow and often long connecting way or path, especially inside a building; **2** a part of a speech or of a piece of writing or music

passenger *noun* a traveller in a vehicle

European Community passport

p

passport *noun* a small book or card with your photograph and information about you in it, which you need if you are travelling to some countries

¹**past** *noun* the time before the present; ⚠ **passed**

²**past** *adjective* to do with or belonging to the past; in the past; ⚠ **passed**

³**past** *preposition, adverb* **1** after: *ten **past** seven*; **2** up to and beyond; ⚠ **passed**

⁴**past** *noun, adjective* talking about an action that has already happened: **past tense**; ⚠ **passed**

pasta *noun* a food made from flour and water that is formed into many different shapes, such as spaghetti

paste *noun* **1** a thin mixture used for sticking paper; **2** a soft mixture that is easily shaped or spread; **paste** *verb*

pastry *noun* a baked mixture of flour, fat, and milk or water that is used for pies

pat *verb* **(patted)** to touch or strike gently with the palm of the hand; **pat** *noun*

patch *noun* **1** a piece of material used to cover a hole or a damaged place; **2** a part of a surface that is different from the space round it; **patch** *verb*

path *noun* a track for walking or riding along

¹**patient** (*say* **payshunt**) *adjective* able to bear trouble without complaining or to wait for something calmly; **patience** *noun*; **patiently** *adverb*

²**patient** (*say* **payshunt**) *noun* a sick person who is being treated by a doctor or nurse

pattern *noun* **1** a regularly repeated arrangement of shapes and colours; **2** something that can be copied and used as a guide for making something

pause *verb* to stop for a short time; **pause** *noun*; ⚠ **paws**

pavement *noun* a hard path at the side of a road

paw *noun* an animal's foot with nails or claws; ⚠ **poor, pore, pour**

¹**pay** *verb* (**pays, paying, paid**) to give money for something bought, work done, etc; **payment** *noun*

²**pay** *noun* money received for work

pea *noun* a round green seed eaten as a vegetable

peace *noun* **1** a state or time in which there is no war or fighting; **2** calmness; quietness; **peaceful** *adjective*; **peacefully** *adverb*, ⚠ **piece**

peach *noun* a round fruit with soft yellowish red skin, sweet juicy flesh, and a large rough seed (**stone**)

peacock

peacock *noun* **1** (*female* **peahen**) the male of a large bird (**peafowl**) whose long tail feathers can be spread out to show beautiful colours and patterns; **2** a butterfly with large colourful wings

peal *noun* a ringing noise, or loud noise: *a **peal** of bells*; **peal** *verb*; ⚠ **peel**

pear *noun* a sweet juicy fruit that is narrower at the stalk end; ⚠ **pair**

pearl *noun* a hard silvery white ball formed inside shellfish, especially oysters, which is very valuable as a jewel

pebble *noun* a small stone

peck *verb* to eat or strike at something with the beak; **peck** *noun*

peculiar *adjective* strange; odd; unusual

¹**pedal** *noun* a part of a machine which can be pressed with the foot to control or move the machine

²**pedal** *verb* (**pedalled**) to work the pedals of a machine; to move a machine, eg a bike, by using pedals

¹**peel** *verb* to remove or lose the peel or an outer covering; ⚠ **peal**

²**peel** *noun* the outer covering of a fruit or vegetable; ⚠ **peal**

peep *verb* to look at something quickly and secretly; **peep** *noun*

¹**peer** *verb* to look at something very carefully or hard

²**peer** (*feminine* **peeress**) *noun* **1** a person of high position, such as an **earl** or a **duke**; **2** a person who has the right to sit in the House of Lords

peg *noun* **1** a short piece of metal, plastic, etc, fixed to a wall or door for hanging coats and hats on; **2** a wooden or plastic clip for fastening wet washing to a line

p

¹**pen** *noun* an instrument for writing or drawing with ink

²**pen** *noun* a small place with a fence round it for keeping animals in

pence *see* PENNY

pencil *noun* a narrow pointed instrument containing a thin stick of lead or coloured material, for writing or drawing

jackass penguin

penguin *noun* a large black and white seabird from cold regions that swims well but cannot fly

penknife *noun* (*plural* **penknives**) a small knife with one or more folding blades

penny *noun* (*plural* **pence** *or* **pennies**) a small coin. In Britain, 100 pence equal one pound

pension *noun* money paid regularly to somebody who has reached the age when he or she can stop working

people *noun* men, women, and children; human beings

pepper *noun* **1** a hot-tasting spice used for flavouring food; **2** a green or red vegetable that can be eaten cooked or raw

per *preposition* for each; during each; ⚠ **purr**

perfect *adjective* of the very best possible kind; without any faults; **perfection** *noun*; **perfectly** *adverb*

perform *verb* **1** to act, dance, play a musical instrument, etc, in front of an audience; **2** to do something; to carry out a piece of work; **performance** *noun*; **performer** *noun*

perfume *noun* **1** a pleasant smelling liquid that is put on the skin; **2** a sweet smell

perhaps *adverb* it may be; possibly

period *noun* a length of time

permanent *adjective* lasting for a long time or for ever; **permanently** *adverb*

permit *verb* (**permitted**) to allow; **permission** *noun*

person *noun* a man, woman, or child; a human being

personal *adjective* belonging to, or for, one person; of your own; private: *a personal letter*; **personally** *adverb*

persuade (*say* **perswade**) *verb* to cause somebody to do or to believe something

pet *noun* **1** an animal you look after and keep in your house; **2** a favourite person

petal *noun* one of the usually coloured leaflike parts of a flower

petrol *noun* a liquid used as a fuel for producing power in car engines

PG *noun, adjective* In Britain, a film that can be watched by anybody but for which you should ask your parents' permission if you are under 15

phantom *noun* a ghost

pharaoh *noun* a ruler of ancient Egypt

pheasant *noun* a large bird with a long tail

p

phone *noun* a machine that you use to speak to someone who is somewhere else. It works by electricity; **phone** *verb*

photograph also **photo** *noun* a picture obtained with a camera and film; **photograph** *verb*; **photographer** *noun*; **photographic** *adjective*

phrase *noun* a group of words that does not make a full sentence

physical *adjective* **1** of or about the body: **physical education**; **2** of or about the natural world

physics *noun* the science of matter and natural forces, such as light, heat, and sound

grand piano

piano *noun* (*plural* **pianos**) a large musical instrument that is played by pressing keys which cause soft little hammers to hit wires; **pianist** *noun*

pick *verb* **1** to choose; **2** to take up or pull off with the fingers

picnic *noun* a meal eaten outside, usually away from home; **picnic** *verb* (**picnicked**); **picnicker** *noun*

picture *noun* **1** a painting, drawing, or photograph; **2 the pictures** the cinema

pie *noun* a pastry case filled with meat or fruit, baked usually in a deep dish

piece *noun* **1** a part of something; a part which is separated from a whole; **2** a single object: *a piece of furniture*; △ **peace**

pig *noun* (*male* **hog**, *female* **sow**, *young* **piglet**) a short-legged animal with a curly tail and thick skin, kept on farms for food

pigeon *noun* a quite large short-legged bird

piglet *noun* a young pig

pile *noun* a heap of things on top of one another; **pile** *verb*

pill *noun* a small ball of solid medicine to be swallowed

pillar *noun* a tall upright usually round post made of concrete, stone, etc

pillow *noun* an oblong cloth bag filled with soft material, for supporting the head in bed: **pillowcase**

pilot *noun* **1** a person who flies an aircraft; **2** a person who guides ships in and out of a harbour; **pilot** *verb*

pimple *noun* a small raised diseased spot on the skin; **pimply** *adjective*; **pimpled** *adjective*

pin *noun* a short thin stiff sharp piece of metal for fastening cloth, paper, etc; **pin** *verb*

p

¹**pinch** *verb* **1** to press tightly and often painfully between the thumb and finger or between two hard surfaces; **2** to steal

²**pinch** *noun* an amount that can be picked up between the thumb and a finger; a small amount

¹**pine** *noun* a tall tree with thin sharp leaves (**pine needles**), that bears cones

²**pine** *verb* to become thin and weak slowly, through disease or unhappiness

pineapple

p

pineapple *noun* a large yellow juicy tropical fruit with thin stiff leaves on top

pink *noun, adjective* pale red; **pinkish** *adjective*

pint *noun* a measure of liquid equal to 0.568 of a litre

¹**pip** *noun* a small fruit seed

²**pip** *noun* a short high-sounding note, as given on the radio to tell the time

pipe *noun* **1** a tube for carrying a liquid or gas; **oilpipe 2** a small tube with a bowl-shaped container at one end, for smoking tobacco; **3** a tube-shaped musical instrument, played by blowing

pirate *noun* **1** a person who robs a ship at sea; **2** a person who uses or sells the work of other people such as books or videos without permission or payment; **piracy** *noun*

pistol *noun* a small gun

pit *noun* **1** a hole, usually in the ground; **2** a coal mine

¹**place** *noun* **1** a particular area, part of space, or position; **2** a position in the result of a competition, race, etc; ⚠ **plaice**

²**place** *verb* to put in a certain place or position; ⚠ **plaice**

plaice *noun* a flat bony sea fish; ⚠ **place**

¹**plain** *adjective* **1** easy to see, hear, or understand; **2** simple; without decoration; **plainly** *adverb*; ⚠ **plane**

²**plain** *noun* a large area of flat land; ⚠ **plane**

plait (*say* **plat**) *noun* a length of something, especially hair, made by twisting three or more pieces over and under one another; **plait** *verb*

plan *noun* **1** a carefully worked out arrangement for something to be done in the future; **2** a drawing of a building or room showing the shape, measurements, etc; **plan** *verb*

plane *noun* a flying vehicle that has wings and at least one engine; ⚠ **plain**

planet *noun* a large body in space that moves round a sun

planetarium *noun* a building containing a machine that throws spots of light onto a surface to show the movements of the stars and planets

plant *to* plug

¹**plant** *verb* to put plants or seeds in the ground to grow

²**plant** *noun* **1** a living thing that has leaves and roots and grows, usually in the ground; **2** the buildings and machines used in making something; a factory

leg in plaster cast

plaster *noun* **1** a soft mixture that hardens when dry and is spread on walls to give a smooth surface; **2** a piece of sticky tape put on the body to protect a wound; **3** also **plaster cast** a special covering for protecting a broken bone in an arm, leg, etc, while it heals

plastic *noun* a man-made material that can be made into different shapes

plate *noun* **1** a flat dish from which food is eaten or served; **2** a flat thin piece of metal

platform *noun* **1** a raised floor or stage; **2** a raised surface along the side of the track at a railway station

¹**play** *verb* **1** to have fun; to take part in a game: **playground**; **2** to perform a part in a film or play; **3** to make sounds on a musical instrument; **4** to reproduce the sounds recorded on a record, cassette, etc; **player** *noun*; **playful** *adjective*; **playfully** *adverb*

²**play** *noun* a story performed in a theatre or on the radio or television

pleasant *adjective* enjoyable; nice; **pleasantly** *adverb*

please *verb* **1** to make somebody happy; **2** used to make a request more polite; **pleasure** *noun*

plenty *noun* a large quantity or number; enough; **plentiful** *adjective*

plough (*say like* **cow**) *noun* a farming tool for breaking up and turning over soil and earth; **plough** *verb*

pluck *verb* **1** to pull the feathers off a bird; **2** to play a musical instrument by pulling the strings and letting go quickly

an eastern musical instrument played by plucking – a sitar

plug *noun* **1** a plastic object with metal pieces that connects a television set, iron, vacuum cleaner, etc, to an electrical socket; **2** something used for blocking a hole, especially a round piece of rubber or plastic for stopping water from running out of a sink or bath

plum *noun* a sweet juicy fruit with a smooth skin and large stone; the tree on which this grows

plumber *noun* somebody who fits and mends water pipes, central heating, etc

plus *preposition* with the addition of; and

Pluto *noun* the planet furthest from the sun

p m after midday (short for *post meridiem*)

pocket *noun* a small flat cloth bag sewn into or onto a piece of clothing for putting money, a handkerchief, etc, in

poem *noun* a piece of writing in patterns of lines and sounds, expressing something in powerful or beautiful language, often using rhymes

poet *noun* a person who writes poems; **poetic** *adjective*

poetry *noun* poems

¹point *noun* **1** a sharp end; **2** the importance or purpose of something said or done; **3** an exact moment; **4** a mark or position on a compass, measuring instrument, etc; **5** a single quantity used in deciding the winner in a game, quiz, etc; a mark

²point *verb* to hold out a finger, a stick, etc, in a direction; to show where something is with the finger; **pointer** *noun*

poison *noun* a substance that harms or kills if it is taken into the body; **poison** *verb*; **poisonous** *adjective*

poke *verb* to push a pointed thing into or at somebody or something; **poke** *noun*

French flag flying from a flagpole

¹pole *noun* a long often thin round stick or post: **flagpole, telegraph pole**

²pole *noun* **1** either end of an imaginary straight line (**axis**) round which a solid round mass, such as the Earth, turns: *North* **Pole 2** a point at the ends of a magnet where its power is greatest

police *noun* a body of men and women whose duty is to protect people and buildings, to make everyone obey the law, to catch criminals, etc: **police force, policeman, police station, policewoman**

¹polish *verb* to make something smooth and shiny by rubbing

²polish *noun* a liquid, paste, etc, used in polishing a surface

polite *adjective* having good manners; **politely** *adverb*; **politeness** *noun*

politics *noun* the study of government; how countries should be governed; **political** *adjective*

pond *noun* a small area of water, in a garden, for example

pony *noun* a small horse

pool *noun* **1** a small area of water; a pond; **2** a small amount of any liquid poured or dropped on a surface; **3** a swimming pool

p

116

poor *adjective* **1** having very little money; **2** low in quality or quantity; not good; **3** needing kindness; unlucky; ⚠ **paw, pore, pour**

¹**pop** *noun* a sudden noise like the sound of the top being pulled out of a bottle

²**pop** *noun* modern popular music and songs

³**pop** *verb* **(popped) 1** to make a popping noise; **2** to go: *pop along to the shops*; **3** to put: *pop it on the table*

Pope *noun* head of the Roman Catholic Church

poppy *noun* a plant that has a milky juice in its stem and bright, usually red flowers

popular *adjective* liked by many people

crested porcupine

porcupine *noun* a small short-legged animal that has long stiff prickles and is larger than a hedgehog

pore *noun* any of the tiny holes in the skin through which you sweat, ⚠ **paw, poor, pour**

pork *noun* meat from a pig

porridge *noun* a soft breakfast food made by boiling oats in milk or water

¹**port** *noun* a harbour or a town with a harbour

²**port** *noun* the left side of a ship or aircraft as you face forward

porter *noun* a person who carries luggage at airports, etc

position *noun* **1** the place where somebody or something is or stands; **2** the place where somebody or something belongs; **3** the way in which somebody or something is placed or moves, stands, sits, etc; **4** a condition or state; **5** a job

possess *verb* to have or own **possession** *noun*

possible *adjective* that may exist, happen, or be done; **possibility** *noun*; **possibly** *adverb*

¹**post** *noun* a strong thick upright pole or bar made of wood, metal, etc, fixed into the ground or some other base especially as a support. **gatepost**

²**post** *noun* the system for collecting, carrying, and delivering letters, parcels, etc: **postbox, postman, post office, postwoman**

³**post** *verb* to send something by post

⁴**post** *noun* **1** a special place of duty, especially on guard or on watch; **2** a job

postage stamp *noun* a stamp for sticking on things to be posted

one of the first postage stamps – a Penny Black

postcard *noun* a small card, often with a picture on one side, on which a message may be written and sent by post

poster *noun* a large printed notice or drawing put up in a public place

postpone *verb* to put off until a later time or day; **postponement** *noun*

pot *noun* a container, especially a round one, made from baked clay, metal, etc

potato *noun* (*plural* **potatoes**) a vegetable with a thin usually brown skin that is cooked and served in many ways

pottery *noun* pots, dishes, etc, made from baked clay

pound *noun* **1** a measure of weight equal to 0.454 kilograms; **2** the standard unit of money in Britain, which is divided into 100 pence

pour *verb* **1** to flow or make a liquid flow; **2** to rain hard and steadily; △ **paw, poor, pore**

powder *noun* a substance in the form of very small dry grains; **powdery** *adjective*

power *noun* **1** strength, force, or energy; **2** the ability to do something; **3** a person, group, government, etc, that has control; **powerful** *adjective*

practice *noun* the doing of something, especially again and again to become better at it; △ **practise**

practise *verb* to do something regularly or over and over again, especially in order to become better at it; △ **practice**

praise *verb* to speak well of; to say that you admire; **praise** *noun*

prawn *noun* a shellfish that looks like a large shrimp

pray *verb* to speak, often silently, to God or a god; △ **prey**

prayer *noun* the act of praying; what you say when you are praying

p

a mosque, where Muslims pray

preach *verb* to give a religious talk; **preacher** *noun*

precede *verb* to come before or in front

precious *adjective* very valuable

prefer *verb* **(preferred)** to like better; **preference** *noun*

pregnant *adjective* about to have a baby; **pregnancy** *noun*

prehistoric *adjective* to do with or belonging to time in history before there were written records

prepare *verb* to get ready or make something ready; **preparation** *noun*

preposition *noun* a word like *to, for, on, by,* etc; a word that is put in front of a noun to show where, when, how, etc

¹**present** (*say* **prez-ent**) *noun* a gift

²**present** (*say* **pree-zent**) *verb* to give; to offer

³**present** (*say* **prez-ent**) *adjective* **1** in the place talked of; there; here; **2** existing or happening now

⁴**present** (*say* **prez-ent**) *noun* the present time; this time

⁵**present** (*say* **prez-ent**) *noun, adjective* talking about an action that is happening now: **present tense**

preserve *verb* to keep safe or in good condition; **preservation** *noun*

president *noun* **1** the head of government in many countries that do not have a king or queen: *the **President** of France*; **2** the head of a company, club, etc

¹**press** *verb* **1** to push firmly and steadily; **2** to make flat or smooth, as by ironing; **pressure** *noun*

²**press** *noun* **1** an act of pressing something; **2** newspapers and magazines in general; **3** a machine for printing books, newspapers, etc

pretend *verb* **1** to act in a deceiving way; **2** to imagine as a game

¹**pretty** *adjective* pleasing to look at; **prettily** *adverb*; **prettiness** *noun*

²**pretty** *adverb* quite though not completely; fairly

prevent *verb* to stop something from happening; **prevention** *noun*

prey *noun* an animal that is hunted by another; ⚠ **pray**

price *noun* an amount of money for which a thing is bought or sold

prick *verb* to make a very small hole or wound in something with a sharp-pointed object

echinocactus – it is very prickly

prickle *noun* a small sharp part of a plant or animal; **prickly** *adjective*

pride *noun* **1** the feeling of having a good opinion of yourself or being satisfied with yourself; being proud; **2** a group of lions

priest *noun* a person trained for various religious duties

primary *adjective* earliest; first; most important

primary school *noun* a school for children aged between five and eleven

prime minister *noun* the head of government

primrose *noun* **1** a pale yellow flower that grows in the spring; **2** its colour

prince *noun* the son or grandson of a king or queen

princess *noun* **1** a daughter or granddaughter of a king or queen; **2** the wife of a prince

¹**print** *noun* **1** a mark on a surface showing the shape, pattern, etc, of the thing pressed into it: **footprint**; **2** printed letters; **3** a photograph printed from film

²**print** *verb* **1** to make a book, magazine, etc, by putting words and pictures on paper using a special machine; **2** to make or copy a photograph on paper from film; **3** to write without joining the letters; **4** to make a paper copy of work done on a computer

printer *noun* **1** a person whose job is printing; **2** a machine for making photographic prints; **3** a machine connected to a computer, for printing out paper copies of the writing, pictures, etc

printout *noun* information produced and printed on paper by a computer

prism *noun* a block of clear glass that breaks up light into its separate colours

prison *noun* a large building where criminals are kept locked up; **prisoner** *noun*

private *adjective* belonging to or to do with one person or one group of people; not for everybody; **privacy** *noun*; **privately** *adverb*

privilege *noun* a right or favour which only one person or a small group of people can have

prize *noun* something of value given to the winner of a competition, game, etc; a reward for doing well or for good work

probably *adverb* almost but not quite certainly; likely

problem *noun* a difficulty that needs attention; a question for which an answer is needed

procession *noun* a line of people or vehicles moving slowly forwards

¹**produce** (*say* **pro-**duce) *verb* **1** to show or bring out; **2** to make or cause to exist; **product** *noun*; **production** *noun*

²**produce** (*say* prod-**uce**) *noun* something produced, especially by growing or farming

professor *noun* a senior teacher at a university

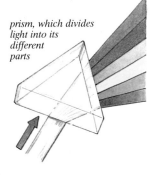

prism, which divides light into its different parts

profit *noun* money you get when you sell something for more than it cost to buy or make; **profitable** *adjective*; ⚠ **prophet**

¹**program** *noun* a set of instructions for a computer; ⚠ **programme**

²**program** *verb* **(programmed)** to provide a computer with a program; ⚠ **programme**

programme *noun* **1** a show, story, etc, on radio or television; **2** a list of things to be done or that will happen; ⚠ **program**

promise *verb* to say that you will or will not do something; **promise** *noun*

pronoun *noun* a word, like *he, she, it, they,* etc, that is used instead of using a noun again

pronounce *verb* to make the sound of a letter or a word; **pronunciation** *noun*

proof *noun* a way of showing that something is true

propel *verb* to drive or push something forward; **propulsion** *noun*

propeller *noun* a set of specially shaped blades that turn rapidly to drive a plane or ship

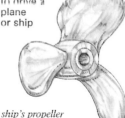

ship's propeller

proper *adjective* suitable; correct; right; **properly** *adverb*

property *noun* **1** something that is owned; **2** land, buildings, or both together

prophet *noun* a person directed by God to make known God's wishes or to teach a religion; ⚠ **profit**

protect *verb* to keep safe; to prevent somebody or something from being hurt or damaged; **protection** *noun*

protein *noun* a substance in food that is needed to build up the body and to keep it healthy

proud *adjective* having a high opinion of yourself or of something connected with yourself; **proudly** *adverb*

prove *verb* to show that something is true

provide *verb* to supply

prune *noun* a dried plum

pub also **public house** *noun* a building where alcohol may be bought and drunk

¹**public** *adjective* for or to do with people in general, for everyone to use

²**public** *noun* **1** people in general; **2 in public** with many people present

pudding *noun* **1** a dessert; **2** a sweet food made with pastry, rice, bread, etc, and served hot; **3** a meat dish boiled with a pastry cover

puddle *noun* a small pool of water, especially rainwater

puff *noun* a sudden rush of air, smoke, etc; **puff** *verb*

pull *verb* **1** to draw something along behind; **2** to move or draw something towards yourself

p

pump *noun* a machine for forcing a liquid or gas into or out of something; **pump** *verb*

bicycle pump

pumpkin *noun* a large round dark yellow vegetable

punch *verb* to strike hard with the fist; **punch** *noun*

puncture *noun* a small hole, especially in a tyre; **puncture** *verb*

punish *verb* to cause somebody to suffer for a fault or crime; **punishment** *noun*

¹**pupil** *noun* a person, especially a child, who is being taught

²**pupil** *noun* the small round opening in the middle of your eye, that looks black and which can grow larger or smaller

puppet *noun* **1** a small toy figure of a person or an animal that can be made to move by pulling wires or strings; **2** also **glove puppet** a hollow cloth figure into which you put your hand to move the figure with your fingers

puppy also **pup** *noun* a young dog

pure *adjective* without anything mixed with it; clean; **purely** *adverb*; **purity** *noun*

purple *noun* a dark colour between red and blue; **purple** *adjective*; **purplish** *adjective*

purpose *noun* a reason for doing something

purr *noun* a low sound produced by a cat when it is pleased; **purr** *verb*; ⚠ **per**

purse *noun* a small bag for carrying money

push *verb* to move somebody or something forward, away, or to a different position as by pressing with your hands; **push** *noun*

pushchair *noun* a light folding chair on wheels for pushing a small child along

put *verb* (**puts, putting, put**) to move, place, or fix somebody or something in, on, or to a certain place

¹**puzzle** *noun* **1** something that you cannot understand or explain; a difficult question to answer; **2** a game or toy in which parts must be fitted together correctly: **crossword puzzle, jigsaw puzzle**

²**puzzle** *verb* to be difficult to understand; **puzzled** *adjective*

pyjamas *noun* a loose shirt and trousers that you wear in bed

pyramid *noun* a solid object or shape with straight flat triangular sides that slope upwards and meet in a point at the top

the Pyramids at Giza, Egypt

Qq

quack *noun* the sound that ducks make; **quack** *verb*

quality *noun* **1** how good something is; **2** something typical of a person or thing

²**question** *verb* **1** to ask a question; **2** to raise doubts about somebody or something; **questioner** *noun*

question mark *noun* the mark (?) used in writing or printing at the end of a sentence that asks a question

queue (*say* **kyoo**) *noun* a line of waiting people, cars, etc; **queue** *verb*; ⚠ **cue**

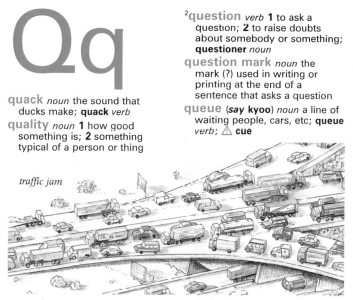

traffic jam

quantity *noun* the amount of something or the number of things

quarrel *noun* an argument; **quarrel** *verb*

quarter *noun* **1** one of four parts of anything; ¼; **2** 15 minutes before or after the hour: *quarter past; quarter to*

queen *noun* **1** a female ruler of a country or the wife of a king; **2** any of the four playing cards with a picture of a queen, that comes between the jack and the king

queer *adjective* strange; unusual; **queerly** *adverb*

¹**question** *noun* **1** a sentence which asks something and needs an answer; **2** a problem; something to be talked about

quick *adjective* fast; not slow; soon finished; **quickly** *adverb*

quiet *adjective* **1** having or making very little noise; **2** calm; peaceful; **quiet** *noun*; **quietly** *adverb*; **quietness** *noun*; ⚠ **quite**

quilt *noun* a thick cover for a bed, often a warm one

quit *verb* to leave a computer program

quite *adverb* **1** rather; **2** completely; perfectly; ⚠ **quiet**

quiz *noun* a competition or game in which questions are asked

quotation mark *noun* either of a pair of marks (" ") or (' ') showing the beginning and end of words said or written by somebody else

Rr

rabbit *noun* (*male* **buck**, *female* **doe**) a small long-eared animal of the hare family that lives in a burrow

¹**race** *noun* a competition to see who can do something fastest

²**race** *verb* **1** to try to run or go faster than somebody else; **2** to go very fast; **racer** *noun*

³**race** *noun* a group of people who have the same colour of skin or other similarities about their faces or bodies; **racial** *adjective*; **racially** *adverb*

racist *noun* someone who hates people of other races; **racist** *adjective*

rack *noun* a frame with bars, hooks, etc, for holding things: **luggage rack**

¹**racket, racquet** *noun* a network, usually of nylon, stretched in a frame with a handle, for hitting the ball in games such as tennis

²**racket** *noun* a loud noise

radar screen

radar *noun* a way of finding the position of solid objects, such as ships, aeroplanes, etc, by using radio waves

radiate *verb* to send out light or heat

radiation *noun* **1** the sending out of heat, light, etc; **2** the giving off of harmful rays from the sun or a radioactive substance

radiator *noun* **1** an object for sending out heat in a house; **2** a machine for cooling the engine of a car

radio *noun* **1** the sending or receiving of sounds through the air by electrical waves; **2** a machine to receive sounds sent out in this way; **radio** *verb*

radioactive *adjective* giving out energy or rays; **radioactivity** *noun*

rag *noun* **1** a small piece of old cloth; **2** an old worn out piece of clothing

rail *noun* **1** a fixed bar to hang things on or for protection; **2** one of the pair of metal bars along which a train runs: **railway**

rain *noun* water falling in drops from the clouds: **raindrop, rainwater**; **rain** *verb*; **rainy** *adjective*; △ **reign, rein**

rainbow *noun* an arch of different colours that sometimes appears in the sky after it has rained

rainforest a thick forest found in hot and wet tropical countries

raise *verb* **1** to lift, push, or move up; **2** to make greater; **raise prices**

raisin *noun* a dried grape

rake *noun* a gardening tool consisting of a row of teeth at the end of a long handle, for levelling soil, gathering up leaves, etc; **rake** *verb*

ram *noun* a male sheep

RAM also **random access memory** *noun* a type of computer memory that holds information and programs

ran *see* RUN

random *adjective* made or done without a fixed plan; by chance; **randomly** *adverb*

rang *see* RING

range *noun* **1** a line of mountains or hills; **2** the distance that a gun can fire; **3** a set of different objects of the same kind

rapid *adjective* very fast; **rapidly** *adverb*

rare *adjective* not happening often; not often seen; **rarely** *adverb*

¹**rash** *noun* a set of red spots on the skin, caused by illness

²**rash** *adjective* acting quickly without thinking enough of what might happen; **rashly** *adverb*

raspberry *noun* a soft sweet red berry; the bush on which this grows

rat *noun* a long-tailed animal with strong sharp teeth, related to but larger than the mouse

a black rat

rather *adverb* **1** a little; quite: *rather* cold weather; **2** sooner; more willingly: I'd *rather* play tennis than swim

¹**rattle** *verb* to make a lot of quick little noises

²**rattle** *noun* a baby's toy that makes a rattling noise when it is shaken

raw *adjective* not cooked; ⚠ **roar**

ray *noun* a line of light, heat, or other form of energy

razor *noun* a sharp instrument for shaving

reach *verb* **1** to stretch out your hand or arm; **2** to be big enough to touch; to stretch out as far as; **3** to get to; to arrive at

read *verb* (**reads, reading, read**) to look at and understand printed or written words; **reading** *noun*; ⚠ **reed**

ready *adjective* **1** prepared; in the right way or order for use; **2** willing; **readily** *adverb*

real *adjective* actual; true; not imagined; ⚠ **reel**

realise *verb* to understand and believe something as a fact; **realisation** *noun*

really *adverb* in fact; truly

reason *noun* **1** what makes you decide to do something; why something happens; **2** the power to think and understand; **reasonable** *adjective*; **reasonably** *adverb*

receipt (*say* ru soot) *noun* a written or printed note saying that something has been paid for or that something has been received

receive *verb* to get something given or sent to you; **receiver** *noun*

recent *adjective* having happened only a short time ago; **recently** *adverb*

recipe (*say* ressipee) *noun* a set of instructions for cooking food

r

recognise *verb* **1** to know again somebody or something you have met before; **2** to agree that something is true; **recognisable** *adjective*; **recognition** *noun*

¹**record** (*say* **re-kord**) *verb* **1** to write down so that it will be known; **2** to keep sounds or pictures on tape, CDs, etc, so that they can be heard or seen again; **recording** *noun*

²**record** (*say* **rek-ord**) *noun* **1** information that is written down and kept; **2** the best yet done; **3** a circular piece of plastic on which sound or music is recorded

recorder *noun* **1** a wooden or plastic musical instrument like a whistle, that is played by blowing; **2** an instrument for recording: **tape recorder, cassette recorder**

descant recorder

red *noun* the colour of blood; **red** *adjective*; **reddish** *adjective*; **redness** *noun*

reduce *verb* to get or make smaller or less; **reduction** *noun*

reed *noun* a tall grasslike plant that grows in wet places; ⚠ **read**

reel *noun* a round object on which cotton, wire, fishing line, recording tape, etc, can be wound; ⚠ **real**

reflect *verb* to throw back light, heat, sound, or a picture; **reflection** *noun*

refrigerator *noun* the full name for a FRIDGE

¹**refuse** (*say* **re-fyooz**) *verb* not to allow; not to accept, do, or give

²**refuse** (*say* **reff-yoos**) *noun* rubbish

register *noun* a list of names; **register** *verb*; **registration** *noun*

regret *verb* (**regretted**) to be sorry about something; **regret** *noun*

regular *adjective* **1** done or happening at fixed times; **2** normal; proper; correct; **regularly** *adverb*

reign (*say* **rane**) *verb* **1** to be king or queen; **2** to exist noticeably: *quietness **reigned**;* **reign** *noun*; ⚠ **rain, rein**

rein *noun* a long narrow band of leather by which a horse is controlled; ⚠ **rain, reign**

reindeer *noun* a deer with long branching horns

reject (*say* **re-ject**) *verb* to refuse to accept; to throw away; **reject** (*say* **ree-ject**) *noun*; **rejection** *noun*

rejoice *verb* to feel or show great joy; **rejoicing** *noun*

related *adjective* of the same family or kind

relation *noun* a member of your family

relative *noun* a relation

relax *verb* **1** to make or become less active; to stop worrying; **2** to make or become less stiff or tight; **relaxation** *noun*

r

release *verb* **1** to set free; to allow to come out; **2** to allow a new film or a record to be shown to or bought by the public; **release** *noun*

reliable *adjective* fit to be trusted; **reliability** *noun*; **reliably** *adverb*

relief *noun* **1** a feeling of comfort at the ending of worry or pain; **2** help for people in trouble: **famine relief**; **relieve** *verb*

religion *noun* **1** belief in one or more gods; **2** a particular set of beliefs and the worship, behaviour, etc, connected with them; **religious** *adjective*

rely *verb* **1** to depend on something or on something happening; **2** to trust somebody or trust somebody to do something

remain *verb* to stay or be left behind after others have gone; **remainder** *noun*

remark *noun* something said; an opinion; **remark** *verb*

remember *verb* to keep in the memory; to not forget

remind *verb* to cause somebody to remember; **reminder** *noun*

remove *verb* to take away; to take off; **removal** *noun*

¹**rent** *noun* money paid for the use of a house or office

²**rent** *verb* **1** to have the use of or allow somebody to use a house, room, etc, in return for money; **2** to pay to use a video for a short time

¹**repair** *verb* to mend

²**repair** *noun* **1** mending; **2 in good/bad repair** in good/bad condition

repeat *verb* to say or do again; **repeat** *noun*; **repetition** *noun*

replace *verb* **1** to put something back in its place; **2** to take the place of somebody or something; **replacement** *noun*

reply *verb* to answer; **reply** *noun*

report *verb* to give the story of; to say what has happened; **report** *noun*; **reporter** *noun*

reproduce *verb* **1** to produce young; **2** to make a copy of; **reproduction** *noun*

a sidewinder snake travels sideways

reptile *noun* a cold-blooded animal, such as a snake, tortoise, or crocodile, that has a body covered in scales

request *verb* to ask politely; **request** *noun*

rescue *verb* to save from harm or danger; to set free; **rescue** *noun*; **rescuer** *noun*

research *noun* the study of a subject, so as to learn new facts; **research** *verb*

respect *noun* **1** admiration; feeling of honour; **2** attention; care; **respect** *verb*

r

response *noun* an answer or reply; an action done in answer to something

responsible *adjective* **1** having the duty of looking after somebody or something, so that you can be blamed if things go wrong; **2** able to be trusted; **responsibility** *noun*; **responsibly** *adverb*

¹**rest** *noun* **1** freedom from anything tiring; sleep; **2** a support; **rest** *verb*; **restful** *adjective*; **restless** *adjective*

²**rest** *noun* what is left

restaurant *noun* a place where food is sold and eaten

result *noun* **1** what happens because of an action or event; an effect; **2** a person's or team's success or failure in an examination, match, etc: *the football results*

retire *verb* to stop working at your job, usually because of old age; **retired** *adjective*; **retirement** *noun*

return *verb* **1** to come or go back; **2** to give or send back; **return** *noun*

revolution *noun* **1** the changing of a government by force, usually by people who have been badly treated; **2** a complete change; something completely new; **3** one complete circular movement round a fixed point; a full turn of a wheel or other object

reward *noun* something received or given for work, service, finding something, etc

rewind *verb* to wind film, tape, etc, back onto a reel; **rewind** *noun*

rhinoceros also **rhino** *noun* a large heavy thick-skinned animal, with either one or two horns on its nose

rhubarb *noun* a garden plant with thick juicy stems that can be eaten

rhyme *noun* **1** a word that ends with the same sound as another; **2** a short and not serious poem or piece of writing, using words that rhyme; **rhyme** *verb*

rhythm *noun* a regular pattern of beats in music, poetry, etc; **rhythmic, rhythmical** *adjective*; **rhythmically** *adverb*

ribbon *noun* a long narrow band of cloth used for tying things, for ornament, etc

rice *noun* a food grain grown in hot wet places, with seeds that can be cooked and eaten

rice growing in paddyfields

rich *adjective* **1** having a lot of money or property; **2** valuable and beautiful; **3** containing a lot of a particular thing; full of goodness and colour: *rich food*; **riches** *noun* (plural); **richly** *adverb*; **richness** *noun*

rid *verb* (**rids, ridding, rid**) **1** to make free of; **2 get rid of** to free yourself from something; to drive or give away

performing dressage at the Spanish Riding School in Vienna

¹**ride** *verb* (**rides, riding, rode, ridden**) **1** to travel along, sitting on a bicycle, in a car, etc; **2** to travel on and control a horse; **rider** *noun*

²**ride** *noun* a journey on an animal, in a vehicle, etc

rifle *noun* a gun fired from the shoulder, with a long barrel

¹**right** *noun, adjective* the side or direction opposite to left; ⚠ **rite, write**

²**right** *adjective* **1** correct; true; **2** good; proper; ⚠ **rite, write**

³**right** *noun* **1** what is good; **2** something a person can have or do because of the law; ⚠ **rite, write**

⁴**right** *adverb* **1** towards the right; **2** directly; straight; **3** properly; correctly; **4** all the way; ⚠ **rite, write**

rind (*say* **rynd**) *noun* the thick outer covering of certain fruits, foods, etc: *lemon* **rind**

¹**ring** *noun* **1** a metal band worn on the finger; **2** a circle; **3** a circular band; something shaped like a circle: **key ring**; **4** any closed-in space where things are shown or performed, as in a circus or for boxing; ⚠ **wring**

²**ring** *verb* to put or make a ring round something; ⚠ **wring**

³**ring** *verb* (**rings, ringing, rang, rung**) **1** to cause a bell to sound; **2** to make a sound like a bell; **3** to phone; **4 ring a bell** to remind you of something; **ring** *noun*; ⚠ **wring**

rinse *verb* **1** to wash in clean water to remove soap, dirt, etc; **2** to colour the hair; **rinse** *noun*

rip *noun* a long tear; **rip** *verb*

ripe *adjective* fully grown and ready to be eaten; **ripen** *verb*

¹**rise** *verb* (**rises, rising, rose, risen**) to go up; to get higher; to increase

²**rise** *noun* **1** an increase in wages, prices, etc; **2** the act of growing greater or more powerful

¹**risk** *noun* a danger; a chance of losing something; **risky** *adjective*

²**risk** *verb* **1** to place in danger; **2** to take a chance

rite *noun* a ceremony, especially one that is religious; ⚠ **right, write**

r

river _noun_ a wide natural stream of water

road _noun_ a smooth broad prepared track for wheeled vehicles; ⚠ **rode**

roar _noun_ a deep loud continuing sound; **roar** _verb_; ⚠ **raw**

roast _verb_ to cook meat or other foods by dry heat in an oven or over a fire

rob _verb_ (**robbed**) to take money, goods, etc, from a person or place when it is not yours; to steal from; **robber** _noun_; **robbery** _noun_

robin also **robin redbreast** _noun_ a fat little bird, with a brown back and a red breast

robot _noun_ **1** a machine that can do some human work; **2** an imaginary machine figure that acts as if alive

robotic arm used in industrial assembly

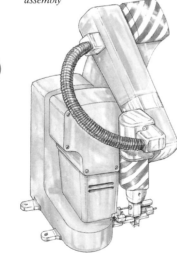

¹**rock** _noun_ **1** stone forming part of the Earth's surface; **2** a large separate piece of stone; **3** a hard sticky sweet made in long round bars; **rocky** _adjective_

²**rock** _verb_ to move backwards and forwards or from side to side

³**rock** _noun_ a kind of popular modern music played on electric instruments and with a strong beat

rocket _noun_ **1** a kind of firework that shoots high into the air and lets out coloured flames; **2** a machine of this kind driven by burning gases, used for spacecraft

rod _noun_ a long thin stiff stick of wood, metal, etc

rode _see_ RIDE; ⚠ **road**

role _noun_ the part taken by somebody in a play or film; ⚠ **roll**

¹**roll** _noun_ **1** a flat piece of some material rolled into a tube shape; **2** a small loaf of bread for one person; ⚠ **role**

²**roll** _verb_ **1** to turn over and over, round and round, or from side to side; **2** to move steadily and smoothly along as if on wheels; **3** to form into a circular shape by curling round and round; **4** to make flat by passing something over and over: **rolling pin**; **5** to make a long deep sound: _the drums_ **rolled**; ⚠ **role**

Roman Catholic _noun_ a member of the branch of the Christian religion (**Roman Catholic Church**) which has the Pope as its head; **Roman Catholic** _adjective_

signature

thatched roofs are sometimes signed by the thatcher in dried grasses

roof *noun* **1** the outside covering on top of a building; **2** the top covering of a tent, vehicle, etc; **3** the bony upper part of the inside of the mouth

room *noun* **1** a place in a building, with its own walls, floor, and ceiling; **2** space which could be filled or is enough for any purpose

root *noun* **1** the part of a plant that grows down into the soil; **2** the part of a tooth, hair, or organ that holds it to the body; ⚠ **route**

rope *noun* a strong thick cord made of twisted threads

¹rose *noun* a sweet smelling flower with prickly stems; the bush on which this grows

²rose *see* RISE

rot *verb* (**rotted**) to decay or go bad; **rot** *noun*; **rotten** *adjective*

rough *adjective* **1** not smooth; **2** not gentle; violent; **3** done or made quickly and not yet in finished form: *a **rough** drawing*; **4** stormy; **roughly** *adverb*; **roughen** *verb*

¹round *adjective* **1** shaped like a circle or a ball; **2** curved

²round *adverb, preposition* **1** with a circular movement or movements; spinning in a circle; **2** in a circular position; surrounding a central point; **3** all over the place; in or into all parts; **4** so as to face the other way; **5 all the year round** during the whole year

³round *noun* **1** one stage, period, or game in a competition or sport; **2** a regular journey to many houses, offices, etc: *a paper **round***; **3** a complete slice of bread

roundabout *noun* **1** a circular machine on which you can ride, usually at a fairground; **2** a circular place where several roads meet or cross

rounders *noun* a ball game in which a player hits the ball and then runs round the sides of a square

route *noun* a way planned or followed from one place to another; ⚠ **root**

¹row (*say like* **no**) *noun* a neat line of people or things side by side

²row (*say like* **now**) *noun* a quarrel; a loud noise; **row** *verb*

³row (*say like* **no**) *verb* to move through the water with oars; **row** *noun*; **rower** *noun*

royal *adjective* for, belonging to, supported by, or connected with a king or queen; **royally** *adverb*

rub *verb* (**rubbed**) to slide something to and fro or round and round against something else; **rub** *noun*

r

rubber _noun_ **1** a substance, made from chemicals or from the juice of a tropical tree, which keeps out water and springs back into position after being stretched; **2** a piece of this substance used for removing pencil marks; **rubbery** _adjective_

rubbish _noun_ **1** waste material to be thrown away; **2** silly remarks; nonsense

rubella _noun_ also **German measles** a disease in which red spots appear for a short time on your body

rucksack _noun_ a cloth bag you carry on your back

rude _adjective_ not polite; **rudely** _adverb_; **rudeness** _noun_

rug _noun_ **1** a thick floor mat; **2** a warm woollen covering to wrap round yourself when travelling

rugby also **rugby football, rugger** _noun_ a type of game played with an oval ball, by teams of thirteen (**rugby league**) or fifteen (**rugby union**) men

ruin _verb_ to destroy and spoil completely; **ruin** _noun_

the ruins of the Inca city Machu Picchu in Peru

¹**rule** _noun_ **1** an order, law, etc, that tells you what you must or must not do; **2** government; **3 as a rule** usually; generally

²**rule** _verb_ **1** to have and use the highest power over a country, people, etc, especially as a government; **2** to draw a straight line

ruler _noun_ **1** a person who rules; **2** a long narrow piece of hard material with straight edges for measuring things or drawing lines

rumour _noun_ something that people tell one another but that may not be true

¹**run** _verb_ (**runs, running, ran, run**) **1** to move on your legs faster than walking; **2** to move quickly; **3** to be in charge of a shop, business, etc; **4** to flow, pour, drip, etc; **5** to stretch; to continue: _The road_ **runs** _beside the river_; **6** to work or cause to work: _The car_ **runs** _well_

²**run** _noun_ **1** the action of running; **2** a journey; **3** a point won in cricket

¹**rung** _noun_ one of the bars that form the steps of a ladder

²**rung** _see_ RING

runway _noun_ an area with a specially prepared hard surface, on which aircraft land and take off

rush _verb_ to hurry; to act quickly; **rush** _noun_

rust _noun_ the reddish brown substance that forms on iron when it has been wet; **rust** _verb_; **rusty** _adjective_

r

Ss

¹**sack** *noun* **1** a large bag used for storing or moving goods: **sackful**; **2** the taking away of someone's job by an employer

²**sack** *verb* to take somebody's job away

sad *adjective* (**sadder**) feeling, showing, or causing sorrow; unhappy; **sadly** *adverb*; **sadness** *noun*

saddle *noun* a leather seat that fits on the back of a horse or on a bicycle, for a rider to sit on; **saddle** *verb*

¹**safe** *adjective* out of danger; not able to be hurt; protected; **safely** *adverb*; **safety** *noun*

²**safe** *noun* a box or cupboard with thick metal sides and a lock, used to protect money, jewellery, etc

safety belt *noun* a belt you wear in a car or plane to protect you if there is a crash

said *see* SAY

¹**sail** *noun* **1** a piece of cloth fixed on a boat to move it through the water by the force of the wind; **2** a short trip in such a boat; **3** **set sail** to begin a trip at sea; ⚠ **sale**

²**sail** *verb* **1** to travel on water; **2** to direct a ship or boat on water; **sailor** *noun*; ⚠ **sale**

salad *noun* a mixture of lettuce, uncooked vegetables, or fruits, served cold

sale *noun* **1** an act of selling; **2** a time when goods are sold at lower prices than usual; ⚠ **sail**

salmon *noun* a large fish of the northern seas with silvery skin and yellowish pink flesh, which swims up rivers to breed

salt *noun* a very common colourless or white solid substance used to improve the taste of food, preserve it, etc; **salt** *verb*; **salty** *adjective*

same *adjective* **1** like something else in every way; not different or changed; **2** being always only one single thing, person etc

sand *noun* a loose material of very small fine grains, found along coasts and in deserts; **sandy** *adjective*

sandal *noun* a light open shoe

sandwich *noun* two slices of bread with some other food between them

sang *see* SING

sank *see* SINK

sardine *noun* a small sea fish used as food

sat *see* SIT

sailing dinghy

jib

mainsail

S

133

satellite *noun* **1** a man-made object that travels round the Earth, moon, etc; **2** a small body moving round a planet

²**saw** *verb* (**saws, sawing, sawed, sawn** *or* **sawed**) to cut with a saw; ⚠ **sore**

³**saw** *see* SEE; ⚠ **sore**

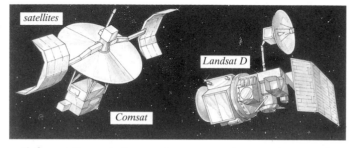

satellites

Landsat D

Comsat

satisfy *verb* **1** to make happy; to please; **2** to be or give enough for; **satisfaction** *noun*; **satisfactory** *adjective*; **satisfying** *adjective*

Saturday *noun* the seventh day of the week

Saturn *noun* a planet surrounded by large rings that is sixth in order from the sun

sauce *noun* any of various kinds of usually cooked liquids put on or eaten with food; ⚠ **source**

saucer *noun* a small plate made for putting a cup on

sausage *noun* a thin eatable tube of animal skin filled with a mixture of meat, cereal, spices, etc: **sausage roll**

save *verb* **1** to make safe from danger; rescue; **2** to keep for later use; **3** to use less; to stop waste; **4** to keep for later use on a computer; **saver** *noun*; **savings** *noun*

¹**saw** *noun* a tool for cutting materials, having a thin flat blade with a row of V-shaped teeth on the edge; ⚠ **sore**

say *verb* (**says, saying, said**) **1** to pronounce a sound, word, etc; to speak; **2** to give an opinion, ask a question, etc, using words; **3 that is to say** also **ie** in other words; **saying** *noun*

scab *noun* a hard mass of dried blood which forms over a wound while it is healing; **scabby** *adjective*

¹**scale** *noun* one of the small nearly flat stiff pieces covering the skin of some animals, especially fish and reptiles

²**scale** *noun* **1** a set of marks on a measuring instrument such as a ruler or a thermometer; **2** a rule or set of numbers comparing measurements on a map or model with actual measurements; **3** a set of musical notes going up or down in order

³**scale** also **scales** *noun* a weighing machine

⁴**scale** *verb* to climb up

scampi *noun* large prawns

scar *noun* a mark remaining on the skin from a wound, cut, etc; **scar** *verb* (**scarred**)

S

scare *verb* **1** to cause sudden fear to somebody; **2** to become afraid; **scare** *noun*; **scared** *adjective*

scarecrow *noun* a figure in the shape of a person; put in a field to keep birds away from the crops

scarf *noun* (*plural* **scarfs** *or* **scarves**) a piece of cloth for wearing round the neck, head, or shoulders

scarlet *noun* a very bright red colour; **scarlet** *adjective*

scatter *verb* **1** to cause a group of people or things to separate widely; **2** to spread widely in all directions

scene *noun* **1** a short part of a play, film, etc; **2** the place where something happens; **3** a view of a place; ⚠ **seen**

scenery *noun* **1** the set of painted backgrounds and other articles used on a theatre stage; **2** a view of the countryside

scent *noun* **1** a liquid with a nice smell; perfume; **2** a smell; ⚠ **cent, sent**

schedule (*say* **shedule**) *noun* a timetable of things to be done or when trains, buses, or planes will come; **schedule** *verb*

¹school *noun* a place where people go to learn: **schoolboy, schoolgirl, schoolwork**

²school *noun* a large group of one kind of fish, whale, etc

science *noun* **1** the study of knowledge which can be made into a system and which usually depends on seeing and testing facts and making general natural laws; **2** a branch of such knowledge, such as chemistry, physics, or biology; **scientific** *adjective*; **scientist** *noun*

scissors *noun* two sharp blades having handles at one end with holes for the fingers, fastened at the centre so that they open in the shape of the letter X and cut when they close: **pair of scissors**

scold *verb* to speak angrily, especially to blame; **scolding** *noun*

scone (*say* **skon** *or* **skohn**) *noun* a small soft round cake

scooter *noun* **1** a child's vehicle, pushed by one foot touching the ground; **2** also **motor scooter** a low bicycle-like vehicle with an engine, two small wheels, and usually a wide curved front to protect the legs

motor scooter

scorch *verb* to burn something slightly, usually so there is a brown mark; **scorch** *noun*

score *noun* the number of points, runs, goals, etc, made in a game, sport, etc; **score** *verb*

135

scrape *verb* **1** to rub with something hard or sharp; **2** to hurt or damage in this way; **scrape** *noun*

¹**scratch** *verb* to rub and tear or mark with something pointed or rough

²**scratch** *noun* a mark or small wound made by scratching

scream *verb* to cry out loudly on a high note; **scream** *noun*

screen *noun* **1** the front surface of a television, computer, or other instrument on which pictures and information can be shown; **2** a flat surface on which films or slides are shown; **3** a covering frame used for protecting people from cold or heat, for hiding something from view, etc

¹**screw** *noun* an object like a nail with a raised edge (thread) going round and round it which helps to hold it in place

²**screw** *verb* **1** to fasten by turning or tightening screws; **2** to move something, such as the top of a jar, in the same way; **3** to make paper, etc, into a small ball

scribble *verb* to write carelessly or in a hurry; **scribble** *noun*

scrub *verb* (**scrubbed**) to clean by hard rubbing, as with a stiff brush; **scrub** *noun*

sea *noun* the great body of salty water that covers much of the Earth's surface: **seabird, seashell, seashore, seaside, seaweed;** ⚠ **see**

¹**seal** *noun* a large fish-eating animal having broad flat limbs (**flippers**) for swimming

²**seal** *noun* a small piece of paper, wax, etc, which is fixed across an opening, and which must be broken in order to open it

³**seal** *verb* **1** to make or fix a seal onto something; **2** to fasten or close tightly and firmly

seam *noun* a line of stitches joining two pieces of cloth, leather, etc, at or near their edges; **seamless** *adjective*; ⚠ **seem**

search *verb* to look at, through, into, etc, to try to find something; **search** *noun*

season *noun* **1** one of the four parts of the year – spring, summer, autumn, or winter; **2** a period of time each year for a particular activity: *the football season*

seat *noun* **1** a place for sitting; **2** a thing to sit on; **3 take/have a seat** please sit down

¹**second** *noun* **1** a length of time equal to 1/60 of a minute; **2** a moment; a very short time

²**second** *adjective, adverb, noun, pronoun* the one after the first; 2nd

elephant seal

S

136

secret *noun* something known to only you or just a few other people; **secrecy** *noun*; **secret** *adjective*; **secretly** *adverb*

secretary *noun* a person with the job of preparing letters, keeping records, arranging meetings, etc, for others; **secretarial** *adjective*

see *verb* (**see, seeing, saw, seen**) **1** to use the eyes; to have or use the power of sight; **2** to look at; **3** to understand or recognise; **4** to visit, call upon, or meet; ⚠ **sea**

the winged seed of a sycamore tree is spread by the wind

seed *noun* the part of a plant from which a new plant can grow; **seedless** *adjective*

seek *verb* (**seeks, seeking, sought**) to make a search for; to try to find or get

seem *verb* to appear to be; ⚠ **seam**

seen *see* SEE; ⚠ **scene**

seesaw *noun* a board for children to sit on at opposite ends, balanced so that when one end goes up the other goes down

self *noun* (*plural* **selves**) your own person

selfish *adjective* thinking only about yourself and not caring for others; **selfishly** *adverb*; **selfishness** *noun*

self-service *noun, adjective* the system in many restaurants, shops, garages, etc, in which customers collect what they want and then pay at special desks

sell *verb* (**sells, selling, sold**) to give to another for money; **seller** *noun*; ⚠ **cellar**

send *verb* (**sends, sending, sent**) to cause or order a person or thing to go or be taken to a place, in a direction, etc; **sender** *noun*

senior *adjective* **1** of higher position or importance; **2** older; **senior** *noun*

¹**sense** *noun* **1** good understanding and reasonable ideas: **common sense**; **2** one of the five powers by which we see, smell, hear, feel, or taste; **sensation** *noun*; **sensitivity** *noun*; **sensitive** *adjective*

²**sense** *verb* to feel; to know through the senses

sensible *adjective* reasonable; having good sense; **sensibly** *adverb*

sent *see* SEND; ⚠ **cent, scent**

sentence *noun* a group of words that forms a statement, question, etc, contains a verb and usually a subject, and (in writing) begins with a capital letter and ends with one of the marks .!?"

¹**separate** (*say* **sepparayt**) *verb* **1** to set or move apart; to go in different directions; **2** to make, become, or keep in different places

S

²**separate** (*say* **sepprut**) *adjective* **1** not the same; different; **2** apart; not joined or shared with another; **separately** *adverb*; **separation** *noun*

September *noun* the ninth month of the year

sergeant (*say* **sar-**junt) *noun* a person in the army or police force

serial *noun* a story appearing in parts; ⚠ **cereal**

series *noun* a group of things coming one after the other

serious *adjective* **1** not cheerful; not joking or funny; **2** important

seriously *adverb* **1** in a serious way; **2** very; extremely: *seriously* rich

servant *noun* a person who works for another as a cook, gardener, maid, etc

serve *verb* **1** to work or do a useful job; **2** to give food to people; **3** to look after somebody buying something; **4** to begin play in tennis, badminton, etc, by hitting the ball to the other player; **5 serve somebody right** to be a fair punishment for somebody

service *noun* **1** work or duty done for somebody; **2** helping customers in a shop or guests in a hotel, restaurant, etc; **3** a religious ceremony; **4** a useful business or job that usually does not produce goods: **postal service, train service**

¹**set** *verb* (**sets, setting, set**) **1** to put in a place; **2** to give a piece of work for somebody to do; **3** to put into a position, arrange: *set the table*; **4** to put into action; to make something happen; **5** to pass downwards out of sight: *The sun is setting*

²**set** *noun* **1** a group of things thought of together; **2** a piece of electrical equipment especially a television

settee *noun* a SOFA

settle *verb* **1** to go and live in a place; **2** to bring or place down, often in a comfortable position; **3** to sink or come down, usually to a position of rest; **4** to decide on; to fix or arrange something; **settlement** *noun*; **settler** *noun*

seven *adjective, noun* the number 7; **seventh** *adjective, adverb*

seventeen *adjective, noun* the number 17; **seventeenth** *adjective, adverb*

seventy *adjective, noun* the number 70; **seventieth** *adjective, adverb*

several *adjective, pronoun* more than two but fewer than many; some but not many

severe *adjective* **1** not kind or gentle; strict; **2** hard; difficult; **severely** *adverb*

sew *verb* (**sews, sewing, sewed, sewn**) to join or fasten cloth, leather, paper, etc, by stitching with thread; to make or mend with needle and thread: **sewing machine**; ⚠ **so, sow**

electric sewing machine

sex *noun* being male or female

¹**shade** *noun* **1** slight darkness; shelter from the sun or other light; **2** something that keeps out light: **lampshade**; **3** a slightly different colour: *light blue and a deeper* **shade**; **shady** *adjective*; **shadiness** *noun*

²**shade** *verb* to shelter from direct light or heat

shadow *noun* a dark shape made by something when it blocks out light

shake *verb* (**shakes, shaking, shook, shaken**) **1** to move quickly up and down and to and fro; **2 shake hands with somebody** to take somebody's right hand in your own for a moment, moving it up and down, as a sign of greeting, goodbye, agreement, etc; **3 shake your head** to move your head from side to side to show 'no' or disapproval; **shake** *noun*; ⚠ **sheikh, sheik**

shall *verb* (**should, shan't**=shall not) **1** used with *I* and *we* when asking a question or offering to do something: *Shall I get you a chair?* **2** sometimes used instead of *will* with *I* and *we* to say what is going to happen: *I* **shall** *have finished my work by next Friday.*

shallow *adjective* not deep; not far from top to bottom

shame *noun* the painful feeling you have when you have done something wrong or silly; **shame** *verb*

shampoo *noun* a liquid soap used for washing hair; **shampoo** *verb*

shan't *see* SHALL

shape *noun* the appearance or form of something seen; **shape** *verb*; **shaped** *adjective*; **shapeless** *adjective*

¹**share** *noun* **1** the part belonging to or done by a person; **2** a part of a company that many people can buy

²**share** *verb* **1** to use, pay, have, take part in, etc, with others or among a group; **2** to divide and give out

shark *noun* a fierce flesh-eating fish that has several rows of sharp teeth, and can be dangerous to people

hammerhead shark

sharp *adjective* **1** having a thin cutting edge; having a fine point; **2** quick and sensitive in thinking, seeing, hearing, etc: **sharp sighted**; **3** sudden and quick: *a sharp pain*; **sharply** *adverb*; **sharpen** *verb*

shave *verb* to cut off hair close to the skin with a razor; **shave** *noun*

she *pronoun* (**her, herself**) that female person or animal

¹shed *noun* a lightly built hut, used for storing things

²shed *verb* (**sheds, shedding, shed**) to let fall or get rid of naturally, things such as leaves, hair, etc

sheep *noun* (*plural* **sheep**) (*male* **ram**, *female* **ewe**, *young* **lamb**) a grass-eating animal kept for its wool and meat

a modern cruise ship

shield *noun* a broad piece of metal, wood, or leather once carried by soldiers to protect them from arrows, blows, etc

¹shine *verb* (**shines, shining, shone**) **1** to give off light; to look bright; **2** to direct a lamp, beam of light, etc

²shine *verb* (**shines, shining, shined**) to polish; to make bright by rubbing; **shiny** *adjective*

¹sheet *noun* **1** a large four-sided piece of cloth used to cover a bed; **2** a piece of paper

sheikh, sheik (*say* **shake**) *noun* an Arab chief or prince;
⚠ **shake**

shelf *noun* (*plural* **shelves**) a flat usually long and narrow board fixed against a wall or in a frame, for putting things on

shell *noun* the hard covering of an animal, egg, nut, etc: **shellfish**

¹shelter *noun* anything that protects, especially a building

²shelter *verb* to protect from harm; to give shelter to

shepherd (feminine **shepherdess**) *noun* a person who takes care of sheep in a field

ship *noun* a large boat

shirt *noun* a piece of clothing for the upper body, usually of light cloth with a collar and sleeves

shiver *verb* to shake, especially from cold or fear; **shiver** *noun*

shoal *noun* a large group of fish swimming together

¹shock *noun* **1** the strong feeling caused by something unexpected and usually very unpleasant; **2** the sudden violent effect of electricity passing through the body; **3** a violent force, as from a hard blow, crash, explosion etc

²shock *verb* **1** to cause unpleasant or angry surprise to somebody; **2** to give an electric shock to

S

*15th century shoes
with long points*

shoe *noun* an outer covering for the foot, usually having a hard sole and a support under the heel

shone *see* SHINE

shook *see* SHAKE

¹**shoot** *verb* (**shoots, shooting, shot**) **1** to fire a weapon at and hit something or somebody; **2** to go fast or suddenly; **3** to kick, throw, etc, a ball in order to score in a game; **4** to make a photograph or film

²**shoot** *noun* a new growth from a plant, especially a young stem and leaves

shooting star *noun* a small meteor from space which burns brightly as it passes through the Earth's air

¹**shop** *noun* **1** a room or building where goods are regularly kept and sold: **shopkeeper**; **2** a place where things are made or repaired

²**shop** *verb* (**shopped**) to buy things; **shopper** *noun*; **shopping** *noun*

shore *noun* the land along the edge of a large stretch of water; ⚠ **sure**

short *adjective* **1** not far from one end to the other; little in distance, length, or height; **2** lasting only a little time; **shortage** *noun*; **shorten** *verb*

shorts *noun* trousers ending above the knees

¹**shot** *noun* **1** an action of shooting a weapon; **2** a kick, throw, etc, of a ball intended to score a point; **3** a sending up of a space vehicle or rocket; **4** a chance to do something; a try

²**shot** *see* SHOOT

should *verb* (**shouldn't**) to have a duty to; ought to

shoulder *noun* **1** the part of the body at each side of the neck where the arms join; **2** either edge of a road outside the travelled part: **hard shoulder**

shout *verb* to speak or say very loudly; **shout** *noun*

shovel *noun* a long-handled tool with a broad blade for lifting and moving loose material such as earth or coal; **shovel** *verb*

¹**show** *verb* (**shows, showing, showed, shown**) **1** to offer for seeing; to allow or cause to be seen; **2** to appear; to be in or come into view; **3** to go with and guide or direct; **4** to explain; to make clear to by words or actions

²**show** *noun* **1** a performance in a theatre, on radio or television, etc; **2** a collection of things for looking at

shower *noun* **1** a short fall of rain or snow; **2** a fall of many small things or drops of liquid; **3** a washing of the body by standing under an opening from which water comes out in many small streams; the thing used for this; **shower** *verb*

S

141

shown *see* SHOW

shrank *see* SHRINK

shrimp *noun* a small sea creature with long legs and a tail shaped like a fan

shrink *verb* (**shrinks, shrinking, shrank, shrunk** *or* **shrunken**) to make or become smaller, as from the effect of heat or water

shrug *verb* (**shrugged**) to lift and drop your shoulders, especially to show you do not know or do not care; **shrug** *noun*

shut *verb* (**shuts, shutting, shut**) to close; to move into a covered, blocked, or folded-together position

shuttle *noun* **1** a spacecraft that can fly into space and return to Earth: *space* **shuttle**; **2** a plane, train or bus that goes on short journeys from one place to another

shuttlecock *noun* a small light object (*see* picture on page 12) for hitting across a net in a game of badminton

shy *adjective* (**shyer** *or* **shier, shyest** *or* **shiest**) nervous in the company of others; **shyly** *adverb*; **shyness** *noun*

sick *adjective* **1** ill; having a disease; **2** upset in the stomach so that the food comes back out through your mouth; **sickness** *noun*

side *noun* **1** a more or less upright surface of something, not the top, bottom, front, or back; **2** the right or left part of the body, from the shoulder to the top of the leg; **3** an edge; **4** either of the two surfaces of a thin flat object; **5** a sports team

sideways *advcrb, adjective* **1** with one side, and not the front or back, forward or up; **2** to or towards one side

sigh *verb* to let out a deep breath slowly and with a sound, usually showing that you are tired, sad, pleased, etc; **sigh** *noun*

sight *noun* **1** the sense of seeing; the power of the eye; **2** something that is seen; **3** something worth seeing, especially a place visited by tourists; ⚠ **site**

¹**sign** *noun* **1** a mark, symbol, or object which is seen and which means something to the person who sees it; **2** a board or other notice giving information, warning, directions, etc: **signpost**; **3** also **sign of the zodiac** any of the twelve divisions of the year named after groups of stars

signs of the zodiac

PISCES ARIES

TAURUS GEMINI

LEO

CANCER

VIRGO LIBRA

SAGITTARIUS

AQUARIUS

SCORPIO

CAPRICORN

²**sign** *verb* to write your name; **signature** *noun*

¹**signal** *noun* **1** a sound, action, movement, or apparatus meant to warn, command, or give a message; **2** a sound, picture, or message sent by waves, as in radio or television

²**signal** *verb* (**signalled**) to give a signal

silence *noun* the state of not speaking or making a noise: complete quiet; stillness

silent *adjective* **1** not speaking; not using spoken expression; **2** free from noise; quiet; **silently** *adverb*

silk *noun* a fine thread which is produced by a type of caterpillar (**silkworm**) and made into thread for sewing or into cloth; the smooth soft cloth made from this; **silky** *adjective*

silkworm building its cocoon

silly *adjective* not clever or reasonable; foolish; not serious; **silliness** *noun*

silver *noun* **1** a soft whitish precious metal that is used in ornaments and coins; **2** the colour of this metal; **silver** *adjective*; **silvery** *adjective*

similar *adjective* like or alike; of the same kind; partly or almost the same; **similarly** *adverb*; **similarity** *noun*

simple *adjective* **1** easy to understand or do; not difficult; **2** of the ordinary kind; not complicated; plain; **simply** *adverb*

sin *noun* something people think is a very bad act; something your religion teaches you is wrong; **sin** *verb*

since *adverb, preposition, conjunction* at a time between then and now; from then until now: *I haven't seen her since her illness*

sing *verb* (**sings, singing, sang, sung**) to make music, musical sounds, songs, etc, with the voice; **singer** *noun*

¹**single** *adjective* **1** the only one; not double; **2** not married; **3** for the use of only one person: *a single room*

²**single** *noun* a CD or tape with only one song on it

¹**sink** *noun* a large basin in a kitchen, for washing dishes, clothes, vegetables, etc, in

²**sink** *verb* (**sinks, sinking, sank, sunk**) to go down below a surface, out of sight, or to the bottom

sip *verb* (**sipped**) to drink, taking only a little at a time into the front of the mouth; **sip** *noun*

sir *noun* a polite way of talking or writing to a man

sister *noun* **1** a girl or woman with the same parents as another girl or woman; **2** a nurse in charge of a hospital ward

sit *verb* (**sits, sitting, sat**) to rest in a position with the upper body upright and your bottom on a chair, the ground, etc: **sitting room**

site *noun* **1** a place where something was or happened; **2** a piece of ground for building on; ⚠ **sight**

six *adjective, noun* **1** the number 6; **2** a cricket hit that counts as six runs; **sixth** *adjective, adverb*

sixteen *adjective, noun* the number 16; **sixteenth** *adjective, adverb*

sixty *adjective, noun* the number 60; **sixtieth** *adjective, adverb*

size *noun* the bigness or smallness of anything

skate *noun* a special shoe or boot fitted with a metal blade or small wheels: **ice skates, roller skates**; **skate** *verb*; **skater** *noun*

skateboard *noun* a piece of wood or plastic with wheels that you stand on and go along on

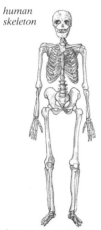

human skeleton

skeleton *noun* the bones in a human or animal body

ski (*say* **skee**) *noun* (*plural* **skis**) a long thin narrow piece of wood, plastic, or metal, curving up in front, that is fastened to a boot for travelling on snow or that you stand on to ski over water (**waterski**); **ski** *verb*; **skier** *noun*; **skiing** *noun*

skill *noun* the ability to do something well; **skilful** *adjective*; **skilfully** *adverb*; **skilled** *adjective*

skin *noun* **1** the natural outer covering of an animal or human body, from which hair may grow; **2** a natural outer covering of some fruits and vegetables; peel

skinny *adjective* thin; without much flesh

skip *verb* (**skipped**) **1** to move in a light dancing way, as with quick steps and jumps; **2** to pass over or leave out something; **3** to jump over a rope which is made to swing over your head and under your feet; **skip** *noun*

skirt *noun* a piece of women's clothing that hangs from the waist

skull *noun* the bones of the head

sky *noun* (*plural* **skies**) the upper air; the space above the Earth where clouds and the sun, moon, and stars appear

slap *verb* (**slapped**) to strike quickly with the flat part of the hand; **slap** *noun*

slave *noun* a person owned by another; a servant without freedom

sledge *noun* a small vehicle made for sliding along snow or ice; **sledge** *verb*

¹**sleep** *noun* the natural resting state of unconsciousness of the body; the state of not being awake; a period of time of this; **sleepy** *adjective*; **sleepily** *adverb*

S

²**sleep** *verb* **(sleeps, sleeping, slept)** to rest in sleep; to be naturally unconscious, as at night

sleeve *noun* a part of a piece of clothing for covering an arm; **sleeveless** *adjective*

slice *noun* a thin flat piece cut from something; **slice** *verb*

¹**slide** *verb* **(slides, sliding, slid)** to go smoothly over a surface

²**slide** *noun* **1** a slipping movement over a surface; **2** a track or apparatus for sliding down; **3** a square piece of framed film for passing light through to show a picture on a surface; **4** a small piece of glass to put an object on for seeing under a microscope

slight *adjective* small; not important; **slightly** *adverb*

¹**slip** *verb* **(slipped) 1** to slide out of place or fall by sliding; **2** to make a slight mistake

²**slip** *noun* **1** an act of slipping or sliding; **2** a slight mistake; **3** a small or narrow piece of paper; **4** a piece of women's underwear not covering the arms or neck

slipper *noun* a light shoe with the top made from soft material, for wearing indoors

slippery *adjective* difficult to hold or to stand, drive, etc, on without slipping

slit *verb* to make a long narrow cut or opening in; **slit** *noun*

slope *noun* a surface that slopes; a piece of ground going up or down; **slope** *verb*

¹**slow** *adjective* **1** not moving or going on quickly; **2** taking a long time or too long; **3** not good or quick in understanding;

4 showing a time that is earlier than the true time; **slowly** *adjective*; **slowness** *noun*

²**slow** *verb* to make or become slower

slug

slug *noun* a small plant-eating creature, like a snail but with no shell, that often does damage to gardens

smack *verb* to strike loudly, as with the flat part of the hand; **smack** *noun*

small *adjective* little in size, weight, force, importance, etc; **smallness** *noun*

smart *adjective* **1** neat and stylish in appearance; **2** clever; good or quick in thinking; **smartly** *adverb*

smash *verb* to break into pieces

¹**smell** *verb* **(smells, smelling, smelled** *or* **smelt) 1** to have or use the sense of the nose; **2** to notice, examine, discover, or recognise by this sense; **3** to have a particular smell

²**smell** *noun* **1** the power of using the nose; **2** something that we discover through the nose

smile *noun* an expression of the face with the mouth turned up at the ends and the eyes bright, that shows amusement, happiness, etc; **smile** *verb*

¹**smoke** *noun* gas mixed with very small bits of solid material that can be seen in the air and is usually given off by burning; **smokeless** *adjective*; **smoky** *adjective*

S

²**smoke** *verb* **1** to suck or breathe in smoke from cigarettes, a pipe, etc; **2** to give off smoke

smooth *adjective* having an even surface without sharply raised or lowered places, points, lumps, etc; not rough; **smooth** *verb*; **smoothly** *adverb*

snail *noun* a small animal with a soft body, no limbs, and a hard spiral shaped shell on its back

snake *noun* a reptile that has a long body with no limbs, a large mouth, and a fork-shaped tongue, sometimes with a poisonous bite

snatch *verb* to get hold of something quickly

sneeze *verb* to push air and liquid out of your nose and mouth suddenly, making a noise, as when you have a cold; **sneeze** *noun*

sniff *verb* to draw air into the nose with a sound, often to discover a smell in or on something; **sniff** *noun*

snooker *noun* a billiards game played on a table with six pockets, with fifteen red balls and six balls of other colours

snore *verb* to breathe heavily and noisily through the nose and mouth while asleep

snow *noun* water frozen into small flat flakes that fall like rain in cold weather and may cover the ground thickly: **snowball, snowflake, snowman**; **snow** *verb*

¹**so** *adverb* **1** in this way or that way; in the way shown or described; **2** in the same way; also; ⚠ **sew, sow**

²**so** *conjunction* **so that, so as to** in order that; therefore; ⚠ **sew, sow**

soak *verb* to remain or leave in a liquid, to become soft or completely wet; **soak** *noun*; **soaked** *adjective*; **soaking** *adjective, adverb*

soap *noun* **1** a substance made from fats or oils, for use with water to wash the body or other things; **2** also **soap opera** a TV programme that goes on for a long time, telling a story about the same group of people; **soapy** *adjective*

sock *noun* a covering of soft material for the foot and part of the lower leg

socket *noun* an opening, hollow place, or machine part that forms a holder or into which something fits: *an electric light socket*

sofa *noun* a comfortable seat with raised arms and a back and wide enough for usually two or three people

soft *adjective* **1** not hard or stiff; not firm against pressure; giving in to the touch; **2** smooth and pleasant to the touch; **3** quiet; not making much noise; **soften** *verb*; **softly** *adverb*; **softness** *noun*

software *noun* programs which control the way a computer works

snowflake

soil *noun* the top covering of the ground, in which plants grow

solar *adjective* **1** of the sun; **2** using the power of the sun's light and heat

solar system *noun* the sun together with all the bodies, such as the moon, planets, etc, going round it

sold *see* SELL

soldier *noun* a person in an army

¹**sole** *noun* **1** the bottom part of the foot on which you walk or stand; **2** the flat bottom part of a shoe not including the heel; ⚠ **soul**

some *adjective, pronoun, adverb* **1** a little, few, or small number or amount; **2** used when speaking about people or things without saying exactly which ones: *Come back some other time*; ⚠ **sum**

somebody also **someone** *pronoun* a person; some but no particular or known person

somehow *adverb* by some means; in some way not yet known

somersault (**say summer-sollt**) *noun* a jump or rolling backward or forward movement in which the feet go over the head before the body returns upright

turning somersaults in the air

²**sole** *noun* a flat fish often eaten as food; ⚠ **soul**

solemn *adjective* done, made, etc, seriously; **solemnly** *adverb*

solid *adjective* **1** keeping its shape; not liquid or gas; **2** having the inside filled up; not hollow; **3** made of one material all the way through; **solid** *noun*

solve *verb* to find the answer to a puzzle, problem, etc; **solution** *noun*

something *pronoun* a thing which is not known or not named

sometime *adverb* at some time in the past or future

sometimes *adverb* at times; now and then; occasionally

somewhere *adverb* in, at, or to, some place

son *noun* a person's male child; ⚠ **sun**

song *noun* **1** a short piece of music with words for singing; **2** the music-like sound of a bird

soon *adverb* within a short time

soot *noun* a black powder produced by burning, and carried into the air and left on surfaces by smoke; **sooty** *adjective*

soothe *verb* **1** to make less painful; **2** to make less angry, excited, or worried; to comfort or calm; **soothing** *adjective*

sore *adjective* painful or aching from a wound, infection, or hard use; **sore** *noun*; **soreness** *noun*; ⚠ **saw**

sorrow *noun* sadness; a cause of unhappiness

sorry *adjective* used to say you are ashamed or unhappy because of things you have done and wish that you had not done them, or that you are sad because you cannot do what is wanted

¹**sort** *noun* a group of people, things, etc, all having certain qualities; a type; a kind; ⚠ **sought**

²**sort** *verb* to put things in order; to arrange; ⚠ **sought**

sought *see* SEEK; ⚠ **sort**

soul *noun* the part of a person that is not the body and is thought not to die; ⚠ **sole**

¹**sound** *noun* what is or may be heard; something that causes a sensation in the ear

²**sound** *verb* **1** to make a sound; to produce an effect that can be heard; **2** to seem: *to* **sound** *interesting*

soup *noun* a liquid cooked food often containing small pieces of meat, fish, or vegetables

sour *adjective* having a taste that is not sweet

source *noun* where something comes from; ⚠ **sauce**

south *noun* one of the four main points of the compass; the right of a person facing the rising sun; **south** *adjective, adverb*; **southerly** *adverb*; **southern** *adjective*

southeast *noun* the direction of the point of the compass which is halfway between south and east

southwest *noun* the direction of the point of the compass which is halfway between south and west

¹**sow** (*say* **so**) *verb* (**sows, sowing, sowed, sown** *or* **sowed**) to plant or scatter seeds on a piece of ground; **sower** *noun*; ⚠ **sew, so**

²**sow** (*say like* **how**) *noun* a fully grown female pig

soya *noun* a plant that is grown for food from its seeds (**soya beans**) which are rich in protein

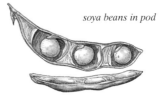

soya beans in pod

space *noun* **1** what is outside the Earth's air; where stars, planets, moons, and other bodies move: **spacecraft, spaceman, spacewoman, spaceship**; **2** an empty or open place; room; **3** an area or distance between objects

space shuttle *noun* a rocket that can return to Earth

astronaut in a spacesuit

spacesuit *noun* a suit for wearing in space, covering the whole body and provided with an air supply

spade *noun* **1** a tool like a shovel for digging earth, with a broad metal blade for pushing with the foot into the ground; **2** a playing card with one or more figures each shaped like a pointed leaf printed on it in black (♠)

spaghetti *noun* a food made of pasta in long strings, usually sold in dry form for making soft again in boiling water

spanner *noun* a metal hand tool for turning nuts and bolts

spare *verb* to be able to give or lend something; **spare** *adjective*

spark *noun* **1** a small bit of burning material thrown out by a fire or by the striking together of two hard objects; **2** a passage of electricity across a space that produces light, also used in car engines; **spark** *verb*

sparkle *verb* to shine in small flashes; **sparkle** *noun*

sparrow *noun* a small brownish bird, very common in many parts of the world

spat *see* SPIT

speak *verb* (**speaks, speaking, spoke, spoken**) to say things; to use the voice; to talk

speaker *noun* **1** a person making a speech; **2** the part on a sound system, TV, or computer where the sound comes from

spear *noun* a pole with a sharp point at one end used for throwing as a weapon

special *adjective* of a particular kind; not ordinary or usual; **specially** *adverb*

speech *noun* **1** the act or power of speaking; **2** a long set of words spoken for people to listen to

speed *noun* how fast something moves

speed *verb* (**speeds, speeding, sped**) to go fast; **speedy** *adjective*

speedometer *noun* an instrument in a vehicle for telling its speed

¹spell *verb* (**spells, spelling, spelt** *or* **spelled**) to name or write the letters of a word in order; **spelling** *noun*

²spell *noun* a condition caused by magical power; the magic words producing this condition

S

spend *verb* **(spends, spending, spent) 1** to give money in payment; **2** to pass or use time

spice *noun* a seed, root, or other part of a plant used to give flavour to food; **spicy** *adjective*

Australian trap spider

spider *noun* a small eight-legged creature which makes thin threads, that it sometimes makes into nets or webs for catching insects to eat

spill *verb* **(spills, spilling, spilt** *or* **spilled)** to pour out accidentally, as over the edge of a container

spin *verb* **(spins, spinning, spun) 1** to make thread by twisting cotton, wool, etc; **2** to produce thread, especially in a mass or net; **3** to turn round and round quickly

spinach *noun* a vegetable whose broad green leaves are usually eaten cooked

spine *noun* **1** also **spinal column** the row of bones in the centre of your back; **2** a stiff pointed part of a plant or animal; a prickle

spiral *noun* a curve that winds round and round, such as a spring or the thread of a screw; **spiral** *adjective*

spirit *noun* **1** the part of you that is not body, and that some people think does not die with your body; **2** a being without a body, such as a ghost; **3** a state of mind: *in high spirits;* **4** a strong alcoholic drink

spit *verb* **(spits, spitting, spat** *or* **spit)** to force liquid from the mouth

spite *noun* **1** not liking and wanting to annoy another person, especially in some small way; **2 in spite of** even though something else happens; **spiteful** *adjective;* **spitefully** *adverb*

splash *verb* to cause a liquid to fall, strike, or move noisily, in drops, waves, etc; **splash** *noun*

splendid *adjective* very fine; excellent; **splendidly** *adverb*

splint *noun* a flat piece of wood, metal or plastic, used for protecting and keeping a damaged part of the body, especially a bone, in position

splinter *noun* a small needle-like piece broken off something, especially of wood

split *verb* **(splits, splitting, split) 1** to break from one end to another, especially with force or by a blow or tear; **2** to divide into separate parts; to share; **split** *noun*

spoil *verb* **(spoils, spoiling, spoiled** *or* **spoilt) 1** to make or become of no use; to ruin; **2** to make a child selfish from having too much attention or being given too much

S

¹**spoke** *noun* a bar which connects the outer ring of a wheel to the centre, as on a bicycle

²**spoke** *see* SPEAK

spoken *see* SPEAK

breadcrumb sponge

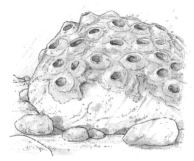

sponge *noun* **1** a sea creature which grows a spreading rubber-like skeleton full of small holes; a piece of this or a substance like it, which is used for washing; **2** also **sponge cake** a soft light sweet cake

spoon *noun* a tool for mixing, serving, and eating food, consisting of a small bowl with a handle: **spoonful, spoonfuls**

sport *noun* games, competitions, or activities done for pleasure

sportsman (feminine **sportswoman**) *noun* a person who plays or enjoys sports

¹**spot** *noun* **1** a part or area different from the main surface, as in colour; a small mark; **2** a particular place; **3** a pimple

²**spot** *verb* (**spotted**) **1** to see; to recognise; **2** to mark with coloured or dirty spots

spout *noun* an opening through which liquid can be poured from a container

sprang *see* SPRING

spray *verb* to scatter liquid in small drops; **spray** *noun*

¹**spread** *verb* (**spreads, spreading, spread**) **1** to put a thin covering on; **2** to open, reach, or stretch out; to be or make longer, broader, wider, etc; **3** to share or divide over an area, period of time, etc

²**spread** *noun* a substance put on bread: *low-fat **spread***

spreadsheet *noun* a computer program to work out money or number problems

¹**spring** *noun* **1** a place where water comes up naturally from the ground; **2** the season between winter and summer; **3** a coil of wire, which goes back to its original shape if you pull it, then let go

²**spring** *verb* (**springs, springing, sprang, sprung**) **1** to move quickly as when jumping; **2 spring a leak** to begin to let liquid through a crack, hole, etc

sprinkle *verb* to scatter in drops or small grains; **sprinkler** *noun*

sprout *verb* **1** to start to grow; **2** to send up new growth, as from a seed or bud; **sprout** *noun*

sprung *see* SPRING

spun *see* SPIN

¹**spy** *noun* a person whose job is to find out secret information, usually from an enemy

²**spy** *verb* **1** to try to get information secretly; **2** to watch secretly

S

square *noun* **1** a shape with four straight equal sides; **2** a piece of material in this shape; **3** an open space surrounded by buildings; **square** *adjective*

¹**squash** *verb* **1** to force or be forced into a flat shape; to press; **2** to push or fit into a small space; to squeeze

²**squash** *noun* **1** an act of squashing; **2** a crowd of people in a small space; **3** a sweet fruit drink; **4** a game played by two or four players, with rackets and a small rubber ball

squeak *verb* to make a high but not loud sound; **squeak** *noun*; **squeaker** *noun*

squeal *verb* to make a long very high sound or cry; **squeal** *noun*

squeeze *verb* to press together from opposite sides; **squeeze** *noun*; **squeezer** *noun*

squirrel *noun* a small four-legged animal with a long furry tail that climbs trees and eats nuts

stable *noun* a building where animals, especially horses, are kept and fed

stadium *noun* a large open building with rows of seats surrounding a sports field

stag *noun* a fully grown male deer

stage *noun* **1** a time or step in a course of events; **2** the raised floor on which plays are performed in a theatre

stain *verb* to make a mark that cannot be taken away; **stain** *noun*; **stainless** *adjective*

stair *noun* any of the steps in a set of stairs; ⚠ **stare**

stairs *noun* a fixed length of steps connecting floors in a building

stake *noun* a pointed piece of wood, metal, etc, for driving into the ground; **stake** *verb*; ⚠ **steak**

stale *adjective* no longer fresh

¹**stalk** *noun* **1** the main upright part of a plant; **2** a long narrow part of a plant supporting one or more leaves, fruits, or flowers; a stem

²**stalk** *verb* to follow or hunt; **stalker** *noun*

stall *noun* a table or open-fronted shop, especially one in a market

¹**stamp** *verb* **1** to strike downwards with the foot; **2** to stick on a stamp

S

Olympic stadium, Atlanta, America

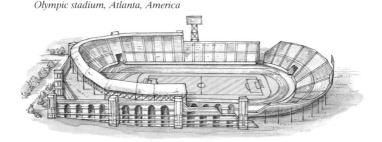

²**stamp** *noun* **1** also **postage stamp** a small piece of paper for sticking on a piece of mail to be sent to show that payment has been made; **2** an instrument or tool for pressing or printing onto a surface

¹**stand** *verb* **(stands, standing, stood) 1** to support yourself on the feet upright; **2** to rise or raise to a position of doing this; **3** to be in or take a particular position; **4** to be able to bear; **5 stand for** to mean; **6 stand a chance** to have a chance; **7 stand on your own (two) feet** to be able to do without help from others

²**stand** *noun* **1** a place or act of standing; **2** a frame, desk, or other piece of furniture for putting something on: **hat stand**; **3** an open building at a sports ground with rows of seats or standing space

¹**standard** *noun* a fixed weight, length, cost, or quality, by which things are measured or judged

²**standard** *adjective* ordinary; of the usual kind

¹**star** *noun* **1** a body, such as the sun or a planet, that appears as a bright point in the sky; **2** a shape with five or more points; **3** a famous or very skilful performer; **starry** *adjective*

²**star** *verb* **(starred) 1** to mark with one or more stars; **2** to have or appear as a main performer

starboard *noun* the right side of a ship or aircraft as you face forward

starch *noun* **1** a white tasteless substance forming an important part of foods such as grain, rice, beans, and potatoes; **2** a powder used for stiffening clothes; **starchy** *adjective*

stare *verb* to look at something with wide-open eyes, for a long time; **stare** *noun*; ⚠ **stair**

starfish *noun* a flat sea animal with five arms forming a star shape

starling *noun* a common greenish black bird

start *verb* to begin; **start** *noun*

starve *verb* **1** to die because you do not have enough food to eat; **2** to be very hungry; **starvation** *noun*

¹**state** *noun* **1** a condition in which a person or thing is; **2** the government of a country; **3** a small part of a country: **United States of America**

²**state** *verb* to say or put into words

statement *noun* something that is said

station *noun* **1** a building on a railway or bus line where passengers or goods arrive or leave; **2** a building that is a centre for a particular kind of service: **police station**; **3** a company or machine that broadcasts on television or radio

stationary *adjective* standing still; not moving; ⚠ **stationery**

stationery *noun* materials for writing, especially paper; **stationer** *noun*; ⚠ **stationary**

statue *noun* a human or animal figure, made in some solid material, such as stone

stay *verb* **1** to stop and remain; **2** to continue to be; **3** to live in a place for a while; to be a visitor or guest; **stay** *noun*

S

steady *adjective* **1** firm; not shaking or moving; **2** not changing; regular; **steadily** *adverb*; **steadiness** *noun*

steak *noun* a flat piece of meat or fish; ⚠ **stake**

steal *verb* (**steals, stealing, stole, stolen**) **1** to take something that belongs to someone else without asking for it; **2** to move secretly or quietly; ⚠ **steel**

¹**steam** *noun* the whitish cloudy gas produced by boiling water

²**steam** *adjective* using steam under pressure to produce power or heat: **steamroller, steamship**

stem *noun* the central part of a plant above the ground, or the smaller part which supports a leaf or flower

¹**step** *noun* **1** the act of putting one foot in front of the other in order to move along; the sound this makes; **2** a flat surface, especially in a set of surfaces each higher than the other, on which the foot is placed for climbing up and down; a stair, rung of a ladder, etc; **3** an act in a set of actions in making or doing something; **4** a type of movement of the feet in dancing; **5 watch your step** to behave or act carefully

the Mallard, a steam locomotive

steel *noun* a hard strong metal made from iron and used for knives, machines, etc; ⚠ **steal**

steel band *noun* a band playing instruments cut from metal drums and tuned to make particular notes

steep *adjective* rising or falling quickly; **steeply** *adverb*

steeple *noun* a church tower with a top part rising to a high sharp point

steer *verb* to direct or guide a ship, car, bicycle, etc

stellar *adjective* of or concerning the stars

²**step** *verb* (**stepped**) to put one foot down usually in front of the other, in order to move along; to walk

stepchild *noun* (*plural* **stepchildren**) the child of somebody's husband or wife by another marriage: **stepbrother, stepdaughter, stepsister, stepson**

stepparent *noun* the person to whom your mother or father has been remarried: **stepfather, stepmother**

stereo *noun* a cassette player, CD, or radio which gives out sound by means of two or more loudspeakers; **stereo** *adjective*

S

stew *noun* a meal with meat, vegetables, etc, cooked together in liquid; **stew** *verb*

steward (feminine **stewardess**) *noun* a person who serves passengers on a ship or plane

¹**stick** *noun* **1** a long thin piece of wood; **2** a long thin piece of any material

²**stick** *verb* (**sticks, sticking, stuck**) **1** to fix or be fixed with a sticky substance such as glue; **2** to push a pointed object into something

sticky *adjective* made of or containing material which can stick to or round anything else

stiff *adjective* **1** not easily bent; **2** painful when moving or moved; **stiffen** *verb*; **stiffly** *adverb*

stile *noun* steps for climbing easily over a fence or wall; ⚠ **style**

¹**still** *adjective* **1** not moving; **2** quiet or silent; **stillness** *noun*

²**still** *adverb* **1** up to and at this or that time: *Does this dress **still** fit you?*; **2** even so

¹**sting** *verb* (**stings, stinging, stung**) **1** to cause sharp pain to, or to feel such a pain; **2** to prick with a sting

²**sting** *noun* **1** a sharp pain, wound, or mark caused by a plant or insect; **2** a sharp organ used as a weapon by some insects; **3** a substance contained in hairs on a plant's surface, which produces pain

stir *verb* (**stirred**) **1** to move round and mix by means of an object such as a spoon; **2** to move a little: *She **stirred** in her sleep*; **stir** *noun*

¹**stitch** *noun* **1** a thread in sewing or knitting made by moving a needle and thread into cloth at one point and out at another in sewing or by a turn of the wool round the needle in knitting; **2** a sharp pain in the side, caused by running

stitches

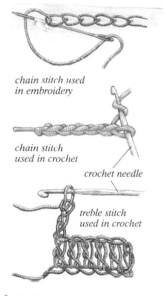

chain stitch used in embroidery

chain stitch used in crochet

crochet needle

treble stitch used in crochet

²**stitch** *verb* to sew; to put stitches in to fasten together or for decoration

stoat *noun* a small brown furry animal

stocking *noun* one of a pair of coverings for the feet and legs

stole *see* STEAL

stolen *see* STEAL

S

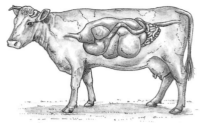

*a cow's stomach has
four separate parts
to help it to digest
the plants it eats*

stomach *noun* a baglike organ in the body into which food goes after it has been swallowed

¹**stone** *noun* **1** a piece of rock; **2** a hard substance; rock; **3** a single hard seed inside some fruits, such as the cherry, plum, and peach

²**stone** *noun* a measure of weight equal to 14 pounds or 6.35 kilograms

stood *see* STAND

stool *noun* a seat without a supporting part for the back or arms

¹**stop** *verb* **(stopped) 1** to finish moving; **2** to prevent something happening, moving, etc; **3** to end; to make an end to; **stopper** *noun*

²**stop** *noun* **1** the act of stopping or state of being stopped; **2** a place on a road where buses or other public vehicles stop for passengers

¹**store** *verb* to put away or keep for future use

²**store** *noun* **1** things kept for future use; **2** a place for keeping things; **3** a large shop

storey *noun* a floor or level in a building

storm *noun* very bad weather, with wind, rain, and often lightning; **stormy** *adjective*

story *noun* **1** a tale about something imaginary that happened; **2** a telling of events

stove *noun* a machine for cooking or heating which works by burning coal, oil, gas, etc, or by electricity

¹**straight** *adjective* **1** not bent or curved; **2** level or upright; **3** tidy; neat; in order; **straighten** *verb*; ⚠ **strait**

²**straight** *adverb* **1** in a straight line; **2** directly: *go straight home*; **3** without waiting: **straightaway**; ⚠ **strait**

strait *noun* a narrow water channel connecting two seas; ⚠ **straight**

strange *adjective* **1** odd or unusual; surprising; **2** not what you are used to; **strangely** *adverb*

stranger *noun* a person you do not know

¹**strap** *noun* **1** a strong narrow band of material, such as leather, used for fastening or holding together; **2** also **shoulder strap** a strap that goes over the shoulder and holds up a piece of clothing, a bag, etc

²**strap** *verb* **(strapped)** to fasten in place with one or more straps

straw *noun* **1** dried stems of grain plants, such as wheat, used for animals to sleep on, for making baskets, mats, etc; **2** a thin tube of paper or plastic for drinking through

strawberry *noun* a red juicy fruit, eaten fresh and in jam; the plant on which this grows

strawberry plant

stream *noun* a natural flow of water, smaller than a river

street *noun* a road with houses or other town buildings on one or both sides

strength *noun* the quality or power of being strong or something that provides this; **strengthen** *verb*

stress *noun* a worried feeling about your life or work

stretch *verb* **1** to make or become wider or longer by pulling; **2** to make as long as possible; **3** to try to reach; **4** to straighten the legs, arms, or body to full length; **stretch** *noun*; **stretchy** *adjective*

strict *adjective* severe, especially in rules of behaviour; **strictly** *adverb*; **strictness** *noun*

¹**strike** *verb* **(strikes, striking, struck)** **1** to hit; **2** to light by hitting against a hard surface: *strike a match*; **3** to have an effect on; to seem or appear to: *An idea struck me*; **4** to refuse to work

²**strike** *noun* a time when no work is done because of an argument, as over pay or working conditions

string *noun* **1** a strong thread or thin rope used especially for tying things up; **2** a thin piece of material, often one of several, stretched across a musical instrument to give sound; **stringed** *adjective*

¹**strip** *noun* a long narrow piece of something

²**strip** *verb* **(stripped)** **1** to remove the covering or parts of; **2** to undress or be undressed

stripe *noun* a band of colour, among one or more other colours; **striped** *adjective*

¹**stroke** *verb* to pass the hand gently over something

²**stroke** *noun* **1** a blow; a hit; a movement; **2** a sudden illness in part of the brain

strong *adjective* **1** having power or force; **2** powerful against harm; not easily broken, spoilt, moved, or changed; **strongly** *adverb*

struck *see* STRIKE

struggle *verb* to try very hard to do something; to fight; **struggle** *noun*

stubborn *adjective* not changing your mind or doing what others want; **stubbornly** *adverb*; **stubbornness** *noun*

stuck *see* STICK

student *noun* a person who is studying at a school, college, etc

mini-sub – a small submarine used to take people on trips to the seabed

studio *noun* **1** a room in which films or radio or television programmes are made; **2** a room where a painter, photographer, etc, works

¹**study** *noun* **1** the act of studying one or more subjects; learning; **2** a room used for studying and work

²**study** *verb* to spend time in learning about one or more subjects

¹**stuff** *noun* material of any sort, of which something is made

²**stuff** *verb* to fill

stump *noun* **1** the base of a tree left after the rest has been cut down; **2** one of the three upright pieces of wood at which the ball is thrown in cricket

stung *see* STING

stupid *adjective* silly or foolish; not clever; **stupidity** *noun*; **stupidly** *adverb*

style *noun* **1** a way of doing something; **2** fashion, especially in clothes; **3** a type or sort; **stylish** *adjective*; ⚠ **stile**

subject *noun* **1** something studied, as at school, college, etc; **2** something talked or written about; **3** a person who belongs to a country

submarine also **sub** *noun* a ship that can sail under water

substance *noun* a sort of material

subtract *verb* to take a part, number, or amount from something larger; **subtraction** *noun*

succeed *verb* to get what you wanted; to do well

success *noun* **1** the act of succeeding in something; **2** a good result; **3** a person or thing that succeeds or has succeeded; **successful** *adjective*; **successfully** *adverb*

such *adjective, pronoun* **1** so large; so much; so good: *Don't be **such** a fool!* **2** **such as** of the same kind; like: *flowers **such** as roses or daisies*

suck *verb* **1** to draw liquid into the mouth by using the tongue, lips, and muscles at the side of the mouth, with the lips tightened into a small hole; **2** to eat something by holding in the mouth and melting by movements of the tongue; **suck** *noun*

S

158

sudden *adjective* happening, done, etc, quickly and unexpectedly; **suddenly** *adverb*

suffer *verb* to experience pain or difficulty; **suffering** *noun*

sugar *noun* a sweet substance used in food

suggest *verb* to say or write to somebody that something is a good idea; **suggestion** *noun*

¹**suit** (*say* **soot**) *noun* **1** a set of clothes which match, usually including a jacket with trousers or skirt; **2** one of the four sets of cards used in games

²**suit** (*say* **soot**) *verb* **1** to satisfy or please; to be right for; **2** to match or look right with; **suitable** *adjective*

suitcase *noun* a strong hard bag for clothes when you are travelling

suite (*say* **sweet**) *noun* a set of furniture for a room, especially a sofa and two chairs; ⚠ **sweet**

sun *noun* the very hot bright thing in the sky, which the Earth goes round and from which it receives light and heat: **sunlight, sunshine; sunny** *adjective*; ⚠ **son**

sunbathe *verb* to spend time in strong sunlight, usually sitting or lying; **sunbather** *noun*

Sunday *noun* the first day of the week; the day before Monday

sung see SING

sunk see SINK

sunrise also **sun-up** *noun* the time when the sun is seen to appear after the night

sunset *noun* the time when the sun is seen to disappear as night begins

super *adjective* wonderful; very nice or exciting

supermarket *noun* a large shop where you serve yourself with food and goods

Concorde – a supersonic airliner

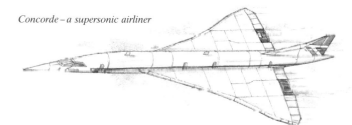

sulk *verb* to be quiet and badtempered; **sulky** *adjective*

sultana *noun* a small seedless kind of raisin used in baking

sum *noun* an exercise in using numbers; ⚠ **some**

summer *noun* the season between spring and autumn when the sun is hot and there are many flowers

supersonic *adjective* faster than the speed of sound

supper *noun* the last meal of the day, taken in the evening

¹**supply** *verb* to give or sell what is needed

²**supply** *noun* a store which can be used; an amount

¹**support** *verb* **1** to hold up; **2** to help, especially with money; **3** to be on the side of; **supporter** *noun*

²**support** *noun* something that holds something else up

¹**suppose** *verb* **1** to think; to guess; **2** to be expected to; ought to

²**suppose** also **supposing** *conjunction* if: *Suppose* it rains, what shall we do?

sure *adjective* having no doubt; certain; **surely** *adverb*; ⚠ **shore**

surface *noun* the outside, flat part, or top of something

surgery *noun* **1** a place where a doctor, dentist, or vet treats his or her patients; **2** the skill and practice of performing medical operations; **3** the performing of such operations, usually including the cutting open of the skin; **surgeon** *noun*

surname *noun* the name you share with the other members of your family; your last name

surprise *noun* an unexpected event; a feeling caused by this event; **surprise** *verb*; **surprising** *adjective*

surround *verb* to be or go all round something; **surrounding** *adjective*

¹**suspect** (*say* su-*spect*) *verb* to think that something is true, though you do not know

²**suspect** (*say* sus-*pect*) *noun* a person the police think did a crime

suspend *verb* **1** to hang from above; **2** to delay or stop

suspense *noun* delay which frightens or excites people

suspicious *adjective* feeling that something is wrong; **suspicion** *noun*; **suspiciously** *adverb*

¹**swallow** *noun* a small insect-eating bird which comes to the northern countries in summer

²**swallow** *verb* to move food or drink down the throat from the mouth

swam *see* SWIM

a swan and her cygnets

swan *noun* (*young* **cygnet**) a large water bird with white or black feathers and a long neck, that lives on rivers and lakes

swear *verb* (**swears, swearing, swore, sworn**) **1** to use very bad language; **2** to promise

sweat *noun* a liquid which comes out from the body through the skin to cool it; **sweat** *verb*; **sweaty** *adjective*

sweater *noun* a warm piece of clothing for the top of the body

sweatshirt *noun* a warm piece of clothing for the upper body, often worn for sport

sweep *verb* (**sweeps, sweeping, swept**) **1** to clean by brushing; **2** to move over or cover quickly

¹**sweet** *adjective* **1** tasting like or containing sugar; **2** pleasant or loving; **sweeten** *verb*; **sweetly** *adverb*; **sweetness** *noun*; ⚠ **suite**

²**sweet** *noun* **1** a small sweet thing, such as a toffee or chocolate, eaten for pleasure; **2** a pudding or dessert; ⚠ **suite**

sweet corn *noun* the yellow seeds of the **maize** plant, eaten as a vegetable

swell *verb* (**swells, swelling, swelled, swollen** *or* **swelled**) to become larger; **swelling** *noun*

swept *see* SWEEP

swerve *verb* to turn suddenly to one side, when moving; **swerve** *noun*

¹**swift** *adjective* fast, short, or sudden; **swiftly** *adverb*

²**swift** *noun* a small bird with long wings

swim *verb* (**swims, swimming, swam, swum**) to move through water by moving your arms and legs; **swimmer** *noun*, **swimming** *noun*

swimming pool *noun* a special pool for swimming in

¹**swing** *verb* (**swings, swinging, swung**) to move backwards and forwards, round and round, or in a curve from a fixed point

²**swing** *noun* a seat on which you can swing

swipe *verb* to move a plastic card with electronic information on it through a special machine, usually to pay for something; **swipe card**

¹**switch** *noun* an apparatus for turning electricity on and off

²**switch** *verb* **1** to turn on or off with a switch; **2** to change for another

swollen *see* SWELL

sword *noun* a weapon with a long blade and a handle

swore *see* SWEAR

sworn *see* SWEAR

swum *see* SWIM

swung *see* SWING

syllable *noun* a part of a word that can be said by itself

symbol *noun* a sign, shape, or object which stands for something else; ⚠ **cymbals**

sympathy *noun* the feeling of sharing or understanding the pain and joy of others; **sympathetic** *adjective*

synthesiser

synthesiser *noun* an electronic musical instrument that can make many different types of sounds

syrup *noun* a thick sweet liquid, especially sugar and water

system *noun* **1** a group of things or ideas working together in one arrangement; **2** a group of computers and the software that runs on them

S

table *noun* **1** a piece of furniture with a flat top supported by legs: **tablecloth**; **2** a list of information

tadpole *noun* the young of a frog or toad

Manx cats are tailless

tail *noun* the movable part growing at the back of an animal's body; **tailless** *adjective*; ⚠ **tale**

tailor *noun* a person who makes clothes to fit you

take *verb* **(takes, taking, took, taken)** **1** to get hold of something; **2** to borrow or use without asking permission or by mistake; **3** to carry something or go with somebody to another place; **4** to eat, drink, breathe in, etc: *take your medicine*; **5** to travel on bus, train, etc; **6** to last: *How long does the flight take?*

tale *noun* a story; ⚠ **tail**

¹**talk** *verb* to use words or make thoughts, ideas, etc, known by means of speech; to speak

²**talk** *noun* a conversation; a speech

tall *adjective* **1** higher than other people or other things; more than average height; **2** having a particular height: *4 feet tall;* **tallish** *adjective*; **tallness** *noun*

¹**tame** *adjective* gentle and not afraid; not fierce or wild; **tameness** *noun*

²**tame** *verb* to train an animal to be tame; **tamer** *noun*

tank *noun* **1** a large container for storing liquid or gas; **2** a large heavy vehicle with guns on it, that moves on two metal belts

¹**tap** *noun* something that you turn to control the flow of water, other liquid or gas from a pipe, barrel, etc

²**tap** *verb* **(tapped)** to strike something lightly; **tap** *noun*

tape *noun* **1** a narrow strip of cloth, paper, etc; **2** a strip of plastic covered with a magnetic material, used for recording sound, pictures, or information

tape recorder *noun* an instrument that can record and play back sound using tape

target *noun* **1** something that is aimed at; **2** an amount you are trying to reach

archery target

¹**tart** *noun* a piece of pastry with fruit or jam cooked on it

²**tart** *adjective* a sharp sour taste

¹**taste** *verb* **1** to test the taste of food or drink by taking a little into the mouth; **2** to experience the taste of; **3** to eat or drink a little of; **4** to have a particular taste; **5** to experience: *to taste freedom*

162

²**taste** *noun* **1** the sense by which you know one food from another by its sweetness, bitterness, etc; **2** the quality special to any food or drink that makes you able to recognise it when it is in your mouth; **3** the ability to judge whether something is good, bad, beautiful, etc; **tasteless** *adjective*; **tasty** *adjective*

taught *see* TEACH

tax *noun* money that is paid to the government

¹**taxi** *noun* a car with its driver, which you pay to take you somewhere

²**taxi** *verb* to go along on a runway before taking off or landing (plane)

tea *noun* **1** a drink made by pouring boiling water onto the dried and cut leaves of the tea bush; these leaves: **teacup**, **teapot**; **2** a meal eaten in the afternoon or early evening

teach *verb* (**teaches, teaching, taught**) to give knowledge or skill of something to a person; to train or give lessons; **teacher** *noun*

team *noun* a group of people who work together or who play on the same side in a game

¹**tear** (*say like* **here**) *noun* a drop of salty liquid from the eye

²**tear** (*say like* **hair**) *verb* (**tears, tearing, tore, torn**) to pull apart or into pieces

³**tear** (*say like* **hair**) *noun* a torn place in cloth, paper, etc

tease *verb* to make fun of playfully or unkindly

teenager *noun* a person aged between thirteen and nineteen

teeth *see* TOOTH

telephone *noun* a phone; **telephone** *verb*

the Hubble space telescope orbits the Earth

telescope *noun* an instrument used for seeing distant objects

television also **TV** *noun* **1** the sending and receiving of pictures and programmes with sound by means of electrical waves; the programmes; **2 TV set** a screen in a box, for receiving these programmes

tell *verb* (**tells, telling, told**) **1** to make something known in words to somebody; to give information or advice; **2** to find out; to decide or know

temper *noun* **1** a particular state of mind; the way you feel; **2 lose your temper** to become angry

temperature *noun* the hotness or coldness of a place, object, etc

temple *noun* a place for worship in various religions

temporary *adjective* only lasting for a short time; not permanent; **temporarily** *adverb*

tempt *verb* to try to make somebody do something wrong; **temptation** *noun*

ten *adjective, noun* the number 10; **tenth** *adjective, adverb*

tennis *noun* a game for two people (**singles**) or two pairs of people (**doubles**) who use rackets to hit a ball over a net

¹**tense** *adjective* **1** full of excitement; **2** tightly stretched

²**tense** *noun* the form of a verb that shows when the action of the verb happens: **present tense** / *go*, **past tense** / *went*, **future tense** / *will go*

tent *noun* a movable shelter made of cloth supported by a framework of poles and ropes

mountaineering tent

term *noun* **1** one of the periods of time into which the school, university, etc, year is divided; **2** a fixed period of time; **3 terms** the conditions by which you agree to do something or pay for something

terrible *adjective* very bad or frightening

terribly *adverb* **1** extremely: ***terribly*** *exciting*; **2** badly: ***terribly*** *injured*

terrific *adjective* excellent; wonderful; **terrifically** *adverb*

terrify *verb* to fill with fear

terror *noun* very great fear

test *noun* a number of questions, things to do, etc, set to measure somebody's ability or knowledge; **test** *verb*

than *conjunction, preposition* used to compare two things or people: *older **than** you*

thank *verb* to say that you are grateful to somebody; **thanks** *noun*

¹**that** *adjective, pronoun* (*plural* **those**) **1** the one described or shown; **2** the one of two or more people or things that is further away; **3** who, whom, or which

²**that** *adverb* so: *I don't like him **that** much!*

³**that** *conjunction* used for joining two parts of a sentence: *It's true **that** he's French*

thaw *verb* to warm to above freezing point and so make or become liquid or soft

the **1** used when it is understood who or what is meant; **2** used with a person or thing that is the only one of its kind

theatre *noun* **1** a special building where plays are performed; **2** also **operating theatre** the room where hospital operations are done

theft *noun* stealing

their *adjective* belonging to them; ⚠ **there**

theirs *pronoun* that or those belonging to them

them *see* THEY

themselves *see* THEY

then *adverb* **1** at that time; **2** next; afterwards; **3** in that case; if that has happened

there *adverb* **1** to, at, or in that place; **2** used as the first word in a sentence or as the second word in a question with a verb such as *be: There is a man at the door;* ⚠ **their**

therefore *adverb* as a result; for that reason; so

thermometer *noun* an instrument for measuring and showing temperature

thief *noun* (*plural* **thieves**) a person who steals

thin *adjective* **1** having little fat on the body; not fat; **2** having a small distance between opposite surfaces; narrow; not thick; **3** watery; flowing easily: *thin gravy;* **4** not closely packed; **thinly** *adverb;* **thinness** *noun*

thing *noun* **1** any object; anything that can be touched or seen; **2** something that exists; an idea, event, organisation, etc

think *verb* (**thinks, thinking, thought**) **1** to use your mind to imagine, understand, believe, or consider something; **2** to form an opinion or have an idea

digital thermometer

these *see* THIS

they *pronoun* (**them, themselves**) those people, animals, or things; the ones being talked about

thick *adjective* **1** having a large distance between opposite surfaces; wide; not thin; **2** measuring a particular amount from side to side or from top to bottom: *ice 5 centimetres thick;* **3** not watery or flowing easily: *thick soup;* **4** difficult to see through: *thick mist;* **5** having many objects set close together; **thicken** *verb;* **thickly** *adverb;* **thickness** *noun*

third *adjective, adverb, noun, pronoun* **1** the one after the second; 3rd; **2** one of three equal parts into which something is divided

thirst *noun* a feeling of dryness in the mouth caused by wanting or needing to drink; **thirst** *verb;* **thirstily** *adverb;* **thirsty** *adjective*

thirteen *adjective, noun* the number 13; **thirteenth** *adjective, adverb*

thirty *adjective, noun* the number 30; **thirtieth** *adjective, adverb*

this *pronoun, adjective (plural* **these**) **1** the one being talked about or considered; **2** the one of two or more people or things that is nearer

thistle *noun* a wild plant with prickly leaves and usually purple flowers

spear thistle

thorn *noun* a prickle growing on a plant

those *see* THAT

though *adverb, conjunction* in spite of the fact

¹thought *noun* **1** the act of thinking; **2** a result of thinking; an idea, opinion, etc; **thoughtful** *adjective*; **thoughtfully** *adverb*; **thoughtless** *adjective*

²thought *see* THINK

thousand *adjective, noun* the number 1000; **thousandth** *adjective, adverb*

¹thread *noun* **1** a long thin piece of cotton, nylon, etc, used for sewing or making cloth; **2** a raised line that winds round the outside of a screw

²thread *verb* to pass one end of a thread through the hole in a needle

three *adjective, noun* the number 3

threw *see* THROW; ⚠ **through**

throat *noun* **1** the tube inside the neck that divides into two, one part taking air to the lungs and the other taking food to the stomach; **2** the front of the neck

through *preposition, adverb* **1** from one side, surface, or end of something to the other; **2** by means of; **3** as a result of; because of; **4** among or between; ⚠ **threw**

¹throw *verb* **(throws, throwing, threw, thrown) 1** to send something through the air by a sudden movement of the arm; **2** to move yourself or part of your body suddenly and with force; **3 throw away** to get rid of something

²throw *noun* an act of throwing

thrush *noun* a brownish bird that sings well

mistle thrush

thumb *noun* the short movable part of the hand that is set apart from the fingers

thunder *noun* the usually loud noise that follows a flash of lightning; **thunder** *verb*

Thursday *noun* the fifth day of the week

thus *adverb* **1** in this way; **2** with this result; so

¹tick *noun* **1** the short regularly repeated sound made by a clock or watch; **2** a mark (✔) put against something to show that it is correct

²**tick** *verb* **1** to make a regularly repeated tick; **2** to show that something is correct by marking with a tick

³**tick** *noun* a small animal that feeds on the blood of sheep, cows, etc

ticket *noun* a piece of paper or card that shows that a person has paid for something, such as a journey on a bus or entrance into a cinema

tickle *verb* to touch a person's skin lightly to produce laughter; **tickle** *noun*; **ticklish** *adjective*

tide *noun* the regular rise and fall of the seas

tidy *adjective* neat; neatly arranged; **tidily** *adverb*; **tidiness** *noun*; **tidy** *verb*

¹**tie** *noun* **1** a band of cloth worn round the neck of a shirt and tied in a knot; **2** an equal score in a game, competition, etc

²**tie** *verb* (**ties, tying, tied**) **1** to fasten with string, rope, etc; **2** to finish a match or competition with equal points

tiger *noun* (*female* **tigress,** *young* **cub**) a large fierce cat that is yellowish with black stripes

tight *adjective* **1** closely fastened, held, knotted, etc; **2** fitting too closely; not looser **tighten** *verb*; **tightly** *adverb*; **tightness** *noun*

tights *noun* a light, very close fitting piece of clothing that covers the legs and lower part of the body

tile *noun* a thin shaped piece of baked clay, plastic, etc, used for covering roofs, floors, etc

¹**till** *noun* a machine in a shop, pub, etc, that adds up the prices of the goods bought and usually has a drawer in it for keeping money

²**till** *preposition, conjunction* until

¹**time** *noun* **1** the passing of the minutes, hours, days, months, or years; **2** a particular point in the day: **bedtime, playtime, teatime**; **3** a period or occasion: *a good* **time**; **4** a number of minutes, hours, etc, needed or available for something; **5** the speed or rhythm or beat of a piece of music

metronome – used by musicians to measure the beat

²**time** *verb* to measure the time taken to do something

times *preposition* multiplied by

timetable *noun* a table of the times at which something happens, such as when buses, trains, etc, arrive and leave or when different lessons begin

tin *noun* **1** a soft metal; **2** a small metal box or container

tiny *adjective* very small

¹**tip** *noun* the end of something

²**tip** *verb* (**tipped**) to lean or cause to lean at an angle; to turn over or cause something to turn over

167

³**tip** *noun* a place where rubbish is left

⁴**tip** *noun* **1** a small amount of money given for a service; **2** a helpful piece of advice

⁵**tip** *verb* **(tipped)** to give a small amount of money to a taxi driver, waitress, etc

tire *verb* to make somebody feel tired; ⚠ **tyre**

tired *adjective* **1** needing rest or sleep; **2** no longer interested; **tiredness** *noun*

tissue (*say tish*-oo) *noun* a paper handkerchief

title *noun* **1** the name of a book, film, etc; **2** a word, such as *Sir* or *Dr*, used in front of a person's name to show his or her position

to *preposition* **1** in the direction of; towards; **2** as far as; **3** reaching or in the state of: *until the lights change* **to** *green*; **4** in a touching position with; against; **5** until: *from midday* **to** *midnight*; **6** compared with: *5 goals* **to** *3*; ⚠ **too, two**

toad *noun* an animal like a large frog that creeps rather than jumps. It usually lives on land, but goes into water for breeding

midwife toad – the male carries the eggs on his back

to and fro *adverb* backwards and forwards; from side to side

¹**toast** *noun* bread made brown by being held in front of heat

²**toast** *verb* to make bread, cheese, etc, brown by holding close to heat

tobacco *noun* the dried leaves of a plant, used in cigarettes, pipes, etc

toboggan

toboggan *noun* a long light sledge; **toboggan** *verb*

today *noun, adverb* **1** this day; **2** the present time

toddler *noun* a child who has just learnt to walk

toe *noun* **1** one of the five movable parts at the end of each foot: **toenail**; **2** the part of a sock, shoe, etc, that fits over the toes; ⚠ **tow**

together *adverb* **1** in or into one group, body, or place; **2** at the same time

toilet *noun* a lavatory

told *see* TELL

tomato *noun* (*plural* **tomatoes**) a red juicy fruit eaten raw or cooked

tomorrow *noun, adverb* **1** the day following today; **2** the future

ton *noun* a measure of weight equal to 2240 pounds or 1016 tonnes

barbecue tongs

tongs *noun* a tool consisting of two movable pieces joined at one end, used for holding or lifting things

tongue *noun* the large movable fleshy part in the mouth

tonight *noun, adverb* the night of today

tonne also **metric ton** *noun* a measure of weight equal to 1000 kilograms or 0.98 tons

too *adverb* **1** also; as well; **2** more than enough or is needed or wanted; ⚠ **to, two**

took *see* TAKE

tool *noun* an instrument for doing a special job

tooth *noun* (*plural* **teeth**) **1** one of the small hard white bony objects growing in the upper and lower mouth of most animals: **toothache, toothbrush, toothpaste; 2** one of the narrow pointed parts that stand out from a comb, saw, etc; **toothed** *adjective*; **toothless** *adjective*

¹**top** *noun* **1** the highest part or point; **2** the upper surface; **3** the most important part of anything; **4** a lid; **5** a piece of clothing worn on the upper part of the body; **top** *adjective*

²**top** *noun* a toy that balances on its point and spins

torch *noun* a small electric light carried in the hand

tore *see* TEAR

torn *see* TEAR

tortoise *noun* a slow-moving reptile that has a body covered by a hard shell into which the legs, tail, and head can be pulled for protection

¹**total** *adjective* complete; whole; **totally** *adverb*

²**total** *noun* the complete amount; everything added together

¹**touch** *verb* **1** to feel with the hands or fingers or another part of the body; **2** to be on or against something; **3** to have no space separating two things

²**touch** *noun* the sense by which an object is felt and by which it is known to be hard, smooth, rough, etc

tour *noun* **1** a journey during which several places of interest are visited; **2** a short trip to or through a place in order to see it; **tour** *verb*; **tourist** *noun*

tow *verb* to pull a vehicle along by a rope or chain; ⚠ **toe**

towards also **toward** *preposition* **1** in the direction of something or somebody; **2** in a position facing something or somebody; **3** for part payment of: £5 **towards** *the present*

towel *noun* a piece of cloth or paper used for drying wet skin, dishes, etc

the Leaning Tower of Pisa, Italy

tower *noun* a tall building standing alone or forming part of a castle, church, etc

town *noun* a large group of houses and other buildings where people live and work

toy *noun* an object for children to play with

¹**trace** *verb* 1 to copy a picture, map, etc, by drawing on thin paper over it: **tracing paper**; 2 to find or discover something or somebody, especially by following up clues or signs

²**trace** *noun* a mark or sign left behind by somebody or something

track *noun* 1 a railway line; 2 a rough path; 3 a special path or road for racing; 4 one of the pieces of music on a CD, record or tape; 5 marks left by a moving person, animal, or vehicle

tracksuit *noun* a loose fitting suit of warm material that is usually worn when exercising

tractor *noun* a powerful motor vehicle used for pulling farm machinery or other heavy objects

¹**trade** *verb* 1 to do business with; to buy or sell goods; 2 to give something in exchange for something else

²**trade** *noun* 1 the buying and selling of goods; 2 a job or particular kind of business

traffic *noun* the cars and other vehicles moving along roads or streets

traffic calming *noun* an arrangement of things, such as roundabouts, in a road to stop people going too fast in cars

traffic lights *noun* a set of coloured lights used for controlling and directing traffic

¹**train** *noun* 1 a line of connected railway carriages drawn by an engine; 2 a part of a long dress that spreads on the ground behind the person wearing it

²**train** *verb* to make yourself, or somebody or something else ready to do something difficult; **trainer** *noun*; **training** *noun*

trainers *noun* sports shoes for running, jogging, etc

transistor *noun* a small part of an electronic circuit for controlling an electric current: **transistor radio**

transparent *adjective* clear; allowing light to pass through so that objects behind can be clearly seen

¹**transport** (*say* trans**port**) *verb* to carry goods, people, etc, from one place to another; **transportable** *adjective*

²**transport** (*say* **trans**port) *noun* 1 the act of transporting goods or people; 2 vehicles, such as cars, lorries, ships, or aircraft, used for transporting goods or people

¹**trap** *noun* 1 a thing for catching and holding an animal; 2 a position in which somebody is caught; a plan for catching a person; 3 a light two-wheeled vehicle pulled by a horse

²**trap** *verb* **(trapped)** to catch in a trap or by a trick

travel *verb* **(travelled)** to go from place to place; to make a journey; **travel** *noun*; **traveller** *noun*

tray *noun* a flat piece of material with raised edges, used for carrying things

treacle *noun* a thick dark sticky liquid made from sugar

treasure *noun* a collection or store of valuable things, such as gold and silver coins

¹**treat** *verb* **1** to act or behave in a particular way towards a person or an animal; **2** to deal with; to handle; **3** to try to cure by giving medicine, **4** to buy or give somebody something special; **treatment** *noun*

²**treat** *noun* something that gives pleasure

¹**treble** *noun* the highest part sung or played in music

²**treble** *adjective, adverb* high in sound

³**treble** *adjective* three times as big, as much, or as many as

tree *noun* a tall plant with a wooden trunk and branches

tremble *verb* to shake without being able to stop, perhaps with fear

triangle *noun* **1** a flat shape with three straight sides and three angles; **2** an instrument made of a piece of metal bent into the shape of a triangle, that is played by being struck with a metal rod; **triangular** *adjective*

tribe *noun* a group of people of the same race, language, habits, etc; **tribal** *adjective*

¹**trick** *noun* **1** an act needing special skill that is done especially to confuse or amuse people; **2** something done to deceive or cheat somebody

²**trick** *verb* to deceive or cheat somebody

trifle *noun* a dish of cake, fruit, and jelly covered with custard and cream

¹**trip** *verb* **(tripped)** to catch your foot and lose your balance

²**trip** *noun* a journey

trombone

trombone *noun* a brass musical instrument with a sliding tube which is pushed out or in to change the note; **trombonist** *noun*

tropical *adjective* to do with or coming from the very hot parts of the world (the **Tropics**) near the Equator

trot *verb* **(trotted)** to move or cause a horse to move at a speed between a walk and a gallop; **trot** *noun*

¹**trouble** *noun* **1** difficulty, worry, or anxiety; **2** **in trouble** in the position where you are blamed for doing something wrong or are thought to have done something wrong

²**trouble** *verb* to cause worry, anxiety, pain, etc, to somebody

trousers *noun* a piece of clothing which covers the body from the waist down and divides into two parts each fitting a leg

truck *noun* **1** a lorry or other motor vehicle for carrying goods; **2** an open cart used on a railway

true *adjective* real; actual; not false; **truly** *adverb*

trumpet *noun* a brass instrument that is played by blowing; **trumpeter** *noun*

trunk *noun* **1** the main stem of a tree; **2** the human body without the head, arms, and legs; **3** a large case or box used for carrying clothes when travelling; **4** the long nose of an elephant

T-shirt *noun* a piece of clothing for the upper part of the body that is made of light material

tub *noun* a large round container

tuba *noun* a large brass instrument that makes a deep sound when blown

tube *noun* **1** a hollow round pipe of metal, glass, plastic, etc; **2** a small soft container for holding toothpaste, paint, etc; **tubular** *adjective*

Tuesday *noun* the third day of the week

¹**tug** *verb* **(tugged)** to pull hard with force or much effort

²**tug** *noun* a sudden strong pull

³**tug** *noun* a small powerful boat used for guiding large ships in and out of a port

tugboat towing barge full of rubbish

trust *verb* to believe in the honesty and goodness of somebody; to have faith in or depend on somebody or something; **trust** *noun*

truth *noun* the true facts; what is true; **truthful** *adjective*; **truthfully** *adverb*; **truthfulness** *noun*

try *verb* **1** to make an effort to do something; **2** to test something; to use, taste, etc, something in order to find out what it is like; **3** to examine a person in a court of law; **try** *noun*

tulip *noun* a garden plant that grows from a bulb

tumble *verb* to fall suddenly; **tumble** *noun*

tumble dryer *noun* a machine in which wet clothing is dried

¹**tune** *noun* a series of musical notes that produces a pleasing pattern of sound; **tuneful** *adjective*

²**tune** *verb* to set the strings of a musical instrument so that it produces the correct notes

tunnel *noun* a passage for a road, railway, etc, through or under a hill, river, the sea, etc

turkey *noun* a large farm bird kept for its meat

¹**turn** *verb* **1** to move round; **2** to change direction or position; **3** to become or make something become different: *to* **turn** *brown*

²**turn** *noun* **1** a single movement completely round a fixed point; **2** a change of direction; **3** a place or time in a particular order: *miss a* **turn**

turnip *noun* a plant that has a large round root which is eaten as a vegetable

green turtle

turtle *noun* an animal that lives mainly in water and has a hard shell into which its soft head, legs, and tail can be pulled

tusk *noun* a long pointed tooth that grows beyond the mouth in some animals, such as the elephant

TV *noun* television

twelve *adjective, noun* the number 12; **twelfth** *adjective, adverb*

twenty *adjective, noun* the number 20; **twentieth** *adjective, adverb*

twice *adjective, adverb* two times

twig *noun* a thin stem going off from a branch

¹**twin** *noun* **1** either of two children born of the same mother at the same time; **2** either of two things very like each other

²**twin** *verb* (**twinned**) to join a town closely with another town in another country

twist *verb* **1** to wind threads together or round something else; **2** to turn; **3** to hurt a joint or limb by pulling and turning sharply; **twist** *noun*; **twisty** *adjective*

two *adjective, noun* the number 2; ⚠ **to, too**

¹**type** *noun* **1** a particular kind, class, or group; **2** a person or thing that is an example of such a group or class

²**type** *verb* to write something with a typewriter or computer keyboard

typewriter *noun* a machine with a keyboard for printing letters on paper

typical *adjective* having the main signs of a particular kind, group, or class; the same as others of a particular kind; **typically** *adverb*

tyre *noun* a thick rubber tube that fits round the outside edge of a wheel; ⚠ **tire**

t

mountain bike tyre in cross section

Uu

U *noun, adjective* a film that anyone of any age may see in a cinema

ugly *adjective* unpleasant to look at; not beautiful; **ugliness** *noun*

umbrella *noun* a piece of cloth or plastic stretched over a frame, used for keeping rain off your head

unable *adjective* not able to do something

uncle *noun* the brother of your father or mother or the husband of your aunt

unclean *adjective* not clean

uncomfortable *adjective* not comfortable; **uncomfortably** *adverb*

unconscious *adjective* not conscious; not knowing what is going on around you and not feeling anything; **unconsciousness** *noun*

under *preposition, adverb* **1** in or to a lower place than; directly below; **2** less than; **3** lower in position than; serving or obeying; **4** beneath the surface of: **underground**; **5** during; in

underneath *preposition, adverb* so as to go under something

understand *verb* (**understands, understanding, understood**) **1** to know or get the meaning of something; **2** to know or feel closely the nature of a person, feelings, etc; **understandable** *adjective*; **understandably** *adverb*

underwear also **underclothes, underclothing** *noun* the clothes worn next to the body under other clothes: **underpants**

undo *verb* (**undoes, undoing, undid, undone**) to unfasten or untie

undress *verb* to take your clothes off

unexpected *adjective* not expected; **unexpectedly** *adverb*

unfasten *verb* to stop being fastened; to undo

unhappy *adjective* not happy; **unhappily** *adverb*; **unhappiness** *noun*

unicorn *noun* an imaginary creature like a horse, with one horn

unicorn

uniform *noun* clothing which all members of an army, etc, wear

uninteresting *adjective* not interesting

unite *verb* to join together

universal *adjective* for all people or every purpose

universe *noun* all space and all the stars, planets, etc, that are in it

university *noun* a place of education at the highest level

unkind *adjective* not kind; cruel or thoughtless; **unkindly** *adverb*; **unkindness** *noun*

unless *conjunction* if ... not; except in the case that

u

unlikely *adjective* not likely to happen or be true; not expected

unlock *verb* to unfasten the lock of

unlucky *adjective* not having or giving good luck

unnecessary *adjective* not necessary; **unnecessarily** *adverb*

unpack *verb* to remove things from boxes, suitcases, etc, where they have been stored

unpleasant *adjective* not nice or pleasant; **unpleasantly** *adverb*

unsteady *adjective* not safe or sure; **unsteadily** *adverb*

untidy *adjective* not tidy; **untidily** *adverb*; **untidiness** *noun*

untie *verb* to undo string, a knot, etc

until also **till** *preposition, conjunction* up to the time that

unusual *adjective* **1** not usual; strange; **2** interesting because different from others; **unusually** *adverb*

up *adverb, adjective, preposition* **1** to, at, or in a higher place or position; above; **2** at an end; so as to be completely finished; **upwards** *adverb*

upon *preposition* on

upper *adjective* in a higher position; further up

upright *adjective* straight up and down

upset *verb* (upsets, upsetting, upset) **1** to knock over; **2** to cause to worry, be unhappy, etc; **3** to make ill, usually in the stomach; **upset** *noun, adjective*

upside down *adverb* with the top turned to the bottom

upstairs *adverb, adjective* at, on, or to the upper floor or floors of a building; **upstairs** *noun*

Uranus *noun* the planet seventh in order from the sun

the planet Uranus

urgent *adjective* needing immediate attention; showing that something important must be done quickly; **urgently** *adverb*; **urgency** *noun*

urn *noun* **1** a large metal container in which large quantities of tea or coffee may be made; **2** a large vase in which the ashes of a dead body are kept; ⚠ **earn**

us *see* WE

¹**use** (*say* yuze) *verb* **1** to do something with; **2** to have a purpose for; **3** use up to finish: *All the paper has been used up*, **4** used to to have done regularly or often: *We used to go there every year*

²**use** (*say* yuse) *noun* **1** using; being used; **2** the purpose or reason for using something; **useful** *adjective*; **usefully** *adverb*; **useless** *adjective*; **uselessly** *adverb*

user-friendly *adjective* easy to use: *a* **user-friendly** *computer program*

usual *adjective* done or happening regularly; normal; **usually** *adverb*

Vv

vacuum *noun* a space that is completely empty of all air or gas

vacuum cleaner *noun* a tool for cleaning floors and floor coverings by sucking up the dirt

vain *adjective* too proud of yourself, especially of what you look like; ⚠ **vane, vein**

valley *noun* **1** the land lying between two lines of hills or mountains; **2** the land through which a river flows

value *noun* what something is worth; **valuable** *adjective*

van *noun* a covered vehicle for carrying goods and sometimes people

vane *noun* **1** one of the blades of a windmill, propeller, etc; **2** also **weather vane** a movable metal apparatus which shows wind direction; ⚠ **vain, vein**

vanish *verb* to go out of sight; to disappear

variety *noun* a lot of different things

various *adjective* several different

vase *noun* a container used either for flowers or as an ornament

VDU also **visual display unit** *noun* the screen of a computer

visual display unit (VDU)

vegetable *noun* a plant that is grown for food

vegetarian *noun* someone who will not eat meat; **vegetarian** *adjective*

vehicle *noun* something in or on which people or goods are carried from one place to another; a car, lorry, train, etc

vein *noun* a tube that carries blood from any part of the body to the heart; ⚠ **vain, vane**

velvet *noun* a fine silky cloth having a short soft thick raised surface of cut threads on one side only; **velvety** *adjective*

Venus *noun* the planet second in order from the sun, and next to the Earth

verb *noun* a word (or words) which tells you what somebody or something does or is: *be, go, carry* are ***verbs***

verse *noun* a set of lines that forms one part of a poem or song, and usually has a pattern that is repeated in the other parts

very *adverb* especially; most

vest *noun* a short piece of underwear for the upper part of the body

vet also **veterinary surgeon** *noun* an animal doctor

viable *adjective* **1** able to live; **2** able to be done; possible

video *noun* **1** film for showing on your TV; **2** also **video recorder**, **VCR** a machine for recording television programmes or playing videos

view *noun* **1** something you see, especially pleasant countryside; **2** a picture or photograph of a piece of scenery, a building, etc; **3** an opinion, idea, etc, about something

village *noun* a small collection of houses and other buildings, smaller than a town

vine also **grapevine** *noun* a type of climbing plant that produces grapes

vinegar *noun* a very sour liquid used for flavouring food

viola *noun* a stringed musical instrument like a violin, but a little larger

violent *adjective* having great force or strength; hurting people; **violence** *noun*; **violently** *adverb*

violet *noun* **1** a small plant with purplish-blue flowers; **2** a purplish-blue colour; **violet** *adjective*

violin *noun* a four-stringed wooden musical instrument, supported between the left shoulder and the chin and played by drawing a bow across the strings; **violinist** *noun*

virus *noun* **1** something that causes an illness; **2** instructions put into a computer secretly, that stops the computer working properly

visit *verb* to go and spend some time in a place or somebody's house; **visit** *noun*; **visitor** *noun*

visual display unit *noun* a VDU

vixen *noun* a female fox

voice *noun* the sound or sounds you produce when speaking and singing

volcano *noun* (*plural* **volcanoes** *or* **volcanos**) a mountain with a large opening (**crater**) at the top through which lava, steam, etc, escape from time to time

volt *noun* a measurement of electricity

volume *noun* **1** the amount of sound something makes; **2** the space inside or filled by something; **3** a large book; one of a set of books of the same kind

vowel *noun* any of the five letters a, e, i, o, u, or their sounds – *compare* CONSONANT

vulture *noun* a large bird with almost no feathers on its head and neck, which feeds on dead animals

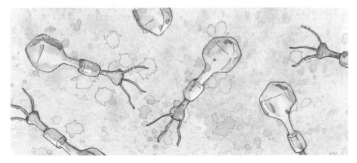

a virus viewed through an electron microscope

Ww

wag *verb* **(wagged)** to shake to and fro; **wag** *noun*

wage *noun* money given to us for the work we do

waggon or **wagon** *noun* a four-wheeled vehicle, drawn by horses, railway engines, etc

wail *verb* to make a long cry showing sadness or pain; **wail** *noun*; ⚠ **whale**

waist *noun* the narrow part of the human body just above the hips; ⚠ **waste**

wait *verb* to stay somewhere without doing anything until somebody comes or something happens; **wait** *noun*; ⚠ **weight**

waiter (feminine **waitress**) *noun* a person who serves food at the tables in a restaurant

wake *verb* **(wakes, waking, woke** or **waked, woken)** to stop or make somebody stop sleeping

¹**walk** *verb* **1** to move along on your feet at a normal speed without running; **2** to take for a walk; **walker** *noun*

²**walk** *noun* a journey on foot

wall *noun* **1** an upright dividing surface, especially of stone or brick, that goes round a house, town, field, etc; **2** the side of a room

walrus *noun* a large animal like a seal, with two long tusks

wander *verb* to move about in no particular direction; **wander** *noun*

want *verb* **1** to wish to have something; **2** to need; **want** *noun*

war *noun* fighting between people, countries, etc

ward *noun* a room of a hospital with beds for patients

warden *noun* a person who looks after a place and people

wardrobe *noun* a room or cupboard in which you hang up clothes

warlock *noun* a male witch

warm *adjective* **1** fairly hot; **2** able to keep in heat: *warm clothes*; **warm** *verb*; **warmly** *adverb*; **warmth** *noun*

warn *verb* to tell of something bad that may happen, or of how to prevent something bad; ⚠ **worn**

the Great Wall of China

W

178

was *see* BE

¹wash *verb* **1** to make clean with water; **2** to flow over or against continually; **washing** *noun*

²wash *noun* **1** washing or being washed; **2** things to be washed

washing machine *noun* a machine for washing clothes

wasn't *see* BE

wasp *noun* a flying stinging insect related to the bee, usually yellow and black

¹waste *verb* to use wrongly, not use, or use too much of; ⚠ **waist**

²waste *noun* **1** an act of wasting; **2** things that are used, damaged, or not wanted. **wastepipe**; ⚠ **waist**

¹watch *verb* **1** to look at; **2** to take care of

²watch *noun* **1** a small clock worn on the wrist or carried in a pocket; **2** one or more people ordered to watch; **3** act of watching

in the 16th century, naval officers used a pocket sundial like this as a watch to tell the time

¹water *noun* the most common liquid, without colour, taste, or smell, which falls from the sky as rain, forms rivers, lakes, and seas, and is drunk by people and animals; **watery** *adjective*

²water *verb* **1** to pour water on, especially onto land or plants: **watering can**; **2** to supply with water

waterfall *noun* water falling straight down over rocks

waterproof *adjective* not allowing water to go through

watt *noun* a measurement of electrical power

¹wave *noun* **1** a raised curving line of water on the surface, especially of the sea; **2** an evenly curved part of the hair; **3** a form in which some forms of energy move: **radio waves**; **wavy** *adjective*

²wave *verb* to move in the air, backwards and forwards, up and down, or from side to side; **wave** *noun*

waveband *noun* a set of waves, especially radio waves

wavelength *noun* **1** a radio signal sent out on radio waves a particular distance apart; **2** the distance between one energy wave and another

wax *noun* a solid material of fats or oils that melts when heated and is used for making candles, polish, crayons, etc

way *noun* **1** a road or path; **2** the right direction to follow; **3** the distance to be travelled to reach a place; **4** how a thing is done or works; ⚠ **weigh**

we *pronoun* (**us, ourselves**) the people speaking or doing

weak *adjective* **1** not strong in body; not strong in character; **2** containing a lot of water: *weak* soup; **weaken** *verb*; **weakly** *adverb*; **weakness** *noun*; ⚠ **week**

wealthy *adjective* rich

w

weapon *noun* a tool for injuring or killing

wear *verb* **(wears, wearing, wore, worn)** **1** to have or carry on the body; **2** to change by continued use; **3** to last; ⚠ **where**

weasel *noun* a small thin furry animal with a pointed face

weather *noun* the condition of wind, rain, sunshine, snow, etc, at a certain time; ⚠ **whether**

weather vane *see* VANE

weave *verb* **(weaves, weaving, wove, woven)** **1** to form threads into material by drawing one thread at a time under and over a set of longer threads on a special machine **(loom)**; **2** to make something by doing this

web *noun* **1** a net of threads spun by spiders and some insects; **2** the skin between the toes of swimming birds and animals; **3** a computer system that allows people all round the world to share information on their computer screens; **webbed** *adjective*

duck's webbed foot

wedding *noun* a marriage ceremony, especially with a party afterwards

Wednesday *noun* the fourth day of the week

weed *noun* a wild plant that grows where it is not wanted

week *noun* **1** a period of seven days and nights, especially from Sunday to Saturday; **2** the period of time during which you work, go to school, etc; **weekly** *adverb*; ⚠ **weak**

weekday *noun* any day except Saturday or Sunday

weekend *noun* Saturday and Sunday

weep *verb* **(weeps, weeping, wept)** to let tears fall from the eyes; to cry

weigh *verb* **1** to find the weight of something, especially by a machine; **2** to have a certain weight; ⚠ **way**

weight *noun* **1** the heaviness of anything; **2** a heavy object for holding something down: **paperweight**; ⚠ **wait**

¹welcome *verb* to greet somebody with pleasure

²welcome *adjective* wanted; happily accepted

³welcome *noun* a greeting when somebody arrives

¹well *adjective* in good health; not ill

²well *adverb* **(better, best)** **1** in a good or satisfactory way; **2** completely; **3** much; quite; **4 as well** also; **5** very

W

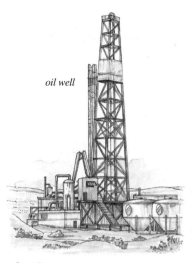

oil well

³**well** *noun* a place where water or oil comes from underground

went *see* GO

wept *see* WEEP

were *see* BE

weren't *see* BE

west *noun* one of the four main points of the compass; the direction in which the sun sets; **west** *adjective, adverb*; **westerly** *adverb*; **western** *adjective*

wet *adjective* **(wetter)** **1** covered in liquid or not dry; **2** rainy; **wet** *verb*; **wetness** *noun*

whale *noun* a very large animal that lives in the sea. Whales look like fish, but are mammals. They breathe air and feed their young with milk; ⚠ **wail**

¹**what** *adjective, pronoun* **1** which thing or person? **2** which? **3** that which; a/the thing that: *I believed **what** he told me*

²**what** *adverb* to what degree?

whatever *adjective, pronoun* **1** anything at all that; no matter what; **2** what?

wheat *noun* a grass plant with grain seeds that are made into flour

wheel *noun* **1** a circular object with an outer frame which turns round an inner part **(hub)** to which it is joined, used for turning machines, making vehicles move, etc; **2** the steering wheel of a car or ship; **wheeled** *adjective*

when *adverb, conjunction* **1** at what time? **2** at the time at which

whenever *adverb, conjunction* **1** at any time at all that; every time; **2** when?

where *adverb, conjunction* **1** at or to what place? **2** at, in, or to which; ⚠ **wear**

wherever *adverb, conjunction* **1** at or to any place at all that; **2** where?

whether *conjunction* **1** if ... or not; **2** no matter if ...; ⚠ **weather**

which *adjective, pronoun* **1** what thing or person? **2** being the one or ones that; **3** which is which? what is the difference between the two? ⚠ **witch**

whichever *adjective, pronoun* **1** any one that; **2** no matter which; **3** which?

while *also* **whilst** *conjunction* during the time that; all the time that

whine *verb* **1** to make a high sad sound; **2** to complain unnecessarily; **whine** *noun*; ⚠ **wine**

W

¹**whip** *noun* **1** a long piece of rope or leather fastened to a handle used for punishing somebody, driving an animal, or spinning a top; **2** a sweet food made of beaten eggs and other foods

²**whip** *verb* **(whipped) 1** to beat with a whip; **2** to beat eggs, cream, etc, until stiff

whirl *verb* to move or make something move round and round very fast; **whirl** *noun*

rat's whiskers

whisker *noun* **1** one of the long stiff hairs near the mouth of a cat, rat, etc; **2 whiskers** hair allowed to grow on the sides of a man's face, not meeting at the chin

¹**whisper** *verb* to speak quietly with noisy breath

²**whisper** *noun* **1** whispered words; **2** a soft windy sound

whistle *noun* **1** a simple musical instrument that makes a high sound when you blow through it; **2** the high sound made by passing air or steam through an instrument, your lips, etc; **whistle** *verb*

white *noun* **1** the colour of snow or milk; the lightest colour; **2** the white part of the eye; **3** the part of an egg that is white after cooking; **white** *adjective*; **whiteness** *noun*; **whitish** *adjective*

who *pronoun* **1** what person or people? **2** that one person; those ones

whoever *pronoun* **1** any person that; **2** no matter who; **3** who?

¹**whole** *adjective* complete; total; not spoilt or divided; ⚠ **hole**

²**whole** *noun* the complete amount, thing, etc; ⚠ **hole**

whom *pronoun* used instead of *who* after words such as *to*, *with*, or *from*: *the man to* **whom** *he talked*

whose *adjective, pronoun* **1** of who or whom? **2** belonging to who or whom

why *adverb, conjunction* **1** for what reason? **2** the reason for which

wicked *adjective* very bad; evil; **wickedly** *adverb*; **wickedness** *noun*

¹**wide** *adjective* **1** large from side to side; **2** fully or completely open; **widely** *adverb*

²**wide** *adverb* completely

width *noun* the distance from one side of something to the other; how wide something is

wife *noun* (*plural* **wives**) the woman to whom a man is married

wild *adjective* **1** living in natural conditions and having natural qualities not produced by human beings; not tame; **2** having strong feelings; **3** great; wonderful; terrific;

w

these wind turbines are modern windmills

¹**will** *verb* (**would; won't; wouldn't**) **1** used to say something about the future: *I will come*; **2** used to ask someone to do something: *Will you come?*; **3** used to show what is possible: *Oil will float on water*

²**will** *noun* **1** the power in the mind to choose what you do; **2** what we want to do; **3** a piece of paper on which a person says who will have his or her property after his or her death

willing *adjective* eager; ready; **willingly** *adverb*; **willingness** *noun*

willow *noun* a tree which often grows near water; the wood of this tree

win *verb* (**wins, winning, won**) **1** to be the best or first in a fight, competition, race, etc; **2** to get as the result of success in a competition, race, or game of chance: *He won a prize*; **winner** *noun*

¹**wind** (*say* wind) *noun* air moving quickly; **windy** *adjective*

²**wind** (*say* wynd) *verb* (**winds, winding, wound**) **1** to turn round and round; **2** to bend and turn; **3** to make into a ball or twist round something; **4** to tighten the working parts of by turning: *to wind a clock*

windmill *noun* **1** a building containing a machine that crushes grain into flour, pumps water, etc, and is driven by large sails turned round by the wind; **2** a toy consisting of a stick with usually four small curved pieces at the end that turn round when blown

window *noun* **1** an opening in the wall of a building to let in light and air, usually with glass in it; **2** a space on a computer screen to look at another program or piece of information

wine *noun* drink made from grapes or other fruit, plants, etc; ⚠ **whine**

wing *noun* **1** one of the two limbs of a bird or insect with which it flies; **2** one of the parts of a plane which support it in flight; **3** any part which stands out from the side: *the west wing of the house*

wink *verb* to close and open one eye quickly; **wink** *noun*

winter *noun* the cold season between autumn and spring; **wintery, wintry** *adjective*

wipe *verb* **1** to pass a cloth over something to remove dirt, liquid, etc; **2** to get rid of; **wipe** *noun*

wire *noun* a thin metal thread

wise *adjective* sensible, clever, and able to understand; **wisdom** *noun*; **wisely** *adverb*

¹**wish** *verb* **1** to want something to happen or to have something; **2** to try to cause a particular thing by magic; **3** to want something or somebody to be or to have: *We wish you a merry Christmas*; **4** to want: *Do you wish to eat alone?*

w

²**wish** *noun* **1** a feeling of wanting; **2** an attempt to make a particular thing happen by magic; **3** what is wished for

witch *noun* a woman who has magic powers; ⚠ **which**

with *preposition* **1** in the company of; beside, near, among, or including; **2** having; **3** using; **4** because of

within *adverb, preposition* in; inside; not beyond or more than

without *adverb, preposition* not having

wives *see* WIFE

wizard *noun* a man who has magic powers

wobble *verb* to move or make something move unsteadily; **wobble** *noun*; **wobbly** *adjective*

woke *see* WAKE

woken *see* WAKE

wolf *noun* (*plural* **wolves**) (*young* **cub**) a wild animal of the dog family, that hunts in a pack

wolf

W

woman *noun* (*plural* **women**) a fully grown human female

won *see* WIN; ⚠ **one**

¹**wonder** *noun* **1** a feeling of surprise and admiration; **2** somebody or something causing this feeling

²**wonder** *verb* **1** to be surprised; **2** to wish to know

wonderful *adjective* unusually good; **wonderfully** *adverb*

won't *see* WILL

carved wooden throne from Tutankhamen's tomb in Egypt

wood *noun* **1** the material of which trunks and branches of trees are made; **2** a place where trees grow, smaller than a forest; ⚠ **would**

wooden *adjective* made of wood

wool *noun* **1** the soft thick hair of sheep and some goats and rabbits; **2** thread or cloth made from this; **woollen** *adjective*; **woolly** *adjective*

word *noun* **1** a letter or letters, a sound or sounds that together make something we can understand; **2** news; a message; **3** a promise

word processor *noun* a computer you use for writing letters, etc, on which you can change the words and the style of the letters on the screen before printing

wore *see* WEAR

¹**work** *noun* **1** activity which uses effort, especially with a special purpose, not for amusement; **2** a job or business; **3** what is produced by work

²**work** *verb* **1** to do an activity that uses effort, especially as employment; **2** to be active; to move or go properly; **3** to make somebody or something work; **worker** *noun*

workman *noun* (*plural* **workmen**) a man who works with his hands

world *noun* **1** the Earth; **2** a planet or star system; **3** all human beings thought of together

worm *noun* a small thin creature with a soft body without bones or legs: **earthworm**

worn *see* WEAR; ⚠ **warn**

¹**worry** *verb* to make or be anxious; **worried** *adjective*

²**worry** *noun* **1** a feeling of anxiety; **2** a person or thing that makes you worried

worse *see* BAD, ILL

worship *verb* (**worshipped**) to pray and show great respect, admiration, etc; **worship** *noun*

¹**worst** *see* BAD, ILL

²**worst** *noun* the most bad thing or part

¹**worth** *preposition* of the value of

²**worth** *noun* value; **worthless** *adjective*; **worthy** *adjective*

would *see* WILL; ⚠ **wood**

wouldn't *see* WILL

¹**wound** (*say* **woond**) *noun* an injury to the body caused by violent means, or an injury to your feelings; **wound** *verb*

²**wound** (*say* **wownd**) *see* ²WIND

wove *see* WEAVE

woven *see* WEAVE

wrap *verb* (**wrapped**) to cover; to fold round; **wrapping** *noun*

¹**wreck** *noun* a ship, car, building, etc, that has been partly destroyed; **wreckage** *noun*

²**wreck** *verb* to destroy or cause to destroy

wren *noun* a very small song bird

wrestle *verb* to fight by holding and throwing a person to the ground; **wrestler** *noun*; **wrestling** *noun*

wriggle *verb* to twist from side to side; **wriggle** *noun*

wring *verb* (**wrings, wringing, wrung**) to twist; to remove water by twisting and pressing; **wring** *noun*; ⚠ **ring**

wrinkle *noun* a line in something which is folded or squashed, especially on the skin; **wrinkle** *verb*; **wrinkly** *adjective*

wrist *noun* the joint between the hand and the lower arm

write *verb* (**writes, writing, wrote, written**) **1** to make letters or words, especially with a pen or pencil on paper; **2** to produce and send a letter; **writer** *noun*; ⚠ **right, rite**

¹**wrong** *adjective* **1** not correct; **2** evil; not good; **3** not suitable; **wrongly** *adverb*

²**wrong** *noun* what is bad

wrote *see* WRITE

wrung *see* WRING; ⚠ **rung**

x-ray *verb* (**x-rays, x-raying, x-rayed**) to photograph, examine, or treat by X-rays

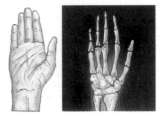

X-ray of a hand

X-ray *noun* (*plural* **X-rays**)
1 a powerful invisible beam of light which can pass through substances that are not transparent, and which is used for photographing conditions inside the body, for treating certain diseases, and for various purposes in industry; **2** a photograph taken using this

xylophone *noun* a musical instrument made of flat bars that produce musical notes when struck with small hammers

xylophone

yacht (*say* **yot**) *noun* a sailing boat; **yachting** *noun*

¹**yard** *noun* a measure of length equal to 3 feet or 0.91 metres

²**yard** *noun* **1** a piece of ground next to a building, with a wall or fence round it; **2** a piece of ground used for a special purpose: **coalyard, shipyard**

yawn *verb* to open the mouth wide and breathe deeply as when tired or bored; **yawn** *noun*

year *noun* a measure of time equal to $365\frac{1}{4}$ days, 52 weeks, or 12 months; the time it takes the Earth to travel round the sun; **yearly** *adverb*

yell *verb* to shout loudly; to cry out; **yell** *noun*

yellow *noun* the colour of butter, gold, or the yolk of an egg; **yellow** *adjective*; **yellowish** *adjective*

yes *adverb* a word used to answer a question, to show that something is true or that you agree with something

yesterday *adverb, noun* the day before this one

yet *adverb* at this moment; then; so far; up to now

yogurt or **yoghourt, yoghurt** *noun* a dessert made from milk treated in a special way to make it thick and a bit sour

yolk (*say* **yoke**) *noun* the yellow central part of an egg

you *pronoun* (**yourself, yourselves**) **1** the person or people being spoken to; **2** one; anyone

¹**young** *adjective* not having lived very long; not old; **youngish** *adjective*; **youngster** *noun*

²**young** *noun* young people or animals

your *adjective* belonging to you; ⚠ **you're**

you're shortened form of you are; ⚠ **your**

yours *pronoun* **1** that or those belonging to you; **2** written at the end of a letter: *yours sincerely*

yourself *see* YOU

yourselves *see* YOU

youth *noun* **1** the time when you are young; **2** a young man; **3** young people as a group; **youthful** *adjective*

yo-yo *noun* a toy made of a round piece of wood, plastic, etc, that can be made to run up and down a string tied to it

Zz

zebra *noun* a wild animal like a horse, that has black or dark brown and white stripes

zebra

zebra crossing *noun* a street crossing marked by black and white lines

zero *noun* (*plural* **zeros** or **zeroes**) the figure 0; a nought; nothing

zigzag *noun* a line shaped like a row of Zs

¹**zip** *noun* **1** also **zip fastener** a fastener that is often used on clothes, and has two sets of teeth which can be joined together; **2** a zipping sound

²**zip** *verb* (**zipped**) **1** to open or fasten with a zip; **2** to make the sound of something moving quickly through the air

zodiac *noun* an imaginary area in space along which the sun and planets appear to travel, divided into twelve signs each named after a special group of stars (*see* page 142)

zoo *noun* a collection of wild animals kept in a park for people to look at or for conservation purposes

zoom *verb* to go or rise quickly

y
z

MEASUREMENTS

WEIGHT

Metric

mg 1000 milligrams = 1 gram
g 1000 grams = 1 kilogram
kg 1000 kilograms = 1 tonne

Imperial (equivalents)

1g = 0.035 ounces
1kg = 2.21 pounds
1 tonne = 0.98 tons

Imperial

oz 16 drams = 1 ounce
lb 16 ounces = 1 pound
st 14 pounds = 1 stone
cwt 8 stones
= 1 hundredweight
112 pounds = 1 cwt
20 cwt = 1 ton

Metric (equivalents)

1 ounce = 28.35 g
1 pound = 0.454 kg
1 stone = 6.35 kg
1 hundredweight = 50.8 kg
1 ton = 1.016 tonnes

LENGTH

Metric

mm 10 millimetres
= 1 centimetre
cm 100 centimetres
= 1 metre
m 1000 metres = 1 kilometre
1 metre = 1000 mm
100 cm

Imperial

in 12 inches = 1 foot
ft 3 feet = 1 yard
yd 220 yards = 1 furlong
8 furlongs = 1 mile
1760 yards = 1 mile
5280 feet = 1 mile

Imperial (equivalents)

1 in = 2.54 cm
1 ft = 30.48 cm
1 yd = 0.91 m
1 mile = 1.609 km

Metric (equivalents)

1 mm = 0.04 in
1 cm = 0.394 in
1 m = 1.09 yd or 3.28 ft
1 km = 0.62 miles
or approx $5/8$ mile